Complete Japanese

Helen Gilhooly

with Mikiko Kurose

First published in Great Britain in 2008 by Hodder Education. An Hachette UK company.

This edition published in 2016 by John Murray Learning

Copyright © Helen Gilhooly 2008, 2010, 2016

The right of Helen Gilhooly to be identified as the Author of the Work has been asserted by her in accordance with the Copyright, Designs and Patents Act 1988.

Database right: Hodder & Stoughton (makers)

The *Teach Yourself* name is a registered trademark of Hachette UK.

British Library Cataloguing in Publication Data: a catalogue record for this title is available from the British Library.

Library of Congress Catalog Card Number: on file.

9781471800498

1

The publisher has used its best endeavours to ensure that any website addresses referred to in this book are correct and active at the time of going to press. However, the publisher and the author have no responsibility for the websites and can make no guarantee that a site will remain live or that the content will remain relevant, decent or appropriate.

The publisher has made every effort to mark as such all words which it believes to be trademarks. The publisher should also like to make it clear that the presence of a word in the book, whether marked or unmarked, in no way affects its legal status as a trademark.

Every reasonable effort has been made by the publisher to trace the copyright holders of material in this book. Any errors or omissions should be notified in writing to the publisher, who will endeavour to rectify the situation for any reprints and future editions.

Cover image © Shutterstock.com

Typeset by Graphicraft Limited, Hong Kong.

Printed and bound in Great Britain by CPI Group (UK) Ltd., Croydon, CR0 4YY.

John Murray Learning policy is to use papers that are natural, renewable and recyclable products and made from wood grown in sustainable forests. The logging and manufacturing processes are expected to conform to the environmental regulations of the country of origin.

Carmelite House
50 Victoria Embankment
London EC4Y 0DZ
www.hodder.co.uk

Acknowledgements

Thank you to all these people for their invaluable comments and feedback in writing this book: my Japanese colleague Mikiko Kurose, Niamh Kelly of Dublin City University and Ginny Catmur at John Murray Learning. And an especially big thanks to John, Rosie and Bonnie for just being there!

Contents

About the author

Helen Gilhooly set up a highly successful Japanese language department in a specialist language secondary school in Derbyshire and taught Japanese there for many years. She has also been a teacher trainer and special lecturer at Nottingham University. She teaches Japanese to people of all ages, has lived and worked in Japan, is a graduate of Churchill College, Cambridge, and has an MA in Japanese. She is author of the following *Teach Yourself* titles: *Get started in Japanese*, *Read and Write Japanese Scripts* and *Speak Japanese with Confidence*, and co-author of the following Michel Thomas Method titles: *Start Japanese*, *Total Japanese* and *Perfect Japanese*. She was also the language consultant and translator for *Fast-track Japanese* (Elisabeth Smith). She is currently a freelance author, speaker and editor.

Mikiko Kurose has given native speaker support during the writing of this book. She was born in Kyoto, Japan, has an MA in Linguistics and is a qualified Japanese secondary-school teacher. She taught for 13 years in state secondary schools and has worked as a translator and interpreter as well as advisor for Sharp in the development of their English—Japanese dictionary software. She has proofread and advised the author on previous *Teach Yourself* books and is the native speaker voice for the Michel Thomas Method Japanese titles. She currently works as a Japanese teacher at the University of Nottingham.

How the course works

Welcome to *Complete Japanese*!

This is an in-depth self-study course that will take you from beginner to intermediate-level Japanese (B1 of the Common European Framework) via a step-by-step approach. This approach will help you to gain confidence and essential skills in understanding and communicating in Japanese. The practical content will enable you to transfer your learning easily to business and social situations both in Japan and in your own country. You will also gain many insights into Japanese culture and the ways in which language and culture influence each other and are closely bonded. You will find *Complete Japanese* useful whether you are planning a trip to Japan, want to communicate better with Japanese colleagues or friends, or simply want the personal satisfaction of mastering Japanese.

AN OPPORTUNITY TO READ JAPANESE

A particular feature of this course is the opportunity to learn to read Japanese, a skill often considered to be the most difficult to acquire when learning Japanese. This book offers a practical and logical approach to reading which breaks down traditional barriers and turns the skill of reading into an enjoyable and achievable challenge. The first part of the course (Units 1–9) is written in both **rōmaji** (Japanese written using the Roman alphabet, a, b, c) for those learners who haven't learned to read Japanese before, and Japanese script for those learners who can already read Japanese script. At the end of each of these units is a reading section which teaches you how to read Japanese. Then in Part 2 the units are written in Japanese script only with the addition of some **rōmaji** passages in the Answer key to support those learners who need it. The teaching approach is very much based on the way the author has learned to read – through visual and pictorial links that help you to break down the script into recognizable parts and make it fun to learn.

How does the course work?

Complete Japanese is divided into two main parts. Part 1 (Units 1–9) teaches the basics of Japanese and employs a primarily topic-based approach with a thorough foundation in structures (the 'nuts and bolts' of the language). A range of language is introduced to help the learner communicate in everyday situations including greetings and introductions, counting, shopping, daily routine, going out, travelling, directions, descriptions, likes, dislikes, hobbies and illness.

Part 2 (Units 10–15) begins to explore the language in more depth and to guide the learner into manipulating the language to express more complex and rich concepts such as opinions, advice, requests and commands. The learner will begin to feel much more confident about saying longer sentences and taking part in conversations on a variety of topics. You will also explore the layers of politeness that are so important and fundamental to Japanese language and society. Although Part 2 includes a lot of important structures, it will still retain a topic-based and practical focus – in other words, you will be learning language that you can use.

INTRODUCING THE MAIN CHARACTERS

There is a storyline running throughout the book involving characters from various backgrounds who eventually all meet or have dealings with one another. The characters are:

▶ *Robert Franks* (British) – married to Rie, living in Tokyo and working as a journalist for *Japan Now* (an English-language newspaper)
▶ *Rie Franks* – married to Robert and working as an English-speaking receptionist in a Japanese hotel
▶ *Tatsuya* and *Naoe Hondo* with their two daughters, *Eri*, aged ten, and *Yuki*, aged 16 – Tatsuya-san works for a Japanese electronics company and Naoe is a full-time mother and carer for her elderly father
▶ *Ian Ferguson* (New Zealander) and *Katie Mears* (American) – Katie teaches English in a private language school and Ian works for a Japanese company
▶ *Roger Wilson* (Australian) – studying Japanese at university in Australia and currently in Japan for one year at Tokyo University
▶ *Miki Sugihara* – has spent five years teaching Japanese in the United States and is a Japanese and English teacher in a private language school in Tokyo
▶ *Takeshi Ishibashi* – studying engineering at Tokyo University and plays in a boy band at weekends.

A note about **furigana**

Furigana are smaller **hiragana** symbols which are placed above **kanji** as a reading aid. They are used in this book above new **kanji** words and **katakana** words but are removed later to encourage you to read **kanji**. You can always check the pronunciation either with the Romanized version or the vocabulary list if you need to.

Learn to learn

The Discovery method

There are lots of philosophies and approaches to language learning, some practical, some quite unconventional, and far too many to list here. Perhaps you know of a few, or even have some techniques of your own. In this course we have incorporated the Discovery method of learning, a sort of DIY approach to language learning. What this means is that you will be encouraged throughout the course to engage your mind and figure out the language for yourself, through identifying patterns, understanding grammar concepts, noticing words that are similar to English, and more. This method promotes language awareness, a critical skill in acquiring a new language. As a result of your own efforts, you will be able to better retain what you have learned, use it with confidence, and, even better, apply those same skills to continuing to learn the language (or, indeed, another one) on your own after you've finished this course.

Everyone can succeed in learning a language – the key is to know how to learn it. Learning is more than just reading or memorizing grammar and vocabulary. It's about being an active learner, learning in real contexts, and, most importantly, using what you've learned in different situations. Simply put, if you figure something out for yourself, you're more likely to understand it. And when you use what you've learned, you're more likely to remember it.

And because many of the essential but (let's admit it!) challenging details, such as grammar rules, are introduced through the Discovery method, you'll have more fun while learning. Soon, the language will start to make sense and you'll be relying on your own intuition to construct original sentences independently, not just listening and repeating.

Enjoy yourself!

How to be successful at learning Japanese

▶ **Create a study habit.** Learning little and often is far more effective than a long session every now and then. So try and put in about 20–30 minutes of regular study (where possible twice or three times per week or more). Try to make it at a regular time so that you can get into the habit of studying 'little and often'.

▶ **Find a balance** between moving through the course and revising what you have already learned so that you can build gradually and effectively on your learning. Set aside one session every now and again (maybe once every five sessions) to look back at previous units and recap on your learning. A good place to start is with the activities – if you have difficulties with a certain structure, look back to the explanation and examples.

▶ **Create an environment conducive to learning.** Find time to study in a quiet room where you can speak out loud. This will help you to focus on building up your speaking and listening skills in an environment where you can concentrate and, literally, hear yourself speak.

- ▶ **Languages settle gradually in the brain** so don't be too harsh on yourself! Learning a language is a gradual and cumulative process and everyone makes mistakes. You mustn't expect to be perfect straightaway and you can't be expected to remember every item of vocabulary and every new structure. Let your learning grow slowly and surely and don't be impatient with yourself.
- ▶ **Resist the temptation to look up every word you don't know.** Read or listen to the same passage several times, concentrating on trying to get the gist of it. If after the third time some words still prevent you from making sense of the passage, look them up.
- ▶ **Maximize your exposure to the language.** You don't have to go to Japan to do this: find out about Japanese societies, join a Japanese class, go to a Japanese restaurant and practise ordering in Japanese (but be careful – people working in Japanese restaurants are not always Japanese), ask a Japanese friend to speak with you in Japanese, visit Japanese shops and areas where you can hear Japanese being spoken around you, watch TV or read online articles and blogs, or see if you can find out Japanese information about a personal hobby or interest.
- ▶ **Learn to cope with uncertainty.** Don't give up if you don't understand, try to guess what is being said and keep following the conversation for a while. The speaker might repeat or paraphrase what you didn't understand and the conversation can carry on.
- ▶ But, most importantly, remember that learning and using a foreign language should be fun!

 00.00

LISTENING TO JAPANESE

- ▶ The audio contains a variety of listening passages to develop different skills such as listening for gist, learning vocabulary, improving pronunciation and listening for specific information. You will find you can listen to and learn parts of the audio such as vocabulary lists and 'learn to say' passages while doing something else such as travelling to work; for other passages such as activities you will need to be more focused. In either case, don't listen for too long otherwise you will probably find you have switched off – **stay focused**.
- ▶ Use the pause button (or on/off button on car systems) to help you to focus on accurate pronunciation and thus to develop your Japanese accent. Use it too when memorizing new words or dialogue – you will have better results if you memorize small chunks at a time.
- ▶ In the listening activities, try to develop the speed of your listening and understanding by listening to the whole activity without using the pause button initially. You won't get all the information the first time, but it will help you to **develop the skill of picking out the essential points** and processing them in your brain more quickly.
- ▶ Once you have listened to the whole activity once or twice, break it down into manageable chunks using the pause button, so that you can complete the information required.

VOCABULARY

▶ Group new words under **generic categories**, e.g. *food, furniture*; **situations** in which they occur, e.g. under post office you can write *stamps, postcards, names of countries*; and **functions**, e.g. *greetings, parting, thanks, apologizing*.

▶ Write the words over and over again. Keep lists on your smartphone or tablet, and switch the keyboard language so you can include special characters and write in Japanese script.

▶ Listen to the audio several times and say the words out loud as you hear or read them.

▶ Cover up the English side of the vocabulary list and see if you remember the meaning of the word. Do the same for the Japanese.

▶ Create flashcards, drawings and mind maps.

▶ Write Japanese words on sticky notes and stick them to objects around your house.

▶ Experiment with words. Look for patterns in words, e.g. words which begin with Japanese-style (**Wa**) and Western-style (**Yō**) such as rooms, food and clothes.

GRAMMAR

▶ Experiment with grammar rules. Sit back and reflect on how the rules of Japanese compare with your own language or other languages you may already speak.

▶ Use known vocabulary to practise new grammar structures.

▶ When you learn a new verb form, try it out with several verbs you already know that follow the same rule.

PRONUNCIATION AND SPEAKING

▶ Practice makes perfect. The most successful language learners know how to overcome their inhibitions and keep going.

▶ Study individual sounds, then full words. Make a list of those words that give you trouble and practise them.

▶ Repeat the conversations line by line and try to mimic what you hear. Record yourself if you can.

▶ When you conduct a simple transaction with a salesperson or waiter, pretend that you have to do it in Japanese, e.g. buying groceries, ordering food, drinks, and so on.

▶ Rehearse the dialogues out loud, then try to replace sentences with ones that are true for you.

▶ Learn from your errors. This is part of any learning process, so don't be so worried about making mistakes to the extent that you won't say anything unless you are sure it is correct. Remember that many errors are not serious as they do not affect the meaning.

▶ Seize every opportunity to speak. If you get stuck for a particular word, don't let the conversation stop; paraphrase or use the words you do know, even if you have to simplify what you want to say.

READING AND WRITING

▶ Don't be impatient with yourself. Eventually you will be able to read **hiragana** confidently but give yourself time.

▶ First of all, get used to reading individual symbols, then words, then group of words. Build your skills gradually and return to earlier reading sections to refresh your brain.

▶ Make mini flashcards of all the symbols and invent fun ways to test yourself such as snap and lucky dip.

▶ Use the many online games, reading tutors and apps which offer hundreds of games and challenges to help you to learn to read Japanese. There are also many Japanese writing tutors available.

▶ Use the audio as you read the dialogues to guide and support you as you learn to read.

▶ As you become more confident, try reading first then listen to the audio to check.

Pronunciation guide

Vowels

 00.01 The Japanese 'alphabet' (it is actually a phonetic system) is made up of a number of sounds created by combining the five Japanese vowels (**a**, **i**, **u**, **e**, **o**) with one of the 19 consonant sounds (letters that are not vowels). Each sound is a single 'beat' or syllable and these are combined to form words. Unlike English with its various pronunciation and spelling rules, in Japanese each sound is always pronounced in the same way. For example, the vowel sound *a* in English can be pronounced:

man   mate   mayor   marsh

However, the Japanese vowel sound **a** is always pronounced as the *a* in *man*. The five Japanese vowels in order are:

a   as in *man*
i   as in *hit*
u   as in *blue*
e   as in *extra*
o   as in *shot*

Here's a bizarre 'headline' to help you remember these sounds:

Man hits two extra shots
   a   i   u   e   o

How to pronounce syllables

 00.02 You are now going to practise pronouncing Japanese using the sound tables of Japanese syllables that follow. Use the audio to listen to a line at a time, then pause and say those sounds out loud.

SOUND TABLES

a あ	i い	u う	e え	o お	
ka か	ki き	ku く	ke け	ko こ	
sa さ	shi し	su す	se せ	so そ	
ta た	chi ち	tsu つ	te て	to と	**tsu** is an unfamiliar sound for English speakers; it is only one syllable (or beat); squash the **t** and **s** together as you say them.

na な	ni に	nu ぬ	ne ね	no の	
ha は	hi ひ	fu ふ	he へ	ho ほ	**fu** is a soft sound, between **f** and **h**. Your front teeth don't touch your lips as you say it; air is let out between your teeth and lips.

ma ま	mi み	mu む	me め	mo も	
ya や		yu ゆ		yo よ	
ra ら	ri り	ru る	re れ	ro ろ	r is a soft sound, somewhere between **r** and **l**, and not like the French 'r' sound.

(o) wo を

wa わ				n ん	n has a full beat. There are examples in the next section
ga が	gi ぎ	gu ぐ	ge げ	go ご	g as in *get* not *gin*.
za ざ	ji じ	zu ず	ze ぜ	zo ぞ	
ba ば	bi び	bu ぶ	be べ	bo ぼ	There is no **v** sound in Japanese and **b** is substituted for foreign words. For example, *Valerie* becomes **Ba-re-ri-i**.

pa ぱ	pi ぴ	pu ぷ	pe ぺ	po ぽ
da だ			de で	do ど

The final set of sounds in the sound tables is made up of a consonant plus **ya**, **yu** or **yo**. These also have a single beat (that is, they are one syllable), although English-speaking people sometimes mistakenly pronounce these sounds with two beats. For example, you may sometimes hear the first sound of the city name **Kyoto** being wrongly pronounced **ki-yo** instead of **kyo**.

Practise saying these sounds carefully:

きゃ **kya**	きゅ **kyu**	きょ **kyo**	
しゃ **sha**	しゅ **shu**	しょ **sho**	
ちゃ **cha**	ちゅ **chu**	ちょ **cho**	*ch* as in *chance*
にゃ **nya**	にゅ **nyu**	にょ **nyo**	
ひゃ **hya**	ひゅ **hyu**	ひょ **hyo**	
みゃ **mya**	みゅ **myu**	みょ **myo**	
りゃ **rya**	りゅ **ryu**	りょ **ryo**	
ぎゃ **gya**	ぎゅ **gyu**	ぎょ **gyo**	
じゃ **ja**	じゅ **ju**	じょ **jo**	*ja* as in *jam*
びゃ **bya**	びゅ **byu**	びょ **byo**	
ぴゃ **pya**	ぴゅ **pyu**	ぴょ **pyo**	

How to pronounce words

 00.03

EQUAL STRESS

Every syllable in Japanese is given equal stress, whereas in English we give more stress to some parts of the word than others. Look at this example:

| (English) | *A-ME-ri-ca* | (the stress is on *me*) |
| (Japanese) | **A-me-ri-ka** | (each syllable has equal stress) |

English-speaking people often add stress to Japanese words. For example:

Hi-ro-SHI-ma   (the stress is on **shi** whereas there should be equal stress)

Hi-ro-shi-ma

So, to make your accent sound more authentic, try not to stress parts of words in the English style; instead, give equal stress to each syllable.

Now listen to the audio for examples.

PITCH

Some Japanese words using identical sounds are distinguished in pronunciation through use of high and low pitch. The word **hashi** can mean either *bridge* or *chopsticks*. **Háshi** means *chopsticks* and **hashí** means *bridge* (the accent above the syllable is my way of showing you where the high pitch is). However, pitch is neither as strong as stress accent nor as complex as in tonal languages such as Chinese.

LONG SYLLABLES

In this course, a macron is used over vowels to indicate long sounds. Here is an example:

Tōkyō   (you hold the sounds with macrons for about twice the normal length)

To-u-kyo-u   (say the word smoothly)

Macrons are not used when the place name appears as part of an English text or translation, only as part of a Japanese dialogue.

THE **N** SOUND

n is a syllable by itself. For example, the greeting *hello* is:

ko-n-ni-chi-wa

When **n** is followed by **p**, **b** or **m** its sound softens to **m**:

gambatte   *good luck*

sampaku   *three nights*

DOUBLE CONSONANTS

 00.04 A double consonant indicates that you should pause slightly before saying it, as you would in these English examples (say them out loud):

headdress   (you pause slightly after *hea* – you don't say *head dress*)

bookcase   (you pause after *boo*)

You will come across these double consonants in Japanese – **kk**, **ss**, **tt**, **pp**.

Listen to the audio and speak out loud:

gambatte   *good luck*

Hokkaidō   north island of Japan

Sapporo   largest city of **Hokkaidō**

massugu   *straight on*

You always build in this slight pause when there is a double consonant.

SILENT VOWELS

 00.05 Sometimes **i** and **u** become almost unvoiced. This is indicated here by bracketing the vowel.

Listen to the audio and say these examples out loud:

des(u)	*it is*
s(u)ki	*I like*
ikimas(u)	*I go*
hajimemash(i)te	*how do you do?*

NON-JAPANESE WORDS

 00.06 Foreign words are adapted to the Japanese sound system.

Look at these examples and listen to the audio: for example, there is no th sound in Japanese, so s is used instead.

Ajia	*Asia*
Sumisu	*Smith*
Robāto	*Robert*
marason	*marathon*
kōhī	*coffee*
hoteru	*hotel*
terebi	*television*

To practise and consolidate your learning so far, listen to the greetings in Unit 1 and practise saying the words in the table out loud. These words cover most of the pronunciation rules you have just learned.

Useful expressions

Here are some useful expressions for you to learn.

SURVIVAL PHRASES

00.07

Mō ichido itte kudasai	*Can you repeat it, please?*
Motto yukkuri itte kudasai	*Speak more slowly, please*
Wakarimasu ka	*Do you understand?*
Wakarimashita	*I understand*
Wakarimasen	*I don't understand*
Shirimasen/wakarimasen (more polite)	*I don't know*
Sō desu ka	*Is that right?*
Hai, sō desu	*Yes, that's right*
Iie, chigaimasu	*No, that's not right*
Eigo/nihongo ga dekimasu ka	*Can you speak English/Japanese?*
Nihongo ga dekimasu ga …	*I speak Japanese but …*
… amari jōzu dewa arimasen	*… not very well*
Sumimasen	*I apologize/excuse me*
Gomennasai	*I am sorry*
Dōmo arigatō	*Thank you*
Ima nanji desu ka	*What time is it now?*
Itadakimasu	*Bon appétit* (said before eating)
Gochisōsama deshita	*That was a feast* (said after eating)

*Note: **ka** is a spoken question mark.

USEFUL EVERYDAY PHRASES

00.08

Ohayō gozaimasu	*Good morning*
Konbanwa	*Good evening*
Hajimemashite	*How do you do?*
Dōzo yoroshiku	*Pleased to meet you*
Konnichiwa	*Hello/Good afternoon*
Oyasumi	*Goodnight* (casual, said to friends and family)
Oyasumi nasai	*Goodnight* (formal, said to superiors and people you don't know well)
Moshi moshi	*Hello* (when answering the phone or making a call)
Ittekimasu	*I'm off now* (as you leave the home)
Tadaima	*I'm back!* (as you arrive home)

Shitsurei shimasu	*Pardon me for interrupting* (as you enter a room at work)
Shitsurei shimashita	*Pardon me for interrupting* (as you leave a room at work)
Ogenki desu ka	*How are you?*
Dōzo	*Go ahead/After you*
Ja mata ne	*See you*
Sayōnara	*Goodbye*

Some features of the Japanese language

It is reassuring to know that there are aspects of the Japanese language that are surprisingly straightforward.

▶ There is no masculine and feminine in Japanese and most words don't have a plural.
▶ Verb endings remain the same regardless of who does the action: **kaimasu** can mean *I buy*, *he buys* or *we buy*.
▶ There are only two main tenses – the past and the present/future: **kaimasu** covers *buy* and *will buy*, **kaimashita** means *bought*.
▶ Pronunciation is relatively easy and very regular.

So you aren't going to be grappling with a lot of complex grammar rules when you start learning Japanese. Of course, much of the vocabulary is new, but even in this aspect there is a pleasant surprise – the Japanese language has always been a great 'word borrower' and it is rich with loanwords from English, for example **aisukuriimu** (*ice cream*), **kompyūtā** (*computer*).

Even if you have never studied Japanese before, because of the huge economic and cultural influence that Japan has had worldwide you will almost certainly already be familiar with many Japanese words and terms, for example **karaoke**, **origami**, **sumō**, **sushi** and **manga**.

There are more challenging aspects to learning Japanese, but this is the case when you learn any language, and it is often these challenges that give the greatest satisfaction. And you certainly won't be alone in your quest to master Japanese – about three million people worldwide are currently learning Japanese. *Complete Japanese* aims to help you to interact with Japanese people through a range of everyday situations. By the end of the course you will feel confident enough to speak, read and understand Japanese in a wide range of practical situations.

Hiragana table

Read these charts column by column, i.e. downwards, starting from the top right corner.

p	b	d	z	g	n	w	r	y	m	h	n	t	s	k		
ぱ	ば	だ	ざ	が	ん	わ	ら	や	ま	は	な	た	さ	か	あ	A
ぴ	び	ぢ	じ	ぎ			り		み	ひ	に	ち	し	き	い	I
ぷ	ぶ	づ	ず	ぐ			る	ゆ	む	ふ	ぬ	つ	す	く	う	U
ぺ	べ	で	ぜ	げ			れ		め	へ	ね	て	せ	け	え	E
ぽ	ぼ	ど	ぞ	ご		を	ろ	よ	も	ほ	の	と	そ	こ	お	O

ry	my	py	by	hy	ny	ch	j	sh	gy	ky	
りゃ	みゃ	ぴゃ	びゃ	ひゃ	にゃ	ちゃ	じゃ	しゃ	ぎゃ	きゃ	A
りゅ	みゅ	ぴゅ	びゅ	ひゅ	にゅ	ちゅ	じゅ	しゅ	ぎゅ	きゅ	U
りょ	みょ	ぴょ	びょ	ひょ	にょ	ちょ	じょ	しょ	ぎょ	きょ	O

Katakana table

Read these charts 'western-style', i.e. row by row, from left to right.

Basic katakana syllables

ア a	イ i	ウ u	エ e	オ o
カ ka	キ ki	ク ku	ケ ke	コ ko
サ sa	シ shi	ス su	セ se	ソ so
タ ta	チ chi	ツ tsu	テ te	ト to
ナ na	ニ ni	ヌ nu	ネ ne	ノ no
ハ ha	ヒ hi	フ fu	ヘ he	ホ ho
マ ma	ミ mi	ム mu	メ me	モ mo
ヤ ya		ユ yu		ヨ yo
ラ ra	リ ri	ル ru	レ re	ロ ro
ワ wa				ヲ wo
ン n	カタカナ Katakana			

Additional sounds

ガ ga	ギ gi	グ gu	ゲ ge	ゴ go	片仮名
ザ za	ジ ji	ズ zu	ゼ ze	ゾ zo	
ダ da	ヂ ji	ヅ zu	デ de	ド do	
バ ba	ビ bi	ブ bu	ベ be	ボ bo	
パ pa	ピ pi	プ pu	ペ pe	ポ po	
キャ kya	キュ kyu	キョ kyo	ギャ gya	ギュ gyu	ギョ gyo
ニャ nya	ニュ nyu	ニョ nyo	ヒャ hya	ヒュ hyu	ヒョ hyo
ビャ bya	ビュ byu	ビョ byo	ピャ pya	ピュ pyu	ピョ pyo
ミャ mya	ミュ myu	ミョ myo	リャ rya	リュ ryu	リョ ryo
ジャ ja	ジュ ju	ジェ je	ジョ jo	チャ cha	チュ chu
チェ che	チョ cho	シャ sha	シュ shu	シェ she	ショ sho

New sounds

ウィ wi	ウェ we	ウォ wo	ティ ti	ディ di	ドュ dyu	フィ fi	フェ fe	フォ fo	フュ fyu
クァ kwa	クィ kwi	クェ kwe	クォ kwo	グァ gwa	ツァ tsa	ツェ tse	ツォ tso	ヴァ va	ヴィ vi
ヴェ ve	ヴォ vo	ヴ vu							

Part 1
Building the foundations

1 はじめまして、ロバート・フランクスと申します

Hajimemashite, Robert Franks to mōshimasu

How do you do? I'm called Robert Franks

In this unit you will learn how to:
▶ *create basic Japanese sentence structure.*
▶ *make introductions, use greetings and farewells.*
▶ *say the words for family members.*
▶ *say it is and it is not.*
▶ *count from one to ten (with actions!).*

CEFR: *(A1) Can establish basic social contact by using the simplest everyday polite forms of greetings and farewells, introductions, etc. (A2) Can understand short, simple texts on familiar matters of a concrete type which consist of high-frequency everyday or job-related language.*

How to address people さん san

You will learn a lot about formal and informal 日本語 **nihongo** (*Japanese language*) throughout this book. In 日本の社会 **nihon no shakai** (*Japanese society*) a distinction is made between the 'in-group' (myself, my family, my work colleagues, my friends) and the 'out-group' (my seniors, people from other families and workplaces). 丁寧語 **Teineigo** (*polite language*) is an important traditional and continuing aspect of Japanese life, especially when speaking to those in the out-group. More informal language is generally used within the in-group.

First of all there is the use of さん **san**. This is attached to the end of a name – either 名前 **namae** (*first name*) or 名字 **myōji** (*surname*) – and is best translated in English as *Mr, Mrs, Miss* or *Ms*. It shows 尊敬 **sonkei** (*respect*) for the person you are addressing but you never use it to refer to yourself or your family.

More casual titles are:

▶ くん **kun**, used to address boys and between male friends (again, never for yourself)
▶ ちゃん **chan**, used for children and between friends, particularly girls, and after nicknames.

Other titles are:

▶ 先生 **sensei**, used for teachers and professors
▶ 様 **sama**, used in more formal situations and when addressing letters.

> **LANGUAGE TIP**
> All titles are attached after the name and it is important to use these titles when talking to other people, whether you address someone by their first name or their surname. If in doubt, it is safest to use the surname and さん **san**.

 How would you address the following? **a** Your friend's son Kenichi; **b** your teacher Mrs Suzuki; **c** your Japanese female friend Hana.

Vocabulary builder

 1 01.01 **Listen to the new vocabulary and practise saying it out loud.**

はじめまして	hajimemash(i)te	*pleased to meet you*
(name) と申します	to mōshimas(u)	*I'm called (name) (formal)*
どうぞよろしく	dōzo yorosh(i)ku	*pleased to meet you*
よろしくおねがいします	yorosh(i)ku onegaishimas(u)	*pleased to meet you* (also used when you feel indebted to someone)
私	watashi	*I*
私の	watashi no	*my*
名刺	meishi	*business card*
です	des(u)	*am, is, are*
ありがとうございます	arigatō gozaimas(u)	*thank you*
会社の営業部長	kaisha no eigyō buchō	*company sales manager*

 2 Try saying these phrases out loud. Say the sounds smoothly.

   a do-u-zo yo-ro-sh(i)-ku
   b yo-ro-sh(i)-ku o-ne-ga-i-shi-mas(u)
   c a-ri-ga-to-u go-za-i-mas(u)

In the early units only, certain letters in **rōmaji** are bracketed to show that they are not pronounced or at most very slightly.

3 Now listen to the audio again and focus on good pronunciation.

Conversation

 01.02 *Robert Franks, a British journalist working for a Japanese newspaper company in Tokyo, is about to interview Tatsuya Hondo who works for an electronics company.*

1 What comment does Robert make as he looks at Mr Hondo's business card?

Robert	はじめして、ロバート・フランクスと申します。どうぞよろし。
Hondō-san	はじめして、本堂たつやと申します。よろしくおねがいします。
Robert	*(Handing over his business card)* 私の名刺です。どうぞ。
Hondō-san	ありがとうございます。*(Hands over his business card)* 私のです。どうぞ。
Robert	ああ、本堂さんは会社の営業部長ですね。お忙しいでしょうね。
Hondō-san	そうですね...
Robert	Hajimemashite, Robāto Franks to mōshimasu. Dōzo yoroshiku.
Hondō-san	Hajimemashite, Hondō Tatsuya to mōshimasu. Yoroshiku onegaishimasu.
Robert	*(Handing over his business card)* Watashi no meishi desu. Dōzo.
Hondō-san	Arigatō gozaimasu. *(Hands over his business card)* Watashi no desu. Dōzo.
Robert	Ā, Hondō-san wa kaisha no eigyō buchō desu ne. Oisogashii deshō ne.
Hondō-san	Sō desu ne . . .

2 In what order does Mr Hondo say his name?

3 How does Robert say 'this is my business card'?

Language discovery

KEY SENTENCES

 1 01.03 The following vocabulary is used in the key sentences in the next exercise. Listen to and repeat out loud the new vocabulary.

ジャーナリスト	jānaris(u)to	*journalist*
家内	kanai	*(my) wife*
の	no	*'s (possessive, to show belonging)*
名前	namae	*name*
家族	kazoku	*family*
五	go	*five*
人	nin	*people (counter)*
息子	musuko	*(my) son*
六	roku	*six*
才（歳）	sai	*years old*
娘	musume	*(my) daughter*

 2 01.04 Next, read and listen to the key sentences a–e that follow. Repeat them out loud for pronunciation practice. You can check the English meanings in the Answer key. Can you work out how the sentences fit together? What words appear repeatedly? Is there a pattern to how they are used?

a 私 はジャーナリストです。 Watashi wa jānaris(u)to des(u).
b 家内の名前はりえです。 Kanai no namae wa Rie desu.
c 家族は五人です。 Kazoku wa go nin desu.
d 息子は六才です。 Musuko wa roku sai desu.
e 娘は十才です。 Musume wa jussai desu.

3 Look at the sentences in the previous exercise again. How you would say the following in Japanese?

a There are six people in my family.
b My daughter is five years old.
c My son is a journalist.
d I am a housewife. (主婦 **shufu**)

1.1 BASIC JAPANESE SENTENCE STRUCTURE

Each of the key sentences used the basic structure 'noun は **wa** noun です **desu**'.

What are nouns? A noun is the word for a person, place, item, idea or emotion. Proper nouns are names and are spelled (in English) with a capital letter (Peter, Tokyo, Mitsubishi). If you can put *the* or *a* in front of the word, then it is a noun.

Grammar markers (also called grammar particles) will be discussed in more detail in later units. They are placed after words and serve to tell you the function of a word in the sentence. So は **wa** tells you that the word it is placed after is the main topic of the sentence.

Here are two examples:

私は営業部長です。 **Watashi wa eigyō buchō desu.** *I am a sales manager.*

息子は六才です。 **Musuko wa roku sai desu.** *My son is six years old.*

This is one of the most basic Japanese structures. The person (or item, place or idea) that is being talked about is followed by the grammar marker は **wa** (this has no meaning in itself). More information is then given about this noun (*sales manager, six years old*), and the sentence ends with です **desu** (*is, am, are*). It ends with ではありません **dewa arimasen** if you want to say *is not/am not/are not*. How is the sentence order different from that of English? (Did you work out that the word for *is* (or *is not*) is spoken at the end of the sentence?)

YOUR TURN Now see if you can say (and write down) these simple sentences in Japanese (look back at the key sentences if you need help).

a I am a journalist.

b My daughter is a company sales manager.

c I am not ten years old.

1.2 WORDS FOR FAMILY MEMBERS (IN-GROUP AND OUT-GROUP)

There are two sets of words for family – my family and other families. Here are some family terms with some gaps. Can you see the pattern and fill in the gaps?

Clue: you are looking for two patterns – one adds to the end of certain words and the other to the start of words:

English	My family	Other family
father	父 chi chi	お父さん otōsan
mother	母 haha	お母さん okāsan
son	息子 musuko	息子さん musukosan
daughter	娘 musume	a 娘_____ b musume _____
husband	主人 shujin	ご主人 goshujin
wife	妻・家内 tsuma/kanai	奥さん okusan
brothers and sisters	兄弟 kyōdai	御兄弟 c _____kyōdai
family	家族 kazoku	御家族 d _____kazoku

So how did you get on? Did you notice that you simply attach さん **san** after some words or the respectful ご **go** at the beginning of other words to make the 'other family' term? Now read out loud these words and refer back to this box when you need to look up family terms.

YOUR TURN In conversation with a Japanese friend, how would you refer to the following?

a her son
b her husband
c your own mother

1.3 FORMAL AND INFORMAL INTRODUCTIONS

Looking back at the conversation, Robert and Mr Hondo used a formal way of introducing themselves.

Here are some phrases showing formal and 'polite but less formal' (neutral polite) ways of introducing yourself and others.

Meaning	Formal	Neutral polite
I am called (name).	(name) と申します (name) **to mōshimasu**	(name) です (name) **desu**
Pleased to meet you. (encompassing the idea of working together and being indebted/tied to each other.)	どうぞよろしくおねがいします **Dōzo yoroshiku onegaishimasu**	どうぞよろしく **Dōzo yoroshiku**
To introduce someone else:	**(out-group)**	**family (in-group)**
this person	こちら **kochira**	こっち **kocchi**
This (person) is Mr Hondo.	こちらは本堂さんです **Kochira wa Hondō-san desu**	
This is my wife. *My wife* (simpler version)		こっちは家内です **Kocchi wa kanai desu** 家内です **Kanai desu**
(This is) my child.		この子 **Kono ko**

YOUR TURN Using the table, how would you say the following in Japanese?

a This is my family.
b This is my father.
c This person is Mrs Suzuki the teacher.

> **LANGUAGE TIP**
> Japanese people say their surname before their first name but they are familiar with the Western order of first name first so you can keep to this but may need to point out which is your surname for clarification.

1.4 GREETINGS AND FAREWELLS

 01.05 In Japanese, there are specific greeting words for different parts of the day and not one general word to cover the meaning *hello*. Listen to the audio and say these new words out loud.

English	Japanese (formal)	Japanese (informal)
good morning	おはようございます **ohayō gozaimas(u)**	おはよう **ohayō**
good afternoon	今日は **konnichiwa**	
good evening	今晩は **konbanwa**	
goodnight	おやすみなさい **oyasumi nasai**	おやすみ **oyasumi**
goodbye	さようなら **sayōnara**	バイバイ・じゃまたね **bai bai/ja mata ne** (*see you*)
when leaving the office	お先に失礼します **osaki ni shitsurei shimasu**	お先に **osaki ni**

YOUR TURN Answer the following questions.
a How do you make the informal versions of *good morning* and *goodnight*?
b Say out loud the informal word バイバイ **bai bai**? Where do you think it might originate?

1.5 SAYING *IT IS* AND *IT IS NOT* (AFFIRMATIVE AND NEGATIVE)

Look at the following table.

am, is, are	am not, is not, are not (formal)	am not, is not, are not (informal and more informal)
です	ではありません	じゃありません （じゃないです）
desu	**dewa arimasen**	**ja arimasen (ja nai desu)**

Have you noticed anything about the use of the word です desu? How is it used compared to the English verb *to be*?

Often you don't need to say *I, you, it, she, he* or *they* (there is more about this in Unit 2). Here are some examples:

ロバートさんはジャーナリストです。
Robāto-san wa jānarisuto desu.
Robert is a journalist.

| です。 | **Shujin desu.** | (He) is my husband. |
| ではありません。 | **Sensei dewa arimasen.** | (She/he) is not a teacher. |

YOUR TURN What do these sentences mean?
a 家族は五人です。 Kazoku wa gonin desu.
b こちらは鈴木先生ではありません。 Kochira wa Suzuki-sensei dewa arimasen.
c 家内じゃありません。 Kanai ja arimasen.

1.6 COUNTING FROM ONE TO TEN (WITH ACTIONS!)

 01.06 It's easy to count from one to ten, especially if you do the actions to help you remember.

1	いち 一	**ichi**	(scratch your shoulder – you have an itch!)
2	に 二	**ni**	(now scratch your knee – itchy knee!)
3	さん 三	**san**	(make a circle with your arms – the sun (pronounce it *san* though!)
4	し 四	**shi**	(point to a girl – she)
5	ご 五	**go**	(do a jogging motion – off you go!)
6	ろく 六	**roku**	(play your air guitar – you're in a rock band)
7	なな 七	**nana**	(pretend to knit like your grandma or nana)
8	はち 八	**hachi**	(lift up the hatchback of your car)
9	きゅう 九	**kyū**	(stand up straight in a queue)
10	じゅう 十	**jū**	(wave your fingers like dew falling on the grass!)

Go through the actions with the numbers backwards, forwards and out of order until you feel confident using them. Then listen to the audio (or read the numbers with the Pronunciation guide in mind) and concentrate on the correct pronunciation. You will find that sometimes the endings of one and six are cut short.

These numbers can be used with counters, that is, words that specify exactly what the number refers to. You have learned two in this unit:

> **LANGUAGE TIP**
> This matching of Japanese numbers to English words is only approximate and may lead to mispronunciation so listen carefully to the correct pronunciation.

Counter	Example	English
にん 人 **nin** (person)	ごにん 五人 **go nin**	*five people*
さい 才 **sai** (years old)	ごさい 五才 **go sai**	*five years old*

Sometimes the number changes or 'squashes' depending on the counter that follows it. For example:

じゅっさい
十才 **jussai**　　*ten years old*　　　　　はっさい
八才 **hassai**　　*eight years old*

よにん
四人 **yonin***　　*four people*

You'll learn more about this in later units.

*****Yo** (**yon**) is another way of saying *four*.

YOUR TURN Using the numbers and counters you have just learned, how would you say the following in Japanese?

a six years old

b seven people

c My son is four years old.

Listening and speaking

 01.07 Naoe Hondo is describing her family to a neighbour.

1 Listen to Naoe and answer these questions.

  a How many people are in her family?

  b How old is Yuki? (Clue: you will hear two numbers – add them together.)

  c How old is Eri?

  d What is Naoe's occupation?

2 Here is Naoe's speech written down. Using this as a guide, introduce your own family.

私 の家族 **Watashi no kazoku** *My family*

家族は四人です。主人の本堂たつやと 娘 のゆきとえりです。ゆきは十六才 です。
そしてえりは十 才です。主人は営 業部 長です。私 は主婦です。よろしくおねが
いします。

**Kazoku wa yonin desu. Shujin no Hondō Tatsuya to musume no Yuki to Eri desu.
Yuki wa jū roku sai desu. Soshite Eri wa jussai desu. Shujin wa eigyō buchō desu.
Watashi wa shufu desu. Yoroshiku onegaishimasu.**

Here are some extra words you may need.

| と | **to** | *and* |
| そして | **soshite** | *and/also* |

3 This time you are going to introduce Naoe Hondo's family.

Remember, you are not part of her in-group so you need to use the other family terms.
And don't forget さん **san** and ちゃん **chan** for other people too. Speak out loud.

Writing

Now write down the introduction you came up with for the previous task in **hiragana** unless
you are still learning this, in which case use **rōmaji** but convert it into **hiragana** when you
are able to.

 Speaking

1 How well do you remember the greetings? Look at each picture and say the greeting out loud.

Good morning   Hello (Good afternoon)   Excuse me

See you!   Goodbye   Good evening   Goodnight

 2 01.08 You meet a Mrs Suzuki Naomi at a business conference. Can you say your side of the conversation out loud?

Use the English prompts to help you. You might find it useful to listen once more to the conversation at the start of the unit before you try this to refresh your memory:

Suzuki-san	はじめまして、鈴木^{すずき}なおみです。どうぞよろしく。
You	**a** Introduce yourself.
Suzuki-san	私^{わたし}の名刺^{めいし}です。どうぞ。
You	**b** Say thank you and hand over your business card.
Suzuki-san	ありがとうございます。
You	**c** Confirm that Mrs Suzuki is a company sales manager.
Optional extra	**d** Comment that she must be busy.
Suzuki-san	Hajimemashite, Suzuki Naomi desu. Dōzo yoroshiku.
You	**a** Introduce yourself.
Suzuki-san	Watashi no meishi desu. Dōzo.
You	**b** Say thank you and hand over your business card.
Suzuki-san	Arigatō gozaimasu.
You	**c** Confirm that Mrs Suzuki is a company sales manager.
Optional extra	**d** Comment that she must be busy.

 ## Reading 1

Read this description of a family and then answer the questions.

Some of the more familiar **kanji** don't have **furigana** above them to encourage you to improve your recognition of **kanji**. You can always check the **rōmaji** version below the questions if you need to.

はじめまして、鈴木なおみと申します。家族は五人です。主人の鈴木けんいちと娘 二人と息子一人です。娘は十才と十二才です。そして息子は八才です。私は営業部長です。よろしくおねがいします。

- **a** What is the name of the person giving the account and what do they do?
- **b** Who is Suzuki Kenichi?
- **c** How many children are there?
- **d** How old are the daughters?
- **e** Who is eight years old?

Rōmaji version: **Hajimemashite, Suzuki Naomi to mōshimasu. Kazoku wa go nin desu. Shujin no Suzuki Kenichi to musume futari to musuko hitori desu. Musume wa jussai to jūni sai desu. Soshite musuko wa hassai desu. Watashi wa eigyō buchō desu. Yoroshiku onegaishimasu.**

Introduction to reading Japanese

The final section of each unit in this book will be devoted to learning how to read Japanese. In the initial stages you may decide that you want to focus on spoken Japanese only. If so, simply leave out this section and move on to the next unit – all the reading sections are independent of the rest of the book. However, the Japanese system of reading is both fascinating and challenging as well as offering an important insight into Japanese culture and the Japanese psyche. So whether you decide to work through the reading sections now or later, give them a try because they will open up a whole new aspect of Japanese language to you.

Described as 'the Devil's tongue' by 16th-century European missionaries, the Japanese reading system has been berated by some as being overcomplicated and cumbersome to learn. Three scripts and the need to learn 2000 Chinese characters to read a newspaper may seem daunting but here are some interesting considerations:

- ► Japan has one of the highest literacy rates in the world.
- ► Japan has the highest readership of newspapers in the world.
- ► **Kanji** (Chinese characters) are very visual – good news for visual learners!
- ► Japanese people are avid readers – you see people reading everywhere in Japan, on trains, buses and in bookshops.
- ► If you visit Japan without being able to read Japanese, it is that much more difficult to be able to get around (there are signs in English, but not always).

A BRIEF HISTORY

Before the 6th century AD Japanese was a spoken language only and **kataribe** (*messengers*) travelled around to convey important information to people orally. The ancient Chinese had developed a writing system in the 14th century BC that spread to the Korean Peninsula and from there to Japan in the 4th and 5th centuries AD (there are also many Korean and Chinese influences on Japanese culture and religion). Both Korea and Japan adapted these **kanji** (*Chinese characters*) to fit their own language because the Chinese language is very different in structure and is not in the same family of languages. Also, over thousands of years, **kanji** in all these countries have been revised, changed, abbreviated and standardized.

AN INTRODUCTION TO THE DIFFERENT SCRIPTS

There are three scripts in Japanese (four, if you include **rōmaji** or romanized script – in other words, the Western alphabet). These three scripts are **kanji**, **hiragana** and **katakana**. Each has its own specific function and the three are used in combination in written texts. You will also find **rōmaji** used for some foreign words and acronyms, for example NATO. In this unit we will look at **kanji**.

漢字 KANJI *CHINESE CHARACTERS*

Kanji are ideographs that convey a specific meaning, word or idea. The simplest and earliest of these were pictographs. These were pictures drawn by the Chinese of the world around them, such as the sun, moon and trees, which were gradually standardized into the **kanji** used today. Here are three examples of this process.

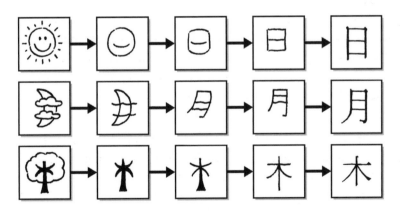

There are **kanji** to represent all aspects of language including concepts, feelings and ideas, and extensive **kanji** dictionaries can have as many as 40,000–50,000 **kanji**. However, in 1981 the Japanese Ministry for Education, **Monbukagakushō**, produced an approved list of 1945 **kanji** for daily use known as the **jōyō kanji**. These are the **kanji** needed to read texts such as newspapers thoroughly. The learning of these 1945 **kanji** is spread over the nine years of compulsory education.

In addition to the 1945 **jōyō kanji**, there are a further 284 more unusual **kanji** that are used in names and Japanese parents may look even beyond these additions to find auspicious **kanji** when naming their children (as parents in the West might consult a naming book to find more unusual names). The rules for writing **kanji** are very precise and the correct order for writing each **kanji** is learned and practised repeatedly at school.

書道 SHODŌ *WAY OF WRITING* OR *CALLIGRAPHY*

書道 **Shodō** was introduced to Japan with **kanji** and many styles have developed since. As in China, it is considered to be one of the fine arts in Japan and the mark of a cultured person.

Styles of calligraphy

In some styles of calligraphy, such as **kaisho**, the characters are easily recognizable but in others, such as **sōsho** (*'grass writing'*), the characters are often abbreviated or linked to each other in a rounded and flowing style. A post-war avant-garde development has produced styles that are totally abstract and bring calligraphy close to the principles of modern art.

Reading 2

You have already been introduced to a number of kanji words and meanings in this unit. Can you match the kanji with their English meanings?

a	日	1	moon
b	月	2	kanji
c	日本	3	tree
d	木	4	ten years old
e	漢字	5	sun
f	十才	6	Japan

 Test yourself

1 How would you do the following in Japanese?

    a Greet a friend in the morning.

    b Say *goodnight* to your teacher.

    c Say *this is my wife/husband/family.*

    d Introduce yourself formally to Mr Hondo.

    e Tell him you are a journalist.

    f Say *I am not a housewife.*

 2 01.09 How well do you remember the numbers? Follow the instructions then listen to the audio to check your answers.

    a Say the numbers from one to ten out loud as quickly as you can.

    b Now say them backwards from ten as quickly as you can.

    c Now say all the even numbers in order – two, four, six …

    d And now the odd numbers – one, three, five …

    e And, finally, teach someone else the numbers with the actions – it'll help you to remember them even better!

SELF CHECK

I CAN...
...make introductions.
...use greetings and farewells.
...say the words for family members.
...say *it is* and *it is not.*
...count from one to ten (with actions).

② りえさんは日本人です
Rie-san wa nihonjin desu
Rie is Japanese

In this unit you will learn how to:
▶ *say the words for countries and nationalities.*
▶ *describe yourself and family using the basic Japanese sentence pattern* **wa/desu.**
▶ *use the link word* **no** *to show ownership between two nouns.*
▶ *use two systems for saying* this, that, that over there.

CEFR: *(A1) Can ask and answer simple questions, initiate and respond to simple statements in areas of immediate need or on very familiar topics. (A2) Can describe people, places and possessions in simple terms.*

TOKYO COMPUTERS
社長 田中　健一
東京コンピューター会社 〒１０３−２０４４東京六本木区２−１９ Phone (03) 1234-5678 Fax　(03) 9876-5432

名刺 Meishi *Business cards*

名刺 **Meishi** (*business cards*) are very important in 日本 **Nihon** (*Japan*) and all 労働者 **rōdōsha** (*working people*) carry them. Their 目的 **mokuteki** (*purpose*) is not simply to provide 名前 **namae** (*name*), 職場 **shokuba** (*workplace*) and other contact details. More importantly, they indicate a person's 地位 **chii** (*status*) and therefore with what level of 尊敬 **sonkei** (*respect*) they should be addressed. Always treat a 名刺 **meishi** with 尊敬 **sonkei** – look at it with interest and then put it carefully away. Don't write on it, bend it or treat it casually – this may 怒らせる **okoraseru** (*cause offence*).

Look at the passage again and answer these questions.

1 What do the following words mean in English and how do you say them in Japanese?
   a 名刺   **b** 名前   **c** 労働者   **d** 職場   **e** 尊敬

2 In Unit 1, Robert handed his 名刺 meishi to Mr Hondo saying 私の名刺です Watashi no meishi desu (*It's my business card*). Using the vocabulary given, how would you say the following?
   a It's my workplace.
   b It's a Japanese business card ('card of Japan').
   c It's my name.

Vocabulary builder

アメリカ	Amerika	America
人	jin	person (nationality)
アメリカ人	Amerikajin	American (person)
フランス	Furansu	France
フランスの	Furansu no	French (items)
ワイン	wain	wine
銀行	ginkō	bank
社長	shachō	company director
これ	kore	this (one)
それ	sore	that (one)
あれ	are	that (one) over there
か	ka	spoken question mark
ではありません	dewa arimasen	is not, am not, are not
こちら	kochira	this (person)
ようこそ	yōkoso	welcome
しつれいします	shitsurei shimasu	excuse me for interrupting
こちらこそ	kochira koso	the pleasure is all mine
あの	ano	hey, erm (used to get attention)
新聞	shinbun	newspaper

Conversation 1

 02.02 *Robert's interview with Mr Hondo is part of his research on the work/home balance for Japanese fathers. As part of this research he meets Mr Hondo's family at home.*

1 How does Mr Hondo introduce his wife?

Hondō-san	ああロバートさん、今日<ruby>今日<rt>こんにち</rt></ruby>は。ようこそ！
Robert	<ruby>今日<rt>こんにち</rt></ruby>は。
Hondō-san	*(Gestures to Naoe)* <ruby>家内<rt>かない</rt></ruby>の<ruby>本堂<rt>ほんどう</rt></ruby>なおえです。
Naoe-san	はじめまして、なおえです。どうぞよろしく。
Robert	はじめまして。こちらこそ。どうぞよろしく。
Hondō-san	Ā, Robāto-san, konnichiwa! Yōkoso!
Robert	Konnichiwa.
Hondō-san	*(Gestures to Naoe)* Kanai no Naoe desu.
Naoe-san	Hajimemashite, Hondō Naoe desu. Dōzo yoroshiku.
Robert	Hajimemashite. Kochira koso. Dōzo yoroshiku.

2 In what order does Mr Hondo's wife say her name?

Conversation 2

 1 02.03 Who does Mr Hondo introduce next?

Hondō-san	この<ruby>子<rt>こ</rt></ruby>は<ruby>娘<rt>むすめ</rt></ruby>のゆきです。この子はえりです。
Yuki and Eri	どうぞよろしく。
Eri-chan	私は十<ruby>才<rt></rt></ruby>です。あの、<ruby>ロバート<rt>ろ ばー と</rt></ruby>さんはアメリカ<ruby>人<rt>じん</rt></ruby>ですか。
Robert	いいえ、イギリス<ruby>人<rt>じん</rt></ruby>です。*Japan Now* <ruby>新聞<rt>しんぶん</rt></ruby>の<ruby>ジャーナリスト<rt>じゃー な り すと</rt></ruby>です。
Hondō-san	Kono ko wa musume no Yuki desu. Kono ko wa Eri desu.
Yuki and Eri	Dōzo yoroshiku.
Eri-chan	Watashi wa jussai desu. Ano, Robāto-san wa Amerikajin desu ka.
Robert	Iie, Igirisujin desu. *Japan Now* shinbun no jānarisuto desu.

2 How old is Eri?

3 Which newspaper does Robert work for?

4 Look at the conversations again. What word does Mr Hondo use to welcome Robert to his house?

5 Look at these examples from the conversation and choose the English phrase that matches the underlined words.

    a <u>この子</u>はえりです。<u>Kono ko</u> wa Eri desu.   **1** This child   **2** That child

    b <u>家内の</u>なおえです。<u>Kanai no</u> Naoe desu.   **1** My wife's   **2** My wife called

Language discovery

KEY SENTENCES

1 02.04 **Read and listen to the key sentences a–e that follow. Repeat them out loud to practise pronunciation. Remember you can check the English meanings in the Answer key. Can you work out how the sentences fit together?**

a ロバートさんはアメリカ人ですか。 Robāto-san wa Amerikajin desu ka.

b いいえ、アメリカ人ではありません。 Iie, Amerikajin dewa arimasen.

c こちらは社長の高橋さんです。 Kochira wa shachō no Takahashi-san desu.

d これはフランスのワインです。 Kore wa Furansu no wain desu.

e あれは東京銀行ですか。 Are wa Tōkyō Ginkō desu ka.

2 Look at the sentences again. Can you work out how you would say the following?

a Is Robert French? (use 'French person')

b Is that over there Japanese wine?

c No, it is not Japanese wine.

2.1 THE PARTICLE (GRAMMAR MARKER) の

The particle の **no** is inserted between two nouns to show some type of ownership or belonging – the first noun 'owns' the second noun; the second noun belongs to the first. Look at these examples:

私のペン	**Watashi no pen**	*my pen* (I own the pen)
りえさんのワイン	**Rie-san no wain**	*Rie's wine* (Rie 'owns' the wine, it belongs to her)

の **no** can also connect a noun with its place of origin or place of work:

フランスのワイン	**Furansu no wain**	*French wine*
アメリカの会社	**Amerika no kaisha**	*American company*
東京銀行の高橋さん	**Tōkyō Ginkō no Takahashi-san**	*Mr Takahashi of the Tokyo Bank*

You can leave out the second noun where it is understood from the context:

私のです	**Watashi no desu**	*It's mine*

YOUR TURN 1 What do these phrases mean?

a りえさんのです Rie-san no desu

b フランスのです Furansu no desu

の **no** is also used when connecting a person's role with their name. For example:

社長の高橋さん	**shachō no Takahashi-san**	*Mr Takahashi, the company director*

YOUR TURN 2 What do these phrases mean?

a 娘のゆきちゃん musume no Yuki-chan

b 家内のりえ kanai no Rie

YOUR TURN 3 Say and write down these phrases.

a American bank

b My wine

c It's Japanese (It's of Japan)

2.2 COUNTRIES

 02.05 **In Japanese the names of many countries sound very close to their pronunciation in their native tongue. Here is a short list in katakana for you to listen to, read and say out loud. Can you work out which countries they are in English? Fill in the gaps in the rōmaji version to complete the table.**

a イングランド

b イタリア

c ニュージーランド

d スペイン

e ポルトガル

f メキシコ

g ブラジル

h ドイツ

i アルゼンチン

j オーストラリア

a Ingurando; _____		**f** _____ : _____	
b _____ : _____		**g** Burajiru; _____	
c Nyū Jīrando; _____		**h** _____ : _____	
d _____ : _____		**i** Aruzenchin; _____	
e Porutogaru; _____		**j** _____ : _____	

Now listen again to the audio and focus on the pronunciation of Portugal, Brazil and Argentina as they are significantly different to the way we say them in English:

Po-ru-to-ga-ru (*Portugal*)   **Bu-ra-ji-ru** (*Brazil*)   **A-ru-ze-n-chi-n** (*Argentina*)

> **LANGUAGE TIP**
> Not all country names in Japanese are derived from their native language; some have a Japanese name. These include: 韓国 **Kankoku** (*Korea*), 中国 **Chūgoku** (*China*) and, of course, 日本 **Nihon** (*Japan*). Some countries have an additional Japanese name as well as their native-tongue-derived name. These include: 米国 **Beikoku** (*America*), 英国 **Eikoku** (*England*). England is most commonly referred to as イギリス **Igirisu**.

2.3 NATIONALITIES

When you add the word 人 **jin** to the end of the word for a country, it indicates a person from that country.

 YOUR TURN 1 02.06 **Listen to the audio and tick off the nationalities as you hear them.**

English	American	Australian	German	Italian

YOUR TURN 2 Read this list of nationalities and work out what they are in English. Then listen to the audio and check your answers.

a アメリカ人

b イギリス人

c ドイツ人

d イタリア人

e オーストラリア人

2.4 LANGUAGES

The suffix 語 **go** at the end of the word for a country changes the meaning so that it refers to the language of that country. The word for *English* (language) is 英語 **Eigo**.

:**YOUR TURN** 02.07 **How do you say the languages of the following five countries in Japanese? Listen to the audio to check your answers.**

a France
b Korea
c China
d Spain
e Portugal

2.5 COUNTRY OF ORIGIN

If you want to talk about the country of origin of an item, you attach の **no** (see 2.1).

The main point being made in explanations 2.2–2.4 is that what is covered by one word in English has three possibilities in Japanese. It all depends on whether you are talking about a person, a language or an item's origin. So *Spanish* could be said in the following ways:

スペイン人	**Supeinjin**
スペイン語	**Supeingo**
スペインの	**Supein no**

By the way, if you want to say *Spanish teacher* you have a choice:

スペイン人の先生	**Supeinjin no sensei**	*a Spanish* (nationality) *teacher*
スペイン語の先生	**Supeingo no sensei**	*a Spanish-language teacher*

It depends on which you want to say but don't forget の **no** connects the two nouns.

2.6 SAYING *THIS*, *THAT* AND *THAT OVER THERE*

02.08 The following table gives you the terms you need to say *this*, *that*, *that one over there* and *which one*.

this (one)	that (one)	that one over there	which one?
これ **kore**	それ **sore**	あれ **are**	どれ **dore**
this	that	that over there	which?
この **kono**	その **sono**	あの **ano**	どの **dono**

Did you notice that as well as *this* and *that*, Japanese also has a word meaning *that over there*? You use this word when the object is near neither the speaker nor the person being spoken to. There are two sets of '*this and that*' words (one set ends in の **no** and the other in れ **re**) and here are examples of their different uses. Can you work out the rule?

これはフランスのワインです。	Kore wa Furansu no wain desu.	*This is French wine.*
このワインはフランスのです。	Kono wain wa Furansu no desu.	*This wine is French.*
それは日本の銀行です。	Sore wa Nihon no ginkō desu.	*That is a Japanese bank.*
あの銀行はフランスのです。	Ano ginkō wa Furansu no desu.	*That bank over there is a French (one).*

Have you worked out how the の **no** and れ **re** set are used differently?

You use れ **re** when you want to say *this one* or *that one* and there is no other word (noun) before は **wa** (technically speaking これ **kore**, それ **sore** and あれ **are** are pronouns taking the place of a noun). Think of them as meaning *this one, that one* and you won't go far wrong.

The の **no** set describes nouns and must be followed immediately by the item (noun) which is being described.

YOUR TURN How well have you understood the difference? Try saying these short sentences in Japanese (you'll need to use the particle **no** in these sentences too).

a   This business card is mine.
b   That one is Robert's.
c   That wine is Italian.
d   That one over there is Spanish.

 Speaking

You are going to play the part of an English to Japanese translator (at a very simple level, of course!). You have a list of English phrases with incomplete Japanese translations. Can you provide the correct missing information in Japanese?

Keep asking yourself if you need nationality, language or country of origin. When you have said the phrases out loud, try writing them down (in Japanese script if you can).

a	American whisky	＿＿＿＿ウイスキー	uisukī
b	a book in French	＿＿＿＿本	hon
c	a Japanese bank	＿＿＿＿銀行	ginkō
d	a newspaper in English	＿＿＿＿新聞	shinbun
e	my Chinese wife	＿＿＿＿家内	kanai
f	a Korean teacher	＿＿＿＿先生	sensei

▶ Writing

The table contains a list of countries. Fill in the columns for nationality and language.

For an extra challenge, complete in Japanese script without looking at the **rōmaji** side of the table.

くに 国	じん 人	ご 語	Country	Nationality	Language
ふらんす フランス			Furansu		
すぺいん スペイン			Supein		
かんこく 韓国			Kankoku		
ちゅうごく 中国			Chūgoku		
べいこく　あ め り か 米国（アメリカ）			Beikoku (Amerika)		

📖 Reading 1

Choose the correct Japanese word for *this* or *that* from the box to complete each of the following sentences.

You can use each word once only so tick it off once you have used it.

その	こっち	この	あの	あれ	こちら
sono	kocchi	kono	ano	are	kochira

a ＿＿＿＿＿＿ほん
　　　　　本は私のです。

　　＿＿＿＿＿＿ hon wa watashi no desu.

　　(*This book is mine.*)

b ＿＿＿＿＿＿せんせい　たかはし
　　　　　先生は高橋先生です。

　　＿＿＿＿＿＿ sensei wa Takahashi-sensei desu.

　　(*That teacher over there is Miss Takahashi.*)

c ＿＿＿＿＿＿うい すきー　　あ め り か
　　　　　ウイスキーはアメリカのではありません。

　　＿＿＿＿＿＿ uisukī wa Amerika no dewa arimasen.

　　(*That whisky is not American.*)

d ＿＿＿＿＿＿は息子のただしです。

　　＿＿＿＿＿＿ wa musuko no Tadashi desu.

　　(*This is my son, Tadashi.*)

e ＿＿＿＿＿＿すずき
　　　　　は鈴木先生です。

　　＿＿＿＿＿＿ wa Suzuki-sensei desu.

　　(*This is Professor Suzuki.*)

f ＿＿＿＿＿＿ちち　かいしゃ
　　　　　は父の会社です。

　　＿＿＿＿＿＿ wa chichi no kaisha desu.

　　(*That over there is my father's company.*)

Reading Japanese – **hiragana** and **katakana**

かな KANA

Hiragana and **katakana** are collectively known as かな **kana**. Both **hiragana** and **katakana** represent the same set of 46 basic sounds (plus other combined and modified sounds) but the symbols are written differently. This is not an alien idea to English speakers for we essentially have two alphabets, capital and lower case, which both represent the same letters. In Japanese, the two **kana** scripts exist for different purposes.

Both scripts are phonetic alphabets or syllabaries. This means that each symbol represents a sound (phoneme). This is different from the Western (Roman) alphabet system, in which each symbol is a letter and letters are grouped into sounds.

For example, in English, the word *goodbye* is made up of seven letters: G-O-O-D-B-Y-E.

In Japanese, *goodbye* is **sayōnara** and is made up of five syllables: SA-YO-U-NA-RA.

These are represented by five **hiragana** symbols: さようなら.

Kana was originally developed in the 9th century in order to be able to write the Japanese language phonetically. The first set of phonetic characters were called **man'yōgana** and these were **kanji** that were chosen because their pronunciation was the same as the sounds of the Japanese language. For example, the sound **ka** is represented by these **kana** symbols:

か (**hiragana**)   カ (**katakana**)

Both symbols were created originally from this **kanji**: 加 (pronounced **ka**).

All **man'yōgana** were gradually simplified into the **hiragana** and **katakana** systems used today. If you look carefully at the **ka** example, you can see that the **hiragana** symbol is a simplification of the whole **kanji** whereas the **katakana** symbol has been developed from part of the **kanji**.

ひらがな HIRAGANA

The word **hiragana** means *rounded* or *easy to use* and indicates both the shape and relative simplicity of the script. It was during the Heian period (794–1185) that **hiragana** developed to allow for a more pure expression of the Japanese language. Before this, written expression had been very limited in Japan, with the use of many Chinese words and phrases restricted mainly to official documents.

It was the Heian Court women who used the **kana** writing system to express themselves through poetry, prose and diaries and so the great creativity in Heian literature was achieved mainly by women. In fact, **hiragana** was also given the name **onnade** meaning *women's hands*. Two famous female authors from this time are Murasaki Shikibu, who wrote the world's first novel, *Tale of Genji*, and Sei Shonagon, who wrote *The Pillow Book*.

Today, **hiragana** symbols are used to write the grammatical parts of words and sentences and Japanese words that have no **kanji**. You will learn more about this in later units.

カタカナ KATAKANA

This word means *partial* because **katakana** symbols were developed from part of **kanji** characters as already shown.

Today, its main use is for writing non-Japanese words that have been introduced into the language. These fall into two main categories:

▶ **Gairaigo** (*loanwords*), for example コンピューター **kompyūtā** meaning *computer*.
▶ Foreign names such as countries, cities and personal names, for example アメリカ **Amerika** meaning *America*.

There are also three ways in which **katakana** is used for writing Japanese words:

▶ to make words stand out, for example in advertising: トヨタ (**Toyota**)
▶ to classify species of plants and animals, for example in botanical gardens
▶ to write onomatopoeic words.

In overall appearance, **katakana** symbols are more angular in shape while **hiragana** are more rounded. Here are the first five sounds of each script (**a**, **i**, **u**, **e**, **o**). Compare these two sets of symbols and see if you can identify these features:

Hiragana	あ い う え お
Katakana	ア イ ウ エ オ

> **LANGUAGE TIP**
> Japanese is traditionally written downwards (**tategaki**) and you begin reading from the top right of a page. This means that books are opened from what we would consider to be the back. Nowadays, however, books, newspapers and magazines are often written Western style, in horizontal lines (**yokogaki**) from left to right and, in these cases, the book is opened from our (Western) understanding of the front.

Reading 2

Here is a short piece of Japanese text. Some parts have been underlined and numbered 1, 2 or 3. Each of these numbers relates to **kanji**, **hiragana** or **katakana**. Can you work out which number relates to which script? Remember: **hiragana** is more rounded, **katakana** is more angular and **kanji** characters are more complex.

In Units 2–8, you will be gradually learning how to read **hiragana**. In Units 9–14, you will learn a total of 82 **kanji** and 52 compound words and finally, in Unit 15, you will be introduced to **katakana**.

1 **How would you say the following in Japanese?**

   a This is my book.

   b That is French wine.

   c That whisky over there is not Japanese.

   d My daughter, Yuki, is Japanese.

   e That (over there) is a Korean bank.

   f My English teacher is American.

2 **Finally, here are some statements taken from the first two units. You have to decide if they are true or false and, therefore, whether です desu (*it is/he is*) or ではありません dewa arimasen (*it is not/he is not*) should complete the end of each sentence.**

   a ロバートさんはイギリス人 _____   Robāto-san wa Igirisujin _____.

   b 本堂さんはジャーナリスト _____   Hondō-san wa jānarisuto _____.

   c ゆきちゃんは十才 _____   Yuki-chan wa jussai _____.

   d なおえさんは本堂さんの奥さん _____

      Naoe-san wa Hondō-san no okusan _____.

   e 本堂さんのご家族は五人 _____   Hondō-san no go-kazoku wa go nin _____.

   f なおえさんは主婦 _____   Naoe-san wa shufu _____.

   g 本堂さんは日本人 _____   Hondō-san wa Nihonjin _____.

SELF CHECK	
	I CAN...
○	...say the words for countries and nationalities.
○	...describe myself and family using the basic Japanese sentence pattern **wa/desu**.
○	...use the particle **no** to link nouns (for example, like *'s* in English).
○	...understand and use the two systems for saying *this, that, that over there*.

3 毎日テレビを見ます
<ruby>毎<rt>まい</rt></ruby><ruby>日<rt>にち</rt></ruby>テレビを<ruby>見<rt>み</rt></ruby>ます

Mainichi terebi o mimasu

I watch TV every day

In this unit you will learn how to:
▸ *talk about your daily routine.*
▸ *use verbs and particles in sentence structures.*
▸ *count from 11 to 99.*
▸ *tell the time ('o'clock').*
▸ *use time expressions.*

CEFR: *(A1) Can understand very short, simple texts a single phrase at a time, picking up familiar names, words and basic phrases and rereading as required. Can give simple descriptions or presentations as a short series of simple phrases and sentences linked into a list. Can handle numbers, quantities, cost and time.*

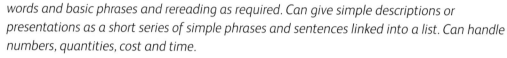 日本の食事 Nihon no shokuji *Japanese meals*
<ruby>日本<rt>にほん</rt></ruby>の<ruby>食事<rt>しょくじ</rt></ruby>

The three main 食事 **shokuji** (*meals*) of the day are 朝ごはん **asagohan** (*breakfast*), 昼ごはん **hirugohan** (*lunch*) and 晩ごはん **bangohan** (*dinner*). ごはん **gohan** (*Rice*) has always been the fundamental component of all traditional 日本の食事 **Nihon no shokuji** (*Japanese meals*), including 朝ごはん **asagohan**, to the extent that the word ごはん **gohan** also means 'meal'. There is such a range of 食べ物 **tabemono** (*food*) and 料理 **ryōri** (*dishes*) in 日本 **Nihon** (*Japan*) that it would be impossible to list them all within this book but 朝ごはん **asagohan** is a good place to start!

The picture shows the typical components of a 日本の朝ごはん **Nihon no asagohan** (*Japanese breakfast*): ごはん **gohan**, みそ汁 **miso shiru** (*bean-paste soup*), 漬物 **tsukemono** (*pickles*) and のり **nori** (*wafers of dry seaweed*). You can also have grilled 魚 **sakana** (*fish*), raw 卵 **tamago** (*egg*) to whisk into the rice, 納豆 **nattō** (*fermented bean curd* – an acquired taste!) and greens such as ほうれん草 **hōrensō** (*spinach*) and 山の幸 **yama no sachi** (*mountain vegetables*). お茶 **ocha** (*Green tea*) is normally served with breakfast.

 1 **What is the common word found in the names of all three meals and what two meanings does it have?**

2 **Asa** means *morning*, **hiru** means *midday* and **ban** means *evening*, so what do the names of the three meals literally mean?

Vocabulary builder

MEALS AND FOOD

朝ご飯	asagohan	*breakfast*
昼ご飯	hirugohan	*lunch*
晩ご飯	bangohan	*evening meal*

トースト	tōsuto	*toast*
卵	tamago	*egg*
レストラン	resutoran	*restaurant*

VERBS

行きます	ikimasu	*go*
起きます	okimasu	*get up*
食べます	tabemasu	*eat*
見ます	mimasu	*watch, look, see*
飲みます	nomimasu	*drink*
話します	hanashimasu	*speak, talk*
します	shimasu	*do, make, play (a sport or instrument)*

ADVERBS

いつも	itsumo	*always*
時々	tokidoki	*sometimes*
一緒に	issho ni	*together*

EXPRESSIONS OF TIME

朝	asa	*morning*
早く	hayaku	*early*
時	ji	*o'clock*
たいてい	taitei	*usually, generally*
たびたび	tabitabi	*many times, over and over again, frequently*
たまに	tama ni	*occasionally*

OTHER USEFUL WORDS AND PHRASES

と	to	*with, and*
ニュース	nyūsu	*news*
それから	sorekara	*and then*
近所の人（と）	kinjo no hito (to)	*neighbour (with)*
に	ni	*(1) at/for/on/in* *(2) to (a place)*
で	de	*at/in (after place)*

3 *Mainichi terebi o mimasu* **I watch TV every day**   29

Conversation

03.02 *Listen as Naoe Hondo describes her morning routine.*

1 Who does she eat breakfast with?

<table>
<tr><td>朝早く起きます。家族と朝ご飯を食べます。いつもテレビニュースを見ます。そして
コーヒーを飲みます。時々近所の人と話します。それから掃除をします。</td></tr>
<tr><td>Asa hayaku okimasu. Kazoku to asagohan o tabemasu. Itsumo terebi nyūsu o mimasu.
Soshite kōhī o nomimasu. Tokidoki kinjo no hito to hanashimasu. Sorekara sōji o shimasu.</td></tr>
</table>

2 Match the Japanese terms to the English.

a コーヒーを飲みます	Kōhī o nomimasu	**1**	sometimes
b 朝早く起きます	Asa hayaku okimasu	**2**	always
c 掃除をします	Sōji o shimasu	**3**	I watch the TV news
d テレビニュースを見ます	Terebi nyūsu o mimasu	**4**	I drink coffee
e いつも	itsumo	**5**	I get up early
f 時々	tokidoki	**6**	I do the cleaning

3 Read the conversation and answer the questions.

a What does Naoe always do as she has breakfast?

b What does she sometimes do in the morning?

c At what time does she get up?

4 Now listen to the conversation line by line and repeat. Try to copy the pronunciation.

 Language discovery

3.1 VERBS

The main objective of this unit is to learn about Japanese verbs, action or 'doing' words in front of which you can put *I, you, she, he, it* or *they*. Japanese verbs have a pattern that is easily recognizable. Look at these verbs that you have already encountered. Can you spot a pattern?

食べます	**tabemas(u)**	*eat*
飲みます	**nomimas(u)**	*drink*
見ます	**mimas(u)**	*watch, look, see*
します	**shimas(u)**	*do, make, play (a sport or instrument)*
話します	**hanashimas(u)**	*speak, talk*

The brackets indicate that the **u** is softly spoken. It doesn't matter who does the action – the ending ます **masu** is always the same.

 03.03 Now listen to the audio and repeat each of the verbs in the table. Notice the way that the final u is softly spoken.

3.2 SENTENCE STRUCTURE

You are going to work out for yourself how to say a full sentence in Japanese. First you need to practise saying four items that you will need to put into your sentences. These have been written with some gaps where you know the item already or it sounds like English.

 YOUR TURN 1 03.04 **Listen, repeat and work out the meanings.**

ご飯 **gohan**	a _____	掃除 **sōji**	*cleaning*
コーヒー **kōhī**	b _____	日本語 **Nihongo**	d _____
テレビ **terebi**	c _____		

Tip: the word **terebi** is a shortened version of the English and is in the title of this unit.

Now you are going to try and say some sentences using these words. Here is an example of a sentence in Japanese:

ご飯を食べます。   **Gohan o tabemasu.**   *I eat rice.*

YOUR TURN 2 03.05 **Following this pattern, can you work out how to say the following sentences?**

- **a** I drink coffee.
- **b** I watch TV.
- **c** I do the cleaning.
- **d** I speak Japanese.

When you have tried these for yourself, listen to and repeat the sentences on the audio.

> **LANGUAGE TIP**
>
> In Japanese, the verb always comes at the end of the sentence – *rice eat*. The を **o** between the item and the verb is called a particle or grammar marker. You will learn more about this later in this unit.

YOUR TURN Key sentences

You are going to build on your work in the previous section.

 1 03.06 **Here are some short sentences in English taken from the conversation. Can you say them in Japanese?**

- **a** I eat breakfast with my family.
- **b** Sometimes I watch the TV.
- **c** I always drink coffee.
- **d** I speak Japanese with my neighbour.
- **e** I do the cleaning in the morning.

Listen to the audio to check your answers and repeat out loud.

2 03.07 **Listen to these Japanese sentences and see if you can work out how the sentences fit together then check the English meanings in the Answer key.**

- **a** 六時に起きます。Rokuji ni okimasu.
- **b** 朝ごはんにトーストと卵を食べます。Asagohan ni tōsuto to tamago o tabemasu.
- **c** ごはんを食べません。Gohan o tabemasen.
- **d** 会社で昼ごはんを食べます。Kaisha de hirugohan o tabemasu.

3.3 MORE VERBS

So far you have learned seven verbs. Now you will learn another seven.

食べます tabemasu	eat		飲みます nomimasu	drink	
します shimasu	do, make, play		話します hanashimasu	talk, speak	
行きます ikimasu	go		見ます mimasu	watch, see, look	
起きます okimasu	get up		聞きます kikimasu	listen	
読みます yomimasu	read		買います kaimasu	buy	
書きます kakimasu	write, draw		働きます hatarakimasu	work	
寝ます nemasu	go to bed		作ります *tsukurimasu	make, build	

*Pronunciation tip: The sound **tsu** is a single syllable (beat) and the **u** is very soft. Your tongue should touch the top of your mouth and the sound almost 'whistles' through. It is very similar to the last sound in the word *cats*.

YOUR TURN Practise what you have learned by saying out loud these sentences in Japanese.

a I eat lunch.

b I sometimes read a newspaper.

c I always listen to the news.

d I draw a picture (*picture* = **e**).

e I make lunch.

f I go to bed early.

g I buy a TV.

h My mother does the cleaning in the morning.

3.4 THE TOPIC OF THE SENTENCE (PARTICLES 1)

母は朝掃除をします。

Haha wa asa sōji o shimasu.   *My mother does the cleaning in the morning.*

This was your final sentence of the previous exercise. You probably missed out the は **wa** after you said 母 **haha** because you hadn't had any practice or explanation of this yet in this unit, but you have met は **wa** in Units 1 and 2. Its function is to mark the topic or subject of the sentence.

In English, the order of the words in the sentence tells us what the subject is (the thing or person that carries out an action) and what the object is (has the action done to it). For example:

My mother drinks coffee.   (*mother* = subject; *coffee* = object)

I do the cleaning.   (*I* = subject; *cleaning* = object)

The sentence order tells us which is the subject and which is the object, with the standard pattern being **subject**, **verb**, **object** (**SVO**).

Here are two examples of Japanese sentence structure.

母はコーヒーを飲みます。   **Haha <u>wa</u> kōhī <u>o</u> nomimasu.**

私は掃除をします。   **Watashi <u>wa</u> sōji <u>o</u> shimasu.**

The order is **subject**, **object**, **verb** (**SOV**).

The grammar markers (particles) indicate subject and object – は **wa** for subject, を **o** for (direct) object.

3.5 SAYING *I*, *YOU*, *SHE*, *HE*, *IT*, *WE* AND *THEY*

These words don't need to be used in Japanese if it is obvious who the subject is or once the subject has been established. They do need to be used to clarify, introduce or emphasize who did what. The following table contains these words for you to learn.

I	私 **watashi** (ぼく **boku** is often used by men)	*he*	かれ **kare**
we	私たち **watashitachi**	*she*	かのじょ **kanojo**
you	あなた **anata** (あなたたち **anatatachi** – plural)	*they*	かれら **karera**

YOUR TURN Now use these words in the following sentences, remembering to say は **wa** after the subject and to put the verb at the end.

a She goes to bed early.

b They get up early.

c We always eat dinner together.

d He watches TV.

e Do you drink coffee?

3.6 に NI (PARTICLES 2)

This particle has different uses – here we will look at two.

1 Meaning と *to* with verbs of movement (for example *go, arrive, return*):

私はフランスに行きます。　(Watashi wa) Furansu ni ikimasu.　　*I go to France.*

2 To say *for* as in *for breakfast*:

朝ごはんにトーストを食べます。

Asagohan ni tōsuto o tabemasu.

I eat toast for breakfast.

> **LANGUAGE TIP**
> Most nouns in a sentence will need a particle, except nouns followed immediately by です **desu**.

YOUR TURN Where is に **ni** placed in the sentence?

In fact, all particles are placed <u>after</u> the word they mark.

3.7 SAYING *WITH, AND* (PARTICLES 3)

と **to** has two meanings – *with* and *and*. Here are two examples you have already come across:

家族と朝ごはんを食べます。

Kazoku <u>to</u> asagohan o tabemasu.　　*I eat breakfast <u>with</u> my family.*

朝ごはんにトーストと卵を食べます。

Asagohan ni tōsuto <u>to</u> tamago o tabemasu.　　*For breakfast I eat toast <u>and</u> egg.*

YOUR TURN Try saying these sentences out loud then check the answers in the Answer key. Remember to put と **to** (*with*) after the noun. と **to** (*and*) works the same as in English.

a In the mornings I always buy a newspaper and a coffee.

b I sometimes watch TV with my brothers and sisters.

c I always make dinner with my mother and my husband.

3.8 します SHIMASU – A USEFUL VERB

します **shimasu** means *do, make, play* depending on the context.

サッカーをします	**sakkā o shimasu**	*play football*
掃除をします	**sōji o shimasu**	*do the cleaning*
電話をします	**denwa o shimasu**	*make a phone call*

Here are ten verbs that use します **shimasu**. Can you work out the meanings where there are gaps?

Japanese		English
掃除をします	sōji (o) shimasu	a
電話をします	denwa (o) shimasu	b
ごろごろします	gorogoro shimasu	*chill out, relax*
勉強します	benkyō (o) shimasu	*study*
仕事をします	shigoto (o) shimasu	*work (do a job)*
サッカーをします	sakkā o shimasu	c
ゴルフをします	gorufu o shimasu	d
食事をします	shokuji (o) shimasu	e
旅行をします	ryokō shimasu	*travel, take a trip*
買い物をします	kaimono (o) shimasu	*shop*

を **o** is in brackets to show that it isn't always spoken or needed but look at the following:

フランスを旅行します。	**Furansu o ryokō shimasu.**	*I travel (in) France.*
日本語を勉強します。	**Nihongo o benkyō shimasu.**	*I study Japanese.*

In these two examples, を **o** is still used to mark the object, in these cases France and Japanese.

3.9 TELLING THE TIME

With 時 **ji** (*o'clock*) you need a particle just as we use in English when we say *at six o'clock*. This particle is に **ni**. Look at these examples:

六時<u>に</u>	**rokuji <u>ni</u>**	<u>*at* six o'clock</u>
日曜日<u>に</u>	**nichiyōbi <u>ni</u>**	<u>*on* Sunday</u>
二月<u>に</u>	**nigatsu <u>ni</u>**	<u>*in* February</u>

So now we have a third use of the particle に **ni** – *for* (for breakfast), *to* (with movement verbs) and *at*, *on* or *in* with precise time expressions.

YOUR TURN How would you say the following in Japanese?
a at one o'clock   **b** at five o'clock   **c** at ten o'clock

Times

 03.08 Listen to the times from one o'clock to 12 o'clock and repeat them out loud. Notice there are changes to three of the numbers:

four o'clock is **yoji** (do you remember that *four people* was **yonin**?)
seven o'clock is **shichiji** (**shichi** is the alternative to **nana** for *seven*)
nine o'clock is **kuji**

3.10 MORE TIME EXPRESSIONS

The following table has some general time expressions (they stand alone – no particle needed) to add to your growing collection. There is a pattern which will make them easier to remember. Can you work out the missing meanings?

	毎 mai ~ (every ~)	今 kon ~ (this ~)	来 rai ~ (next ~)
日 nichi (day)	毎日 mainichi (a _____)	今日 kyō (today)	明日 ashita (tomorrow)
週 shū (week)	毎週 maishū (b _____)	今週 konshū (e _____)	来週 raishū (h _____)
月 getsu/tsuki (month)	毎月 maitsuki (c _____)	今月 kongetsu (f _____)	来月 raigetsu (i _____)
年 nen/toshi (year)	毎年 mainen/maitoshi (d _____)	今年 kotoshi (g _____)	来年 rainen (j _____)

3.11 で DE (PARTICLES 4)

Uchi _de_ bangohan o tabemasu.   *I eat dinner <u>at</u> home.*

When you talk about the place in which an action takes place, you use the particle で **de** after the place word. It means *on* or *at* in English. Look at this example of how you would say *I eat lunch at the company every day*:

私は	毎日	会社で	昼ごはん　を	食べます
Watashi wa	**mainichi**	**kaisha de**	**hirugohan o**	**tabemasu**
I	*every day*	*at the company*	*lunch*	*eat*
Subject	time	place	object	verb

> **LANGUAGE TIP**
> There is some flexibility in Japanese sentence order as long as the subject (where used) is before the object and the verb is at the end. Time expressions generally are placed at or near the beginning of a sentence.

YOUR TURN You're going to say some sentences in Japanese using で **de**.

You need some more place words to do this. Here are two which originate from shortened versions of English words – can you work them out?

デパート　**depāto**　　(clue: different departments under one roof)

スーパー　**sūpā**　　(clue: a shop where you can do ALL your food shopping)

Now try these sentences:

a I drink coffee at the office (use 'company') every day.
b I occasionally buy a newspaper at the supermarket.
c My daughter does her shopping at the department store every week.
d Today I eat with my family at the restaurant.

3.12 HOW WELL DO YOU KNOW THE PARTICLES?

Here is a short summary of the particles you have met so far:

は **wa**	marks the subject of the sentence – the doer of the action:	母は晩ごはんを食べます。 **Haha wa bangohan o tabemasu.** *Mum eats dinner.*
を **o**	marks the object of the sentence – the action is done to this:	母は晩ごはんを食べます。 **Haha wa bangohan o tabemasu.** *Mum eats dinner.*
に **ni**	means *to* with movement verbs:	日本に行きます。 **Nihon ni ikimasu.** *I go to Japan.*
に **ni**	also means *for*:	朝ごはんに **asagohan ni** *for breakfast*
に **ni**	also means *on, in, at* when used with time expressions:	五時に **goji ni** *at five o'clock*
と **to**	means *and, with*:	母と父 **haha to chichi** *Mum and Dad* 母と晩ごはんを食べます。 **Haha to bangohan o tabemasu.** *I eat dinner with my mum.*
で **de**	marks the place where an action happens:	家で母と晩ごはんを食べます。 **Uchi de haha to bangohan o tabemasu.** *I eat dinner with Mum at home.*

3.13 NUMBERS 11 TO 99

You learned 11 and 12 when you learned to tell the time. Did you work out the pattern?

Here it is: 10 + 1 = 11 = 十一 **jū ichi**   10 + 2 = 12 = 十二 **jū ni**

So once you know one to ten you can count to 99 using combinations of these numbers.

YOUR TURN Now using the pattern can you work out and say the following numbers?

a 14

b 16

c 17

d 19

 03.09 **Here are the numbers from 11 to 19. Listen to them on the audio and repeat out loud.**

11	十一	jū ichi		16	十六	jū roku
12	十二	jū ni		17	十七	jū nana (jū shichi)
13	十三	jū san		18	十八	jū hachi
14	十四	jū shi		19	十九	jū kyū
15	十五	jū go				

How would you say 20? If you have a mathematical mind then this pattern may have occurred to you:

2 × 10 = 二十 **nijū**

You need to know that there are alternative numbers for 4 and 7 (you know this already from learning the time):

4 = **shi, yon (yo)**   7 = **shichi, nana**

For 40 and 70 say **yonjū** and **nanajū**.

> **LANGUAGE TIP**
> The word **shi** also means *death* in Japanese, which is why you will never find a room or floor numbered four in a hospital or hotel!

 03.10 **Before you listen to the audio, see if you can count in tens from 20 to 90, then listen and repeat out loud.**

To say 21, 22, 23, you add the single number like this: **nijū ichi**, **nijū ni**, **nijū san**, and so on.

Listening

 03.11 Katie Mears, an American English teacher in Tokyo, is describing her daily routine.

1 Can you pick out these words? What do they mean?

a	朝ごはん	asagohan
b	飲みます	nomimasu
c	近所の人	Kinjo no hito
d	買い物をします	kaimono o shimasu
e	レストラン	resutoran
f	スーパー	sūpā
g	たまに	tama ni
h	仕事をします	shigoto o shimasu

2 Listen again and this time see if you can work out the answers to these questions. There is a vocabulary list after the questions to help you:

- **a** What time does Katie: 1) get up? 2) go to work?
- **b** What does she drink at breakfast time?
- **c** What does she do with her neighbour?
- **d** What does she sometimes do in the afternoon?
- **e** What does she do after she has watched TV?

食べません	**tabemasen**	*don't eat*
が	**ga**	*but*
午後	**gogo**	*afternoon, p.m.*
帰ります	**kaerimasu**	*return, go back to*
それから	**sorekara**	*and then*
夜	**yoru**	*(in the) evening*
から	**kara**	*from*

Speaking

Now you are going to listen to Katie's daily routine again. Listen, pause and repeat as many times as you need to until you feel you are really speaking Japanese.

七時に起きます。朝ごはんは食べませんがいつもコーヒーを飲みます。朝たびたび近所の人とデパートで買い物をします。そしてレストランで食事をします。午後時々スーパーに行きます。そして家に帰ります。たまに家を掃除します。いつもテレビを見ます。それから晩ごはんを作ります。夜七時から仕事をします。

Shichiji ni okimasu. Asagohan wa tabemasen ga itsumo kōhī o nomimasu. Asa tabitabi kinjo no hito to depāto de kaimono o shimasu. Soshite resutoran de shokuji o shimasu. Gogo tokidoki sūpā ni ikimasu. Soshite uchi ni kaerimasu. Tama ni uchi o sōji shimasu. Itsumo terebi o mimasu. Sorekara bangohan o tsukurimasu. Yoru shichiji kara shigoto o shimasu.

Writing

1 Reorder the following Japanese words to make Japanese sentences that match the English meanings. You will need to supply the particles and think about the sentence order.

Example:

For breakfast I eat rice and miso soup.

miso shiru, asagohan, gohan, tabemasu

Asagohan ni gohan to miso shiru o tabemasu.

a For lunch I eat egg and toast. And I drink coffee.

トースト、コーヒー、卵、昼ごはん、飲みます、食べます、そして

tōsuto, kōhī, tamago, hirugohan, nomimasu, tabemasu, soshite

b I get up every day at six o'clock. Then I make breakfast.

朝ごはん、毎日、六時、起きます、作ります、それから

asagohan, mainichi, rokuji, okimasu, tsukurimasu, sorekara

c Tomorrow I will play golf with my neighbour.

ゴルフ、近所の人、明日、します

gorufu, kinjo no hito, ashita, shimasu

d In the afternoons I usually read the newspaper. Sometimes I watch the news.

新聞、午後、たいてい、時々、ニュース、読みます、見ます

shinbun, gogo, taitei, tokidoki, nyūsu, yomimasu, mimasu

e I always return home. Occasionally I eat dinner with my family.

いつも、たまに、家、家族、十時、晩ごはん、帰ります、食べます

itsumo, tama ni, uchi, kazoku, jū ji, bangohan, kaerimasu, tabemasu

2 Using the sentences in the previous exercise as a guide, write a diary entry about your own daily routine.

3 Can you write in the correct particles to complete the sentences? To quickly find words you can't remember, use the vocabulary lists at the end of the course.

a スーパー ＿＿＿＿ 卵 ＿＿＿＿ コーヒー ＿＿＿＿ 買います

Sūpā ＿＿＿＿ tamago ＿＿＿＿ kōhī ＿＿＿＿ kaimasu.

b うち ＿＿＿＿ 主人 ＿＿＿＿ ニュース ＿＿＿＿ 聞きます

Uchi ＿＿＿＿ shujin ＿＿＿＿ nyūsu ＿＿＿＿ kikimasu.

c 六時 ＿＿＿＿ 近所の人 ＿＿＿＿ デパート ＿＿＿＿ 行きます

Rokuji ＿＿＿＿ kinjo no hito ＿＿＿＿ depāto ＿＿＿＿ ikimasu.

d 今日一緒 ＿＿＿＿ レストラン ＿＿＿＿ 食事 ＿＿＿＿ 食べます

Kyō issho ＿＿＿＿ resutoran ＿＿＿＿ shokuji ＿＿＿＿ tabemasu.

e 毎日会社 ＿＿＿＿ 昼ごはん ＿＿＿＿ 作ります

Mainichi kaisha ＿＿＿＿ hirugohan ＿＿＿＿ tsukurimasu.

The first 15 **hiragana**

In this unit, you will learn the first 15 **hiragana**. **Hiragana** is the phonetic script that Japanese children learn first. They then gradually learn **kanji** and, as they do so, replace **hiragana** words or parts of words with these **kanji**. In a similar way, you will first develop your skills in reading **hiragana** before adding some useful everyday **kanji**.

START READING

 03.12 You learned about the phonetic sounds of Japanese in the pronunciation guide at the beginning of this book. Now listen to the first 15 sounds (a–so), and say each sound out loud as you read the table of the 15 hiragana symbols (their pronunciation appears underneath).

あ	い	う	え	お
a	i	u	e	o
か	き	く	け	こ
ka	ki	ku	ke	ko
さ	し	す	せ	そ
sa	shi	su	se	so

HOW TO REMEMBER HIRAGANA SYMBOLS

It really helps if you can create mnemonics to remember each symbol. Mnemonics are sound and picture associations that help you to link the visual symbol with its sound. Here are a few ideas to get you started. Focus on the sounds rather than the letters or spellings.

あ (**a**) is for *apple*

い (**i**) is *igloo*

う (**u**) *ooh!* my back hurts

え (**e**) is *escalator*

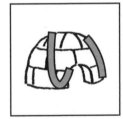
お (**o**) is for *ostrich*

き (**ki**) looks like a <u>key</u>

OTHER IDEAS TO HELP YOU REMEMBER

Make flashcards of each **hiragana** symbol on paper or card. Write the pronunciation on the back then keep testing yourself to see how well you can remember them. Look at the cards every day or on a regular basis to build up your reading skills and recognition of each symbol.

On a large sheet of white paper draw a grid of squares with five squares down and ten squares across. Begin to fill in the table with the first 15 **hiragana**, starting at the top right square and working down the columns from right to left (Japanese order). Fill in the table each time you learn a new set of symbols until you have the complete set. Put the poster up on a wall where you can look at it and practise or test yourself.

SIMILAR-LOOKING HIRAGANA

The following **hiragana** symbols look quite similar and you may find this confusing at times. Here are some clues to help you tell them apart:

あ, お   the loop in あ (**a**) curls around the vertical line whereas the smaller loop in お (**o**) is a continuation of the vertical line

お (**o**) has an extra 'dash' line above the loop

い, こ   い (**i**) is more or less vertical, こ (**ko**) is horizontal

き, さ   き (**ki**) has two horizontal lines whereas さ (**sa**) has only one

Also note that you may come across this alternative way of writing **ki**, **sa** and **so** especially when handwritten: き   さ   そ

 # Reading

Look at the following two columns of hiragana words. The same words are in both columns but in a different order. Can you correctly pair up these words?

a すし	1 えき
b あい	2 あき
c あかい	3 けさ
d あき	4 こえ
e けさ	5 うえ
f えき	6 すし
g こえ	7 すき
h あおい	8 あい
i すき	9 あかい
j うえ	10 あおい

Test yourself

1 Match these verbs with their English meanings.

a 食べます tabemasu

b 起きます okimasu

c 作ります tsukurimasu

d 飲みます nomimasu

e 買い物をします kaimono o shimasu

f 行きます ikimasu

g 見ます mimasu

1 go

2 drink

3 eat

4 see, watch

5 make

6 wake up, get up

7 do the shopping

2 Which particle is being described in each of the statements that follow?

a marks the subject of the sentence

b means *on, in, at* when used with time expressions

c means *and, with*

d means *to* with movement verbs

e marks the place where an action happens

SELF CHECK

	I CAN...
○	...talk about my daily routine.
○	...understand the main points of someone's daily routine.
○	...understand sentence order and the purpose of particles.
○	...use a selection of verbs in my sentences.*
○	...use and understand time expressions and tell the time.
○	...count from 11 to 99.
○	...use the first 15 **hiragana** symbols.

*There is a verb table at the back of this book which includes all the verbs you will encounter in this course. You may find it helpful to refer to this as you work your way through this book.

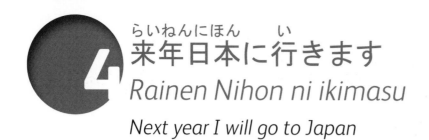

来年日本に行きます
らいねんにほん　　　い
Rainen Nihon ni ikimasu
Next year I will go to Japan

In this unit you will learn how to:
▶ *say* shall we *and* let's.
▶ *say the months of the year.*
▶ *use the future tense.*
▶ *use the negative –* I don't.
▶ *form sentences with verbs of motion.*

CEFR: *(A2) Can use a series of phrases and sentences to describe family, other people, and daily routines. Can make and respond to suggestions. Can use the most frequently occurring connectors to link simple sentences in order to tell a story or describe something as a simple list of points.*

和食 **Washoku** *Japanese cuisine*

寿司 SUSHI

寿司 **Sushi** means *vinegared rice* and is not, as is often thought, raw fish. Sushi rice is made by seasoning cooked ごはん **gohan** (*rice*) with 米酢 **komezu** (*rice vinegar*), 砂糖 **satō** (*sugar*) and 塩 **shio** (*salt*). お茶 **Ocha** (*green tea*) is normally provided with the 寿司 **sushi** but ビール **bīru** (*beer*) or 酒 **sake** (*rice wine*) make good accompaniments too. You dip your sushi into 醤油 **shōyu** (*soy sauce*) mixed with わさび **wasabi** (*hot green mustard*). 握り寿司 **Nigirizushi** (**nigiri** means *squeezed*) is the classic 寿司 **sushi** consisting of rolled ovals of sushi rice with toppings such as raw fish, seafood and omelette-style egg, and a dab of わさび **wasabi** in between. 巻き寿司 **Makizushi** (**maki** means *rolled*) is made by spreading sushi rice on squares of のり **nori** (*dried seaweed*), placing the toppings on top, rolling it all up and cutting it into segments.

刺身 SASHIMI

刺身 **Sashimi** is raw, very fresh, sliced 魚 **sakana** (*fish*). The skill is in the cutting of the 魚 **sakana** and the presentation of the dish with garnishes such as shredded 大根 **daikon** (*Japanese radish*), しそ **shiso** (*Japanese basil*) and わさび **wasabi**. The delight of eating 刺身 **sashimi** is in its texture. It almost melts in the mouth like smoked salmon and does not have the slimy texture or strong smell that many Westerners associate with uncooked fish.

焼き鳥 YAKITORI

焼き鳥 **Yakitori** means *grilled bird* and traditionally was 鶏肉 **toriniku** (*chicken*), dipped in either a sweet-sour soy sauce or in 塩 **shio** (*salt*) and grilled on bamboo skewers over charcoal. Nowadays, grilled pieces of vegetable, beef and pork are also grilled **yakitori**-style.

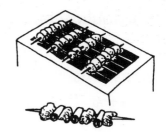

フグ FUGU

Fugu is the highly prized (and highly priced) blowfish which has highly poisonous parts including the liver. Incorrect preparation of the fish has led to a number of deaths and nowadays only specially licensed chefs are allowed to serve it.

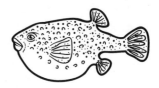

 1 **Look back at the passage and see if you can say these sentences in Japanese using the new vocabulary.**

    a I sometimes eat at a Japanese restaurant.

    b I frequently eat sushi. And I drink green tea. Sometimes I eat raw fish.

    c Japanese people frequently eat fish but they occasionally eat blowfish.

    d Tomorrow I will eat grilled chicken and soy sauce with my family. And I will drink rice wine.

2 **Can you give the English meanings for the Japanese phrases in this passage?**

Eating out in Japan?

Many Japanese restaurants display the food they serve in the form of plastic models in the window. If you are unsure of the name of a dish, take the waiter outside, point to the item and say **a**) あれをください **Are o kudasai**.

When you enter a restaurant, you are greeted with the word **b**) いらっしゃいませ **Irasshaimase**.

To show your appreciation of the meal, say **c**) ごちそうさまでした **gochisōsama deshita** as you leave the **d**) レストラン **resutoran**.

Vocabulary builder

 04.01 Listen to the new vocabulary and practise saying it out loud.

VERB FORMS

食べません	tabemasen	*don't eat*
食べましょう	tabemashō	*let's eat*
行きましょうか	ikimashō ka	*shall we go?*

PLACES AND TRANSPORT

家	uchi	*home*
事務所	jimusho	*office*
コレッジ	korejji	*college*
デパート	depāto	*department store*
スーパー	sūpā	*supermarket*
電車	densha	*train*
電車で	densha de	*by train*

TIME AND OTHER EXPRESSIONS

着きます	tsukimasu	*arrive*
遅く	osoku	*late*
遅くまで	osoku made	*until late*
ごろ	goro	*about* (used with times)
何	nani (nan)	*what*

Conversation

 04.02 *Robert is interviewing Mr Hondo about his daily routine as part of his article on work/home balance.*

1 Generally at what times does he start work and get home?

本堂さん　毎日六時に起きます。朝ごはんにたいていトーストを食べます。そしてコーヒーを飲みます。電車で事務所に行きます。いつも八時に着きます。遅くまで働きます。そして度々事務所の人とレストランで晩御飯を食べます。

ロバートさん　何時に帰りますか。

本堂さん　十時、十一時ごろです。妻とテレビを見ます。そして寝ます。

ロバートさん　日曜日に何をしますか。

本堂さん　時々事務所の人とゴルフをしますがたいてい家族と家でごろごろします。

Mr Hondo　Mainichi rokuji ni okimasu. Asagohan ni taitei tōsuto o tabemasu. Soshite kōhī o nomimasu. Densha de jimusho ni ikimasu. Itsumo hachiji ni tsukimasu. Osoku made hatarakimasu. Soshite tabitabi jimusho no hito to resutoran de bangohan o tabemasu.

Robert　Nan ji ni kaerimasu ka.

Mr Hondo　Jūji, jūichiji goro desu. Tsuma to terebi o mimasu. Soshite nemasu.

Robert　Nichiyōbi ni nani o shimasu ka.

Mr Hondo　Tokidoki jimusho no hito to gorufu o shimasu ga taitei kazoku to uchi de gorogoro shimasu.

2 What time does he get up?

3 What does he frequently do after work?

 4 Look at the conversation again and match these Japanese phrases with the English meanings.

a 遅くまで働きます。	Osoku made hatarakimasu.	**1** I go to the office by train.
b 妻とテレビを見ます。	Tsuma to terebi o mimasu.	**2** I chill out at home.
c 電車で事務所に行きます。	Densha de jimusho ni ikimasu.	**3** I watch TV with my wife.
d 家でごろごろします。	Uchi de gorogoro shimasu.	**4** I work until late.

5 What two items does Mr Hondo have for breakfast (in Japanese and English)?

6 What is his routine on a Sunday (describe in English)?

7 Now listen to the conversation line by line and repeat. Try to copy the pronunciation.

8 Looking at the vocabulary list, can you work out how to say *Let's do something* in Japanese? What do each of the following phrases mean in English?

a 食べましょう   tabemashō

b 飲みましょう   nomimashō

c テレビを見ましょう。   Terebi o mimashō.

d 日本語を話しましょう。   Nihongo o hanashimashō.

e 掃除をしましょう。   Sōji o shimashō.

9 How do you change the end of a verb so that its meaning changes from *let's* to the question *shall we*? Can you convert the verbs in the table into *let's* and *shall we* forms?

Verb (ます)	Verb (masu)	Let's	Shall we
食べます	tabemas(u)		
飲みます	nomimas(u)		
見ます	mimas(u)		
します	shimas(u)		

KEY SENTENCES

1 04.03 Here are some sentences that demonstrate the key grammar points you will learn in this unit. You can check the English meanings in the answer key. Can you work out how the sentences fit together? What words appear repeatedly? How are they used?

a あのレストランで晩御飯を食べましょう。

Ano resutoran de bangohan o tabemashō!

b 明日フランスに行きます。

Ashita Furansu ni ikimasu.

c 一緒にレストランに行きましょうか。

Issho ni resutoran ni ikimashō ka.

YOUR TURN 2 Now look at the key sentences again and see if you can work out how you would say the following (the changes you need to make are underlined).

a Let's eat <u>lunch</u> at <u>this</u> restaurant.

b <u>On Sunday</u> I will go to <u>America</u>.

c Shall we <u>eat</u> together <u>at home</u>?

 Language discovery

4.1 GOING, COMING AND RETURNING – VERBS OF MOTION

Verbs that describe movement don't have a direct object – instead you talk about the places you *go to*, *return from* or *come to*. In English, the word *to* or *from* is usually required to convey the movement; in Japanese, we use に **ni** or へ **e** for *to* and から **kara** for *from*.

The three verbs you are going to use are: 行きます **ikimasu** (*go*); 帰ります **kaerimasu** (*return*) and 来ます **kimasu** (*come*).

For example:

明日日本に行きます。 **Ashita Nihon ni ikimasu.** *Tomorrow I will go to Japan.*

> **LANGUAGE TIP**
> When you go to your home, home town or the country you come from, you should use 帰ります **kaerimasu** (*return*) and not 行きます **ikimasu** (this has the meaning more of *go out/go away from home*).

YOUR TURN How would you say these sentences in Japanese? (Say them out loud if you can.)
a I will go to the office tomorrow.
b I will go to the supermarket with my son.
c I sometimes go (return) home early.
d My father will come to college in the morning.
e I will return to Japan tomorrow.

4.2 SAYING *I DON'T*

Saying *I don't* (*she/he doesn't* and so on) is easy – change ます **masu** to ません **masen**:
ご飯を食べません。 **Gohan o tabemasen.** *I don't eat rice.*

Often in negative sentences the particle を **o** is changed to は **wa** to emphasize the thing that is not done, especially if there is no other は **wa** in the sentence:
コーヒーは飲みません。
Kōhī wa nomimasen.
I don't drink coffee. (but there are lots of things I do drink)

YOUR TURN Try these sentences:
a I don't play golf.
b My wife doesn't clean the house.
c He doesn't work.

4.3 MONTHS OF THE YEAR

The months are easy to say and remember in Japanese because rather than having names such as *January* and *February* they are numbered from 1 to 12 so they literally mean *one month, two month, three month*, using the word 月 **gatsu** for *month*.

1 Here is a table with some months filled in. Can you work out what would go in the gaps?

Script	Rōmaji	English
いちがつ 一月	ichigatsu	January
a	b	February
c	d	March
しがつ 四月	shigatsu	April
ごがつ 五月	gogatsu	May
e	f	June

Script	Rōmaji	English
しちがつ 七月	shichigatsu	July
はちがつ 八月	hachigatsu	August
くがつ 九月	kugatsu	September
g	h	October
i	j	November
じゅうにがつ 十二月	jūnigatsu	December

 2 04.04 **Listen and copy the pronunciation of the months of the year.**

 # Speaking

How would you say the following? Where appropriate use particle を o rather than は wa but remember that は wa can be used instead for emphasis.
Example:

You don't watch TV in the evenings. (evenings = 夜 よる yoru)

夜テレビを見ません　　**Yoru terebi o mimasen.**

a You don't have meals with your family.
b You don't talk to your neighbour.
c You don't drink coffee for breakfast.
d You don't clean the house.
e You don't go to work early.

📖 Reading 1

1 Here are some questions in Japanese about Mr Hondo's daily routine using 何時 **nanji** (*what time?*) and 何 **nani** (*what?*). Can you match them with their correct English meaning?

a 何時に家に帰りますか。
なんじ うち かえ
Nan ji ni uchi ni kaerimasu ka.

b 何時に起きますか。
なんじ
Nan ji ni okimasu ka.

c 何時まで働きますか。
はたら
Nan ji made hatarakimasu ka.

d 日曜日に何をしますか。
にちようび なに
Nichiyōbi ni nani o shimasu ka.

e 朝ごはんに何を食べますか。
なに
Asagohan ni nani o tabemasu ka.

1 What time does he get up?

2 What does he have for breakfast?

3 What time does he work until?

4 What time does he go home?

5 What does he do on Sundays?

Check your answers and then see if you can reply to the questions in Japanese. Refer back to the conversation for help.

2 Can you match the Japanese month to its English equivalent?

a 七月 shichigatsu
b 九月 kugatsu
c 八月 hachigatsu
d 四月 shigatsu
e 一月 ichigatsu
f 十一月 jūichigatsu
g 二月 nigatsu
h 五月 gogatsu
i 十二月 jūnigatsu
j 三月 sangatsu
k 六月 rokugatsu
l 十月 jūgatsu

1 January
2 February
3 March
4 April
5 May
6 June
7 July
8 August
9 September
10 October
11 November
12 December

3 Look at the calendar pages and see if you can work out:

a which months they are for
b the first day of the week, as listed.

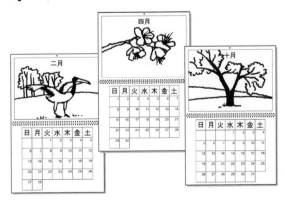

Practising reading **hiragana**

Here is a table containing the first 15 **hiragana** you have already learned with spaces to add new **hiragana** as you learn them. It is written in Japanese reading order, reading down each column from right to left. Create your own table and fill in the new **hiragana** as you learn them. Can you remember what these say?

					さ	か	あ
					し	き	い
					す	く	う
					せ	け	え
					そ	こ	お

Reading 2

1 04.05 **Now you are going to try reading some hiragana words. These are also on the audio so you can listen and repeat, or try reading them yourself first and then check your answers.**

a え picture
b あい love
c あう meet
d うえ above
e かお face
f あおい blue
g あかい red
h あき autumn
i えき station
j くさ grass

k けさ this morning
l こえ voice
m すし sushi
n せき seat
o そこ over there
p すき like
q せかい world
r せいき century
s おおきい big
t おいしい tasty

2 **The words from the previous activity are all contained in the following word search. Can you find them?**

あ	い	け	く	こ	う	う	え
え	う	あ	さ	お	か	え	き
く	す	き	け	せ	か	い	こ
さ	し	し	す	い	せ	そ	こ
お	そ	あ	い	き	う	え	え
お	お	せ	か	き	あ	い	く
け	え	き	こ	さ	か	お	し
お	い	し	い	す	い	せ	い

3 **Here, in random order, are the 15 hiragana symbols that you have learned in Units 3 and 4. Can you read them all? Speak out loud.**

か し う く さ　　　き そ あ お け　　　え す い こ せ

 Test yourself

1 **How would you say the following in Japanese?**
   a Shall we eat at a restaurant?
   b Let's eat at a restaurant!
   c Let's go to that department store over there.
   d Let's buy sushi in this supermarket.
   e Shall we go (return) home?
   f I will go to Japan next year.
   g My mother does not eat sushi.

2 **How many verbs can you remember from this unit without looking back? What are the ます masu (*I do/will do*) and ません masen (*I don't/won't*) forms of each? (Clue – here are the verbs in English: drink, eat, see/watch/look, listen, speak/talk, write, read, work, make, buy, go, return, come, do, get up, go to bed, play golf, chill out, study, play football, do the shopping, travel, have a meal, make a phone call.)**

SELF CHECK	
I CAN...	
⚪	...recall and use a number of useful verbs in ます **masu** form.
⚪	...understand and use the particles に **ni**, へ **e** and から **kara** with verbs of motion.
⚪	...make suggestions using *shall we* and *let's*.
⚪	...say sentences in the negative form.
⚪	...read and say the months of the year.

買い物をしましょう！
Kaimono o shimashō!

Let's do some shopping!

In this unit you will learn how to:
▶ *use essential phrases for shopping.*
▶ *use counters with nouns.*
▶ *say where things and people are.*
▶ *use more question words.*
▶ *say money amounts and count above 100.*

CEFR: *(A2) Can ask about things and make simple transactions in shops, post offices and banks. Can give and receive information about quantities, numbers, prices, etc. Can make simple purchases by stating what is wanted and asking the price.*

買い物 **Kaimono** *Shopping*

The pictures show some of the typical 日本のお土産 **Nihon no omiyage** (*Japanese souvenirs*) that you can buy relatively inexpensively in Japan or in 日本の店 **Nihon no mise** (*Japanese shops*) around the world. Wooden こけしの人形 **kokeshi no ningyō** (*kokeshi dolls*) are made in many styles and often decorated with symbols, pictures and stories from the regions where they are made. The more expensive ones are usually handmade, with the artist's signature on them.

円 **en** (*yen*) is the Japanese currency. To give you an idea of value, コーヒー **kōhī** (*a cup of coffee*) costs between 三百円 **sambyaku en** (*300 yen*) and 五百円 **gohyaku en** (*500 yen*), a meal out at a moderately priced レストラン **resutoran** (*restaurant*) would cost between 千円 **sen en** and 二千円 **nisen en** (*1000–2000 yen*) per person.

How would you say the following money amounts in Japanese?

a 500 yen **b** 200 yen **c** 800 yen **d** 8000 yen

Vocabulary builder

 05.01 **Listen to the new vocabulary and practise saying it out loud.**

ESSENTIAL SHOPPING PHRASES

すみません。	Sumimasen.	*Excuse me* (to get attention), *sorry*
Xがありますか。	X ga arimasu ka.	*Do you have any X?*
X を売っていますか。	X o utteimasu ka.	*Do you sell X?*
いくらですか。	Ikura desu ka.	*How much is it?*
Xはいくらですか。	X wa ikura desu ka.	*How much is X?*
Xをみせてください。	X o misete kudasai.	*Please show me X.*
Xをください。	X o kudasai.	*May I have X?*

USEFUL ITEMS AND GENERAL TERMS

時計	tokei	*watch (clock)*
切手	kitte	*stamps*
浴衣	yukata	*cotton kimono*
せんす	sensu	*folding fan*
お酒	o-sake	*rice wine*
かばん	kaban	*bag*
はがき	hagaki	*postcard*
新聞	shinbun	*newspaper*
クリスマスカード	Kurisumasu kādo	*Christmas card(s)*
百	hyaku	*100*
千	sen	*1000*
いいえ	iie	*no*
じゃあ	jā	*right, OK, in that case*
何も	nani mo	*nothing, not anything*
二階	nikai	*second floor*

WORDS USED BY SHOPKEEPERS

いらっしゃいませ	irasshaimase	*welcome, may I help you?* (used to greet customers)
かしこまりました	kashikomarimashita	*certainly* (used by shop assistants, tradespeople)
全部で	zembu de	*altogether, in total*

> **LANGUAGE TIP**
> Where you see a double consonant (or a **hiragana** symbol preceded by a small っ) you should pause slightly on the first consonant or っ. Listen again to the pronunciation of **utteimasu ka** and **irasshaimase** and try to copy these correctly.

Conversation 1

05.02 *Rie Franks, Robert Franks' wife, is shopping at her local* 売店 **baiten** *(kiosk).*

1 What two items does she buy and how much does she pay altogether?

Shop assistant	いらっしゃいませ！
Rie	それはイギリスの新聞ですか。
Shop assistant	いいえ、これはアメリカのです。これはイギリスのです。
Rie	いくらですか。
Shop assistant	四百円です。
Rie	じゃあ、これをください。そしてこのクリスマスカードを二枚ください。
Shop assistant	かしこまりました。全部で千円です。
Shop assistant	Irasshaimase!
Rie	Sore wa Igirisu no shinbun desu ka.
Shop assistant	Iie, kore wa Amerika no desu. Kore wa Igirisu no desu.
Rie	Ikura desu ka.
Shop assistant	Yon hyaku en desu.
Rie	Jā, kore o kudasai. Soshite kono kurisumasu kādo o ni mai kudasai.
Shop assistant	Kashikomarimashita. Zembu de sen en desu.

2 How much is the first item she buys?

3 How many of the second item does she buy?

Conversation 2

05.03 *Tatsuya Hondo is at the* 郵便局 **yūbinkyoku** *(post office).*

1 How much is one postcard? How much is one stamp?

Shop assistant	いらっしゃいませ。
Hondō Tatsuya	すみません、はがきを売っていますか。
Shop assistant	はい、あそこです。
Hondō Tatsuya	ああ、そうですか。いくらですか。
Shop assistant	一枚、百円です。
Hondō Tatsuya	じゃあ、このはがきを三枚と七十五円の切手も三枚ください。
Shop assistant	かしこまりました。全部で五百二十五円です。
Shop assistant	Irasshaimase.
Hondō Tatsuya	Sumimasen, hagaki o utteimasu ka.
Shop assistant	Hai, asoko desu.
Hondō Tatsuya	Ā, sō desu ka. Ikura desu ka.
Shop assistant	Ichi mai, hyaku en desu.
Hondō Tatsuya	Jā, kono hagaki o san mai to nanajū go en no kitte mo san mai kudasai.
Shop assistant	Kashikomarimashita. Zembu de gohyaku nijū go en desu.

2 How many postcards does he buy? How many stamps?

3 How much is it altogether?

4 Find the Japanese for these phrases from the conversations and say them out loud:

  a Is that an English newspaper?

  b May I have two of these Christmas cards, please?

  c Excuse me, do you sell postcards?

  d May I have three of this postcard and also three of the 75 yen stamps, please?

5 Using the vocabulary given in the Vocabulary builder and the conversation, can you work out how you would say the following sentences?

  a Do you have any postcards?

  b Excuse me, do you sell cotton kimono?

  c How much is this folding fan?

  d May I see that newspaper?

  e May I have this rice wine?

  f May I have this watch and this bag?

> **LANGUAGE TIP**
>
> Make sure you remember to say the item first followed by the phrase. For example:
>
> *Do you have any folding fans?*
> せんすがありますか
> **Sensu ga arimasu ka.**
>
> *How much are these postcards?*
> このはがきはいくらですか
> **Kono hagaki wa ikura desu ka.**

6 Can you work out how to say these numbers using the following examples to help you?

  Examples: 450　四百五十（よんひゃくごじゅう）**yon hyaku gojū**　　2500　二千五百（にせんごひゃく）**ni sen go hyaku**

  a 700　　　　　　　　　　　　　**d** 750

  b 4000　　　　　　　　　　　　**e** 5500

  c 240　　　　　　　　　　　　　**f** 7575

KEY SENTENCES

05.04 Here are some sentences to demonstrate the key grammar points you will learn in this unit. Can you work out how the sentences fit together? What words appear repeatedly? Is there a pattern to how they are used? (Clue: があります **ga arimasu** also means *there is*.)

a この新聞（しんぶん）はいくらですか。
  Kono shinbun wa ikura desu ka.

b このクリスマスカードを二枚（にまい）ください。
  Kono kurisumasu kādo o nimai kudasai.

c すみません、フランス（ふらんす）の新聞がありますか。
  Sumimasen, Furansu no shinbun ga arimasu ka.

d 二階（にかい）にテレビ（てれび）やコンピューター（こんぴゅーたー）があります。
  Nikai ni terebi ya kompyūtā ga arimasu.

e 二階に何（なに）もありません。
  Nikai ni nani mo arimasen.

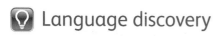

Language discovery

5.1 COUNTERS (SYSTEM A)

In Japanese you rarely use the numbers one to ten by themselves, you normally add a counter word. We do this sometimes in English (two *loaves* of bread; six *portions* of rice; three *slices* of toast; one *bottle* of wine) but not always, whereas in Japanese there is a counter word for everything.

This system of counting involves using the numbers **ichi**, **ni**, **san** and adding a specific counter depending on the type of item. There are many, many of these in Japanese. Here is a list of some of them.

Counter word	Type of item	Examples
mai	square-ish, flat-ish	shirts, folded clothes, stamps, paper, tickets, pizza, CDs
dai	large machinery	cars, lorries, televisions, computers
hon (pon, bon)	long, cylindrical items	bottles, films, pens, trees
kai, gai*	floors, number of times	
hiki (piki, biki)*	small animals	dogs, cats, fish, mice
tō*	large animals	cows, horses, elephants
nin	people	
ko	round objects	apples, sweets, round fruit, eggs, soap
satsu	books	magazines, comic books, notebooks
soku*	pairs (footwear)	shoes, socks, boots

Note: The counters marked * are not really used in this course, but they are useful to know. Don't worry about remembering all the counters – refer back to this table when you need to.

As we mentioned in Unit 1, with some counters the pronunciation of the number or counter changes slightly. The most common change is the 'squashing' or shortening of the numbers 1, 6, 8 and 10. For example, counters beginning with **k** have these changes to 1, 6 and 10:

いっかい	**ikkai**	*first floor*	いっこ	**ikko**	*one round item*
ろっかい	**rokkai**	*sixth floor*	ろっこ	**rokko**	*six round items*
じゅっかい	**jukkai**	*tenth floor*	じゅっこ	**jukko**	*ten round items*

And counters beginning with **s** have these changes to 1, 8 and 10:

いっさつ	**issatsu**	*one book*	いっそく	**issoku**	*one pair*
はっさつ	**hassatsu**	*eight books*	はっそく	**hassoku**	*eight pairs*
じゅっさつ	**jussatsu**	*ten books*	じゅっそく	**jussoku**	*ten pairs*

For three pairs you may hear さんぞく **sanzoku**, but it is fine to use さんそく **sansoku**.

Finally, counters beginning with **h** have these changes to 1, 3, 6, 8 and 10:

いっぽん	**ippon**	*one cylindrical item*	いっぴき	**ippiki**	*one animal*
さんぼん	**sanbon**	*three cylindrical items*	さんびき	**sanbiki**	*three animals*
ろっぽん	**roppon**	*six cylindrical items*	ろっぴき	**roppiki**	*six animals*
はっぽん	**happon**	*eight cylindrical items*	はっぴき	**happiki**	*eight animals*
じゅっぽん	**juppon**	*ten cylindrical items*	じゅっぴき	**juppiki**	*ten animals*

When you say 4 or 7, by the way, with all these counters use **yon** and **nana**.

 YOUR TURN 05.05 Look at items a–g and see if you can work out which counter to use. Then listen to the audio and see if you can work out how many of each item there is. Finally, listen again and say the items and numbers out loud, focusing on the sentence order and pronunciation.

Example: *three bottles of beer* (**bīru** + **hon** counter) = (ビール三本 び ー る さんぼん **bīru sanbon**)

a pairs of shoes (靴 くつ kutsu)

b apples (りんご ringo)

c bottles of rice wine (お酒 さけ sake)

d bottles of beer (ビール bīru)

e cotton kimono (浴衣 ゆ か た yukata)

f televisions (テレビ て れ び terebi)

g books (本 ほん hon*)

Note: This is the same **kanji** as the counter for bottles.

5.2 COUNTERS (SYSTEM B)

 05.06 This system uses an alternative way of counting from one to ten. It is used for the many items that don't have a special counter (especially items that don't have a particular shape) and you can, in fact, use it even for items that do have a special counter, although you will then sound less authentic. As you listen to the audio, speak out loud:

1	=	一つ	**hitotsu**		6	=	六つ	**muttsu**
2	=	二つ	**futatsu**		7	=	七つ	**nanatsu**
3	=	三つ	**mittsu**		8	=	八つ	**yattsu**
4	=	四つ	**yottsu**		9	=	九つ	**kokonotsu**
5	=	五つ	**itsutsu**		10	=	十	**tō**

> **LANGUAGE TIP**
> The reason that there are two systems for counting in Japanese is because both the imported Chinese system (一、二、三、四 **ichi**, **ni**, **san**, **shi** ...) and the native Japanese system (ひと **hito**, ふた **futa**, み **mi**, よ **yo**) are used. These have become intermingled and adapted into the Japanese language.

Here are some hints for remembering System B:

▶ The words for *four* and *seven* items are familiar because they use よ **yo** and なな **nana**.

▶ 1–9 all end in the item counter つ **tsu**.

▶ *Ten* (**tō**) sounds rather like the English word *toe* – and you have ten of these!

▶ *Two* (二つ **futatsu**) has a sound not unlike *foot* (**futa**) and you have two of these!

YOUR TURN Now practise using this system with the following items: *mobile phones* (携帯電話 **keitai denwa**); *cakes* (ケーキ **kēki**); *cups of coffee* (コーヒー **kōhī**); *bag* (かばん **kaban**); *watch* (時計 **tokei**).

a three cups of coffee

b ten bags

c two mobile phones

d four watches

e one cake

5.3 USING COUNTERS IN FULL SENTENCES

Do you remember how to say *may I have* or *I'd like*? To ask for a number of items you say the counter after the item and between the particle を **o** and ください **kudasai**. For example:

かばんを三つください。	**Kaban o <u>mittsu</u> kudasai.**	*May I have <u>three</u> bags?*
ビールを一本ください。	**Bīru o <u>ippon</u> kudasai.**	*May I have <u>a</u> bottle of beer?*

YOUR TURN Ask for the following using System B (**tsu**).

a two bags

b five watches

c four cups of coffee

Ask for the following using System A (counter in brackets, underlined if changes).

d two (**hon**) bottles of rice wine お酒 (**o-sake**)

e six (**hon**) bottles of beer ビール (**bīru**)

f three (**ko**) apples りんご (**ringo**)

g five (**mai**) stamps 切手 (**kitte**)

h three (**satsu**) notebooks ノート (**nōto**)

5.4 SAYING *THERE IS* AND *THERE ARE*

You have learned how to say *it is, I am, they are* using the word です **desu** and its negative (*isn't, am not*) using ではありません・じゃありません・じゃない **dewa arimasen** (**ja arimasen, ja nai**). Now you are going to learn how to say *there is, there are* using あります **arimasu** and います **imasu**.

Look at these two examples and see if you can work out when you use each one:

<ruby>ジャーナリスト<rt>じゃーなりすと</rt></ruby>がいます。 **Jānarisuto ga <u>imasu</u>.** *There is a journalist.*
(There are journalists.)

かばんが<u>あります</u>。 **Kaban ga <u>arimasu</u>.** *There is a bag. (There are bags.)*

Did you spot that one is used for non-living things (inanimate) while the other is for living things (people and animals)?

YOUR TURN Should these sentences end in います **imasu** or あります **arimasu**?
a 母が _____ haha ga _____
b <ruby>時計<rt>とけい</rt></ruby>が _____ tokei ga _____
c <ruby>木<rt>き</rt></ruby>が _____ ki (tree) ga _____

5.5 PARTICLE が **GA**

Did you spot the new particle? You can think of it as meaning *a* or *some* in this type of sentence. As you have probably come to expect, you say it after the item.

YOUR TURN Say these sentences in Japanese:
a There is a book. (<ruby>本<rt>ほん</rt></ruby> **hon**)
b There are some apples. (りんご **ringo**)
c The neighbour is not there.

The particle が **ga** often changes to は **wa** with negative sentences to add emphasis:
<ruby>イギリス人<rt>いぎりす</rt></ruby>はいません。 **Igirisujin wa imasen.**
There are no <u>English people</u> (but there are <u>Americans</u>).

5.6 MORE ABOUT THE PARTICLE NI

You learned in Unit 3 that you use particle で **de** to say <u>where</u> an action took place:
家<u>で</u>晩御飯を食べます。 **Uchi <u>de</u> bangohan o tabemasu.** *I eat dinner <u>at</u> home.*

When you use あります **arimasu** and います **imasu** there is no action – these are known as verbs of existence; in other words, you are saying what there is rather than what is happening. So with these two verbs you use particle に **ni** after the place where there is someone or something.

YOUR TURN What do these sentences mean?
a 家に母がいます。 Uchi ni haha ga imasu.
b <ruby>二階<rt></rt></ruby>に<ruby>テレビ<rt>てれび</rt></ruby>があります。 Nikai ni terebi ga arimasu.

You can translate に ni as *in*, *on* or *at*. Say the place at the beginning of the sentence. Now try these:
c My family are at home.   d On the third floor is a supermarket.
e There are French and English journalists in that office (over there).

5.7 MORE ABOUT QUESTION WORDS

You have already learned these question words:

何時ですか。	**Nanji desu ka.**	*What time is it?*
何時に起きますか。	**Nanji ni okimasu ka.**	*What time do you get up?*
<ruby>日曜日<rt>にちようび</rt></ruby>に<u>何</u>をしますか。	**Nichiyōbi ni <u>nani</u> o shimasu ka.**	*What do you do on Sundays?*

To answer these questions, you simply replace なん **nan** or なに **nani** with the appropriate information and repeat the sentence, leaving off か **ka** at the end.

YOUR TURN 1 Answer the questions given in the examples with this information:

   a It is one o'clock.

   b You get up at seven.

   c You play golf (on Sundays).

2 **a** Using あります **arimasu** how would you ask: *What is on the second floor?*
     (Clue: order is *second floor on, what is there?*)

   b Give this reply: *There are TVs and clocks.*

3 **Can you work out how to ask these questions using the question word** *who* だれ **dare?**

   a Who is in the office?

   b Who is at home?

   c Who is on the third floor?

5.8 MORE ABOUT なに NANI AND だれ DARE

Building on the question words なに **nani** and だれ **dare** you can now learn how to ask:
Is there anyone? Is there anything?

To do this, you add か **ka** after the question word (you don't need the particle が **ga**).

二階になに<u>か</u>ありますか。	**Nikai ni nani <u>ka</u> arimasu ka.**	*Is there anything on the second floor?*
家にだれ<u>か</u>いますか。	**Uchi ni dare <u>ka</u> imasu ka.**	*Is there anyone at home?*

YOUR TURN 1 How would you say the following in Japanese?

   a Is there anybody in this office?

   b Is there anything on the first floor?

   c Is there anyone at home?

How would you reply *yes there is* **(start with** はい **hai** *(yes)***)?**

   d Yes, there is somebody.

   e Yes, there is something.

2 **Looking at these examples, can you work out the rules for answering in the negative?**

二階になにもありません。	**Nikai ni nani mo arimasen.**	*There is nothing on the second floor.*
家にだれもいません。	**Uchi ni dare mo imasen.**	*There is nobody at home.*

3 **How would you say the following in Japanese?**

   a There is nobody in this office.

   b There is nothing on the first floor.

   c There is no one at home.

5.9 HUNDREDS (百 HYAKU) AND THOUSANDS (千 SEN)

When talking about money in Japan you will often use *hundreds* (百 **hyaku**) and *thousands* (千 **sen**). As you have seen, you use the number system 一、二、三 **ichi, ni, san** and attach 百 **hyaku** and 千 **sen**. The numbers 'squash' and change by the same rules as you learned for the counters. There is a full list in the Appendices with audio to listen to so you can practise saying the numbers.

You say numbers in the same order as you would in English:

220　二百二十　**nihyaku nijū**　　　　2220　二千二百二十　**nisen nihyaku nijū**

YOUR TURN 1 Following the example, give these prices:

Example: *The coffee is 200 yen* = コーヒーは二百円です **kōhī wa nihyaku-en desu**

a　The chopsticks are 500 yen.
b　The newspaper is 350 yen.
c　The cotton kimono is 4400 yen.
d　The doll is 6800 yen.
e　This camera is 9999 yen.

 2　05.07 Now listen to the audio to check your answers and practise these amounts again.

5.10 COUNTING BEYOND 9999

The Japanese have an additional unit for 10,000 called **man**.

10,000　一万　**ichiman**　　　　20,000　二万　**niman**

You say these amounts by stating the units of 10,000 then saying the rest of the amount. Here is an example:

45,163 yen　4 × 10,000, 5 × 1000, 163　四万、五千、百六十三円

yonman, gosen hyaku rokujū san en

> **LANGUAGE TIP**
> If you count four decimal points from the right end of the number, then everything to the left of that is counted in **man**:
> 4 | 5163　　to left of line remains 4 so 四万 **yonman** (40,000)
> 65 | 7800　　to left of line remains 65 so 六十五万 **rokujū goman** (650,000)

YOUR TURN How would you say these prices in Japanese?
a　35,600 yen
b　356,600 yen
c　356,666 yen

5.11 DIFFERENT WAYS TO SAY *AND*

There are a number of ways to say *and* in Japanese. Let's focus on the use of *and* between two nouns (books *and* pens, boys *and* girls, peace *and* quiet).

朝ごはんにトーストと卵を食べます。

Asagohan ni tōsuto <u>to</u> tamago o tabemasu.

I eat toast <u>and</u> eggs for breakfast.

Another way of saying *and* is や **ya**.

二階にテレビやコンピューターなどがあります。

Nikai ni terebi <u>ya</u> kompyūtā ga arimasu.

On the second floor are TVs and computers.

You use と **to** when the list is exhaustive (you list everything there is) and や **ya** to give a few examples from a longer list. You can add など **nado** to say *etc./and so on.*

1 What do you think this sentence means?

二階にテレビやコンピューターなどがあります。

Nikai ni terebi ya kompyūtā nado ga arimasu.

If you are listing only two items and want to say *both … and*, you use the particle も **mo**.

ビールもお酒もあります。　　**Bīru <u>mo</u> o-sake <u>mo</u> arimasu.**

There is both beer and rice wine.

2 What do you think this sentence means?

朝ごはんにご飯もトーストも食べます。

Asagohan ni gohan <u>mo</u> tōsuto <u>mo</u> tabemasu.

YOUR TURN Add the missing *and* word to these sentences:

a 一階にせんす ＿＿＿ 浴衣 ＿＿＿ があります。 Ikkai ni sensu ＿＿＿ yukata ＿＿＿ ga arimasu. (*There are fans, cotton kimono and so on on the first floor.*)

b 母 ＿＿＿ 父 ＿＿＿ この会社で働きます。 Haha ＿＿＿ chichi ＿＿＿ kono kaisha de hatarakimasu. (*Both my mum and dad work in this company.*)

Listening

でございます	de gozaimasu	polite form of **desu**
キロ	kiro	*kilo*

 1 05.08 **You are going to listen to three short conversations. For each one, listen for the following information:**
  - What item(s) does the shopper buy?
  - How many of each item do they buy?
  - How much is each item?
  - What is the total cost?

 2 05.09 **Listen to the conversations and choose the correct time, price, number or month from the possible answers provided.**

a i   ii   iii

b i   ii   iii

c 1 200 yen   **2** 2000 yen   **3** 1000 yen

d 1 31,000 yen   **2** 32,000 yen   **3** 72,000 yen

e 1 September   **2** May   **3** June

🗾 Speaking

1 Practise asking for the items in the pictures using the question *May I have?*
You need to use the correct counter and put the counter word in the correct place
(between を **o** and ください **kudasai**). You can use System B if you aren't sure
of the correct counter to use.

Example:

せんすを六_むつください。

Sensu o muttsu kudasai.

Example   **1**   **2**

3   **4**   **5**

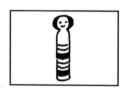  

2 05.10 Listen to the dialogue 'At the post office' then learn to say the customer's
part by pausing after the assistant's part and saying your part out loud. Listen to
the audio to check.

Post office assistant	いらっしゃいませ。	Irasshaimase!
You	すみません、はがきを売っていますか。	Sumimasen, hagaki o utteimasu ka.
Assistant	はい、あそこです。	Hai, asoko desu.
You	ああ、そうですか。いくらですか。	Ā, sō desu ka. Ikura desu ka.
Assistant	一枚_{いちまい}、百_{ひゃくえん}円です。	Ichimai, hyaku en desu.
You	じゃあ、このはがきを三枚_{さんまい}と七十五円_{ななじゅうごえん}の切手_{きって}も三枚_{さんまい}ください。	Jā, kono hagaki o san-mai to nanajū go en no kitte mo sanmai kudasai.
Assistant	かしこまりました。全部_{ぜんぶ}で五百二十五円_{ごひゃくにじゅうごえん}です。	Kashikomarimashita. Zembu de gohyaku nijū go en desu.

Writing

1 **The following sentences have gaps requiring either** あります **arimasu or** います **imasu (or the negative). You also need to add the particles** に **ni and** が **ga in the correct place.**

   a 二階 ___ テレビやコンピューター ___ ___。Nikai ___ terebi ya kompyūtā ___ ___. (There are TVs, computers etc. on the second floor.)

   b あのデパート ___ 母 ___ ___。Ano depāto ___ haha ___ ___. (My mother is in that department store over there.)

   c レストラン ___ だれも ___。Resutoran ___ dare mo ___. (There <u>isn't</u> anyone in the restaurant.)

   d そのスーパー ___ だれ ___ ___ か。Sono sūpā ___ dare ___ ___ ka. (Who is there in that supermarket?)

   e このかばん ___ カメラ ___ ___。Kono kaban ___ kamera ___ ___. (There <u>isn't</u> a camera in this bag.)

2 **You have also learned how to say** *someone* **or** *something* **using dare ka and nani ka, and** *no one* **or** *nothing* **using dare mo and nani mo plus the negative. Put in the correct words to complete these sentences.**

   a 家に Uchi ni ___ ___ ___. (There is someone in the house.)

   b 家に Uchi ni ___ ___ ___. (There is no one in the house.)

   c 三階に Sangai ni ___ ___ ___ か ka. (Is there anything on the third floor?)

   d いいえ Iie, ___ ___ ___. (No, there isn't anything.)

   e あの事務所に Ano jimusho ni ___ ___ ___ か ka. (Is there anyone in that office?)

   f はい Hai, ___ ___ ___. (Yes, there is somebody.)

Fifteen more **hiragana** symbols

START READING

05.11 **Look back at the pronunciation guide in the Introduction. Focus on the middle 15 sounds (ta–ho). Here are those 15 hiragana symbols with their pronunciation underneath. Look at them and say each sound out loud. Listen to the audio to reinforce the sounds.**

た	ち	つ	て	と
ta	chi	tsu	te	to
な	に	ぬ	ね	の
na	ni	nu	ne	no
は	ひ	ふ	へ	ほ
ha	hi	fu	he	ho

HOW TO REMEMBER **HIRAGANA** SYMBOLS

Try to think of some more mnemonics to help you remember these new symbols. Focus on the sounds of the words you choose, not the spellings. Here are a few ideas to get you started:

た (**ta**) looks like the letters **t** and **a**

ち (**chi**) is a *chee*rleader

と (**to**) is the *toe* of a shoe

ね (**ne**) Loch *Ness* Monster

ふ (**fu**) Mount *Fuji* (Japan's highest mountain)

Here are some other ideas that might work for you:

つ	(**tsu**)	looks like a nose and someone sneezing 'ātsu!'
て	(**te**)	looks like a <u>t</u>able (pronunciation not spelling)
な	(**na**)	is a <u>na</u>nny pushing a pram
に	(**ni**)	is a <u>kne</u>e
ぬ	(**nu**)	looks like two chopsticks picking up <u>noo</u>dles
の	(**no**)	is a <u>kno</u>t
は	(**ha**)	could be made to look like a <u>h</u>ouse
ひ	(**hi**)	looks like a mouth laughing – <u>hee</u> hee
へ	(**he**)	turn into a <u>h</u>elicopter
ほ	(**ho**)	make it look like a thermometer – <u>ho</u>t

OTHER IDEAS TO HELP YOU REMEMBER

Add the new **hiragana** to your flashcards. Mix them in with the first 15 symbols and keep testing yourself. Then try this game. Spread all the cards out, **hiragana** side up. Collect 'families' such as all symbols ending in **a** and all symbols ending in **i**. Continue this for **u**, **e** and **o**.

Now spread the cards out again and try families beginning with **k**, **s**, **t**, **n** and **h**.

Add the next 15 **hiragana** symbols to your table. It should look like this:

				は	な	た	さ	か	あ
				ひ	に	ち	し	き	い
				ふ	ぬ	つ	す	く	う
				へ	ね	て	せ	け	え
				ほ	の	と	そ	こ	お

SIMILAR-LOOKING HIRAGANA

The following **hiragana** symbols look quite similar and you may find this confusing at times. Here are some clues to help you tell them apart:

ぬ, ね	ぬ (**nu**) has two 'vertical' lines at the top and two loops whereas ね (**ne**) has only one of each.
さ, ち	さ (**sa**) leans to the left; ち (**chi**) looks like the number 5 (the top has slipped).
け, は, ほ	け (**ke**) has no loop at the bottom; は (**ha**) has one horizontal line; ほ (**ho**) has two horizontal lines.

Note that, depending on the font, you may come across this alternative form of ふ **fu**: ふ

Reading

 1 05.12 Try reading some **hiragana** words containing the new **hiragana** symbols only. These are also on the audio so you can either listen and repeat or try reading them yourself first and then check your answers with the audio.

a たて vertical
b なに what
c ふね ship
d ちち father
e ひとつ one item
f ふたつ two items
g ななつ seven items
h はは mother

i へた poor at
j ぬの cloth
k ほね bones
l て hand
m なつ summer
n はな nose
o ひと person

 2 05.13 Now see if you can read the following **hiragana** words which contain combinations of all the **hiragana** symbols you have learned so far. You can also listen to the words on the audio.

a とけい clock
b へそ navel
c かた shoulders
d さいふ purse
e あに older brother
f あね older sister
g おとうと younger brother
h うち house
i かない wife
j あした tomorrow

k おはし chopsticks
l おさけ rice wine
m ほほ cheeks
n せなか back
o たいてい generally
p ふつう usual
q いつつ five items
r ここのつ nine items
s とう 10 items
t いくつ how many items?

3 Each of the following rows of **hiragana** symbols includes an 'odd man out'. Can you find it and identify what the correct symbol would be?

a あ か し た な は
b け ひ ふ へ ほ
c ほ の と そ こ あ
d か さ く け こ

e う く す つ ね ふ
f ひ に ち し き こ
g た さ つ て と

READING CHALLENGE

Here, in random order, are the 30 **hiragana** symbols that you have learned so far. Can you read them all? Speak out loud:

た ぬ か ひ し つ
う ほ く な さ ち
き へ そ て あ ふ
お と け え に す
は い の こ ね せ

❓ Test yourself

1 Read the ten Japanese sentences and match them with their English meanings.

a かばんを三つください。Kaban o mittsu kudasai.

b 二階に何がありますか。Nikai ni nani ga arimasu ka.

c 一階にせんすや浴衣^{ゆ か た}などがあります。Ikkai ni sensu ya yukata nado ga arimasu.

d お酒を売っていますか。O-sake o utteimasu ka.

e このお酒はいくらですか。Kono o-sake wa ikura desu ka.

f すみません、はがきがありますか。Sumimasen, hagaki ga arimasu ka.

g あの人形^{にんぎょう}を見せてください。Ano ningyō o misete kudasai.

h 家にだれかいますか。Uchi ni dare ka imasu ka.

i 母も父もこの会社で働きます。Haha mo chichi mo kono kaisha de hatarakimasu.

j 二階に何もありません。Nikai ni nani mo arimasen.

   1 May I see that doll over there?

   2 Is there anyone at home?

   3 There is nothing on the second floor.

   4 There are fans, cotton kimono, etc. on the first floor.

   5 Both my mum and dad work in this company.

   6 May I have three bags?

   7 Do you sell rice wine?

   8 What is there on the second floor?

   9 Excuse me, do you have any postcards?

  10 How much is this rice wine?

2 Can you do the following?

a Count in blocks of 100 from 100 to 900.

b Count in blocks of 1000 from 1000 to 10,000.

c Do both of these backwards.

d Say the year you were born in.

SELF CHECK

	I CAN...
⦿	...use essential phrases for shopping.
⦿	...use a variety of counter words to say numbers of items.
⦿	...say where things and people are.
⦿	...use question words to ask and answer questions.
⦿	...use question words with か **ka** or も **mo** to say *anyone, anything, no one, nothing*.
⦿	...understand money amounts and count above 100.
⦿	...use different words to say *and*.
⦿	...read 30 **hiragana** symbols.

6 映画館はどこにありますか
Eigakan wa doko ni arimasu ka
Where is the cinema?

In this unit you will learn how to:
▶ *give the location of places, items and people.*
▶ *give and follow directions.*
▶ *arrange to meet someone.*
▶ *speak in the past* (I did, I didn't).
▶ *make, accept and refuse suggestions.*
▶ *talk about what you want to do.*
▶ *say days of the week.*
▶ *tell the time* (five past, ten to).
▶ *talk about hobbies and leisure activities.*

CEFR: *(A2) Can make arrangements to meet, decide where to go and what to do. Can discuss what to do next, making and responding to suggestions, asking for and giving directions. Can ask for and give directions referring to a map or plan.*

 ## 趣味や興味 **Shumi ya kyōmi** *Hobbies and leisure activities*

Belonging to clubs and having a variety of 興味 **kyōmi** (*interests*) and 趣味 **shumi** (*hobbies*) are an important element of Japanese society and you may well be asked: 趣味は何ですか **Shumi wa nan desu ka** (*What is your hobby?*). To answer this question you simply reply 趣味は ____ です **Shumi wa ____ desu** (*My hobby is ____*).

Some popular Japanese 興味 **kyōmi** and 趣味 **shumi** are 折り紙 **origami** (*paper folding*), 生け花 **ikebana** (*flower arranging*) and 書道 **shodō** (*calligraphy*).

The word 武道 **budō** covers all types of martial arts practised in Japan, some of the better known being 柔道 **jūdō**, 剣道 **kendō** (*fencing with bamboo swords*), 弓道 **kyūdō** (*archery*), 合気道 **aikidō** and 空手 **karate**. The word 道 **dō** by itself means *path* or *way* and it is a Buddhist term attached to arts that help you to achieve a meditative and harmonious state of mind.

---

 1 Using the phrases from the passage, ask and answer the question 'What is your hobby?' for each of these pictures:

2 How many words ending in 道 **dō** can you find in the passage? What does this ending mean?

Vocabulary builder

06.01 Listen to the new vocabulary and practise saying it out loud.

MORE HOBBIES

茶道	sadō	*tea ceremony*
琴	koto	*Japanese harp*
武道	budō	*martial arts*
野球	yakyū	*baseball*
サッカー	sakkā	*soccer, football*
庭仕事	niwa shigoto	*gardening*

DIRECTIONS

後ろ	ushiro	*behind*
の後ろ	_____ no ushiro	*behind the* _____
信号	shingō	*traffic lights*
右にまがって	migi ni magatte	*turn right* (**migi** = *right*)
まっすぐ行って（ください）	massugu itte (kudasai)	*(please) go straight ahead* (**massugu** = *straight ahead*)
交差点	kōsaten	*crossroads*
左（側）	hidari (gawa)	*left (side)*
まがると	magaru to	*if you turn*
右（側）	migi (gawa)	*right (side)*
隣	tonari	*next to*
前	mae	*in front of*
バス停	basutei	*bus stop*
橋	hashi	*bridge*
歩道橋	hodōkyō	*footbridge*
横断歩道	ōdan hodō	*pedestrian crossing*
角	kado	*corner*
道路	dōro	*street, road*
道	michi	*road, way*
一つ目	hitotsu me	*first*
二つ目	futatsu me	*second*
次	tsugi	*next*

PLACES

映画館 <small>えいがかん</small>	eigakan	*cinema (**eiga** = film)*
会社 <small>かいしゃ</small>	kaisha	*company*
学校 <small>がっこう</small>	gakkō	*school*
郵便局 <small>ゆうびんきょく</small>	yūbinkyoku	*post office*
銀行 <small>ぎんこう</small>	ginkō	*bank*
美術館 <small>びじゅつかん</small>	bijutsukan	*art gallery*
博物館 <small>はくぶつかん</small>	hakubutsukan	*museum*
劇場 <small>げきじょう</small>	gekijō	*theatre*
喫茶店 <small>きっさてん</small>	kissaten	*coffee shop*
ボーリング場 <small>ぼーりんぐじょう</small>	bōringu jō	*bowling alley*
ニュー東京ホテル <small>にゅーとうきょうほてる</small>	Nyū Tōkyō hoteru	*New Tokyo Hotel (**hoteru** = hotel)*

MORE USEFUL PHRASES

今週 <small>こんしゅう</small>	konshū	*this week*
ご存知ですか <small>ぞんじ</small>	gozonji desu ka	*do you know? (respectful)*
知っています <small>し</small>	shitteimasu	*I know*
ね	ne	*isn't there, isn't it, right? (used when you expect agreement from the other person)*
わかりました	wakarimashita	*I've understood, I've got it*
いいです	ii desu	*it's OK, it's fine*
半 <small>はん</small>	han half	*half past*
じゃあ木曜日に <small>もくようび</small>	jā mokuyōbi ni	*well, on Thursday*

 06.02 The phrase X はどこにありますか **X wa doko ni arimasu ka means** *Where is X?* **Look at the title of this unit for an example of this then ask this question using the 12 place words in the vocabulary list. Check your answers by listening to the audio and use it to learn correct pronunciation of the new words.**

Conversation 1

 06.03 *Katie Mears, an American English teacher in Tokyo, has arranged to meet Rie Franks at the hotel where Rie works.*

1 The New Tokyo Hotel is behind which building?

Katie	あの、すみません。
Passer-by	はい？
Katie	ニュー東京ホテルはどこにありますか。ご存知ですか。
Passer-by	ニュー東京ホテル...はい、知っています。あそこに東京美術館がありますね。
Katie	はい。
Passer-by	ニュー東京ホテルは美術館の後ろにあります。あの信号を右にまがって、まっすぐ行ってください。
Katie	はい、わかりました。ありがとうございます。

Katie	Ano, sumimasen.
Passer-by	Hai?
Katie	Nyū Tōkyō hoteru wa doko ni arimasu ka. Gozonji desu ka.
Passer-by	Nyū Tōkyō hoteru…Hai, shitteimasu. Asoko ni Tōkyō bijutsukan ga arimasu ne.
Katie	Hai.
Passer-by	Nyū Tōkyō hoteru wa bijutsukan no ushiro ni arimasu. Ano shingō o migi ni magatte, massugu itte kudasai.
Katie	Hai, wakarimashita. Arigatō gozaimasu.

2 How does Katie ask the passer-by *Do you know it*?

3 Where should Katie turn right?

Conversation 2

 06.04 Miki Sugihara, a Japanese teacher, and Roger Wilson, an Australian who is studying Japanese in Tokyo, are both friends of Rie Franks. Miki and Roger arrange by phone to have an evening out.

1 What does Miki suggest they do?

Miki	今週どこかに行きましょうか。
Roger	いいですね。どこに行きましょうか。
Miki	そうですね。喫茶店でコーヒーとケーキを食べましょうか。
Roger	喫茶店ですか。喫茶店はちょっと … ボーリングはどうですか。
Miki	ボーリングですか。私はボーリングが下手ですがボーリングをしましょう！
Roger	じゃあ、明日はどうですか。
Miki	明日は水曜日ですね。水曜日はちょっと … 木曜日はどうですか。
Roger	木曜日はいいです。何時に会いましょうか。
Miki	七時半はどうですか。
Roger	はい、七時半に「グリーンランド」ボーリング場の前で会いましょう。

Miki	Konshū doko ka ni ikimasen ka.
Roger	Ii desu ne. Doko ni ikimashō ka.
Miki	Sō desu ne. Kissaten de kōhī to kēki o tabemashō ka.
Roger	Kissaten desu ka. Kissaten wa chotto … Bōringu wa dō desu ka.
Miki	Bōringu desu ka. Watashi wa bōringu ga heta desu ga bōringu o shimashō!
Roger	Jā, ashita wa dō desu ka.
Miki	Ashita wa suiyōbi desu ne. Suiyōbi wa chotto … Mokuyōbi wa dō desu ka.
Roger	Mokuyōbi wa ii desu. Nanji ni aimashō ka.
Miki	Shichiji han wa dō desu ka.
Roger	Hai, shichiji han ni 'Gurīn rando' bōringu jō no mae de aimashō.

2 How does Roger react to Miki's suggestion?

3 On which day and at what time do they agree to meet up?

Conversation 3

 06.05 *Miki isn't sure where 'Greenland' bowling alley is and asks Roger for more information.*

1 Where is the bowling alley?

Miki	あの、すみません。「グリーンランド」ボーリング場はどこにありますか。
Roger	ニュー東京劇場をご存知ですか。
Miki	はい、知っています。
Roger	劇場の前に信号があります。その信号を右にまがって、まっすぐ行ってください。左側に映画館があります。映画館の後ろに「グリーンランド」ボーリング場があります。
Miki	映画館の後ろですね。わかりました。じゃあ、木曜日に。さようなら。
Roger	さようなら。
Miki	Ano, sumimasen. 'Gurīn rando' bōringu jō wa doko ni arimasu ka.
Roger	Nyū Tōkyō gekijō o gozonji desu ka.
Miki	Hai, shitteimasu.
Roger	Gekijō no mae ni shingō ga arimasu. Sono shingō o migi ni magatte, massugu itte kudasai. Hidarigawa ni eigakan ga arimasu. Eigakan no ushiro ni 'Gurīn rando' bōringu jō ga arimasu.
Miki	Eigakan no ushiro desu ne. Wakarimashita. Jā mokuyōbi ni. Sayōnara.
Roger	Sayōnara.

2 Where are the traffic lights that Roger mentions?

3 What should Miki do at the traffic lights?

4 Focus on the position words 後ろ **ushiro** (*behind*) (Conversation 1) and 前 **mae** (*in front*) (Conversation 3). Where are they in relation to the point or place they describe? How does this compare to word order in English?

KEY SENTENCES

Use the new vocabulary and conversations to work out the meaning of these sentences.

> **LANGUAGE TIP**
> Japanese sentences are often 'backwards' to English ones, so once you have found the subject marked by **wa** (if there is one) start from the end of the sentence and work back.

a Massugu itte kudasai. まっすぐ行ってください。

b Shingō o migi ni magatte kudasai. 信号を右にまがってください。

c Bijutsukan wa hoteru no tonari ni arimasu. 美術館はホテルの隣にあります。

d Kono chikaku ni (*near here*) yūbinkyoku ga arimasu ka.
この近くに (*near here*) 郵便局がありますか。

e Depāto no mae ni basutei ga arimasu. デパートの前にバス停があります。

Language discovery

6.1 GIVING A LOCATION

In English we say the location word known as a preposition and then the place while in Japanese we do the reverse.

Behind the art gallery is 美術館の後ろ **bijutskan no ushiro.**

And did you notice the small word の **no** between the place and the preposition?

YOUR TURN Say these location points out loud using ushiro and mae.

a in front of the hotel
b behind the department store
c in front of the bank
d behind the art gallery
e behind the restaurant

6.2 PREPOSITIONS

 06.06 **Now you're going to expand your collection of prepositions. Listen to the audio and practise saying them:**

後ろ	ushiro	*behind*
前	mae	*in front (of)*
隣	tonari	*next to, next door*
そば	soba	*alongside, by*
横	yoko	*beside, side*
上	ue	*above, on top*
下	shita	*below, under*
近く	chikaku	*near to*
中	naka	*inside, in*
向かい側	mukaigawa	*opposite*

YOUR TURN How would you say the following in Japanese?

a next door to the restaurant
b to the side of the bank
c by the school
d above the museum
e below the department store
f in the theatre
g opposite the post office

6.3 GIVING A LOCATION IN A COMPLETE SENTENCE

Look at this sentence from the conversation:

ニュー東京ホテルは美術館の後ろにあります。

Nyū Tōkyō Hoteru wa bijutsukan no ushiro ni arimasu.

The New Tokyo Hotel is behind the art gallery.

Can you see how it is all put together?

Place (subject) は **wa** point of location にあります **ni arimasu** (**imasu** for people and animals).

YOUR TURN What do these sentences mean?

a バス停は銀行の横にあります。

　Basutei wa ginkō no yoko ni arimasu.

b 私の家は学校のそばにあります。

　Watashi no uchi wa gakkō no soba ni arimasu.

c りえさんは劇場の中にいます。

　Rie-san wa gekijō no naka ni imasu.

d ケイティさんは私のそばにいます。

　Katie-san wa watashi no soba ni imasu.

6.4 REPLACING NI ARIMASU/NI IMASU WITH DESU

Using です **desu** gives the meaning *is* rather than *is located*. For example, *The post office is opposite the bank* could be either of these:

郵便局は銀行の向かい側にあります。　Yūbinkyoku wa ginkō no mukaigawa ni arimasu.

郵便局は銀行の向かい側です。　　　　**Yūbinkyoku wa ginkō no mukaigawa desu.**

However, when you want to say *there is* or *there are* you must use あります・います **arimasu/imasu**:

家に新聞があります。　**Uchi ni shinbun ga arimasu.**　　*There is a newspaper in the house.*

In this case, using **desu** would make no sense:

家に新聞です。　　　　**Uchi ni shinbun desu.**　　　*In the house, it is newspaper.*

6.5 DIFFERENT MEANINGS OF NAKA (*INSIDE*)

You can say either of the following to describe where someone (or something) is:

りえさんは劇場の中にいます。　**Rie-san wa gekijō <u>no naka ni</u> imasu.**　　*Rie is in the theatre.*

りえさんは劇場にいます。　　　**Rie-san wa gekijō ni imasu.**　　　　　*Rie is at the theatre.*

Using 中 **naka** makes the location more specific: *she is inside.* It is not always necessary to make this clear, in which case you don't need to use 中 **naka**.

りえさんは家にいます。　**Rie-san wa uchi ni imasu.**　　*Rie is at home/in the house.*

6.6 MORE QUESTION WORDS

You already know three question words: どこ、**doko**, なに、**nani**, だれ **dare** (*where, what, who*). If you want to ask where the post office is, you can say either of these:

郵便局はどこにありますか。	**Yūbinkyoku wa doko ni arimasu ka.**
郵便局はどこですか。	**Yūbinkyoku wa doko desu ka.**

The reply could be:

郵便局は銀行の隣にあります。

Yūbinkyoku wa ginkō no tonari ni arimasu.

The post office is next door to the bank.

1 If you wanted to avoid repeating post *office*, what would you say in Japanese? (*It's next door to the bank*.)

You can also use なに **nani** and だれ **dare** (*what, who*) with あります **arimasu** and います **imasu**:

銀行の隣に何がありますか。

Ginkō no tonari ni nani ga arimasu ka.

What is (there) next to the bank?

2 What does this mean?

銀行の前にだれがいますか。	**Ginkō no mae ni dare ga imasu ka.**

Look at how these sentences are constructed. Can you pick out the location part at the beginning followed by the question part: *bank next to, what is there?*?

YOUR TURN 3 How would you say the following in Japanese?

a What is there behind the bank?

b What is there by the school?

c Who is opposite the post office?

To reply, you replace the question word with the information required. To answer question **a**, you can say:

銀行の後ろにスーパーがあります。

Ginkō no ushiro ni sūpā ga arimasu.

Behind the bank is a supermarket.

Or simply:

スーパーがあります	**Sūpā ga arimasu.**	*There is a supermarket.*

6.7 GIVING AND FOLLOWING DIRECTIONS

To give directions you use a special form of verb which in this book is called the て **te** form. You will learn about this in detail later – here it is used for giving directions.

 1 06.07 Listen to the audio of the directions given. Can you work out what would go in the gaps in the English translations?

まっすぐ	massugu	*straight ahead*
まっすぐ行って	massugu itte	*go straight ahead*
まっすぐ行ってください。	Massugu itte kudasai.	*Go straight ahead, please.*
まがってください	magatte kudasai	*a) _____ turn*
右_{みぎ}にまがってください。	Migi ni magatte kudasai.	*Please b) _____ (to the) right.*
左_{ひだり}にまがってください。	Hidari ni magatte kudasai.	*Please c) _____ (to the) left.*
交差点_{こうさてん}を右にまがってください。	Kōsaten o migi ni magatte kudasai.	*Please turn d) _____ at the crossroads.*
信号を右にまがってください。	Shingō o migi ni magatte kudasai.	*e) _____ turn right at the traffic lights.*
渡_{わた}ってください。	Watatte kudasai.	*Please cross.*
橋_{はし}を渡ってください。	Hashi o watatte kudasai.	*Please f) _____ the bridge.*
歩道橋_{ほどうきょう}を渡ってください。	Hodōkyō o wattate kudasai.	*Please cross the footbridge.*
道_{みち}を渡ってください。	Michi o watatte kudasai.	*Please cross the road.*
一つ目_めの信号を左にまがってください。	Hitotsūme no shingō o hidari ni magatte kudasai.	*Please turn g) _____ at the first h) _____ _____.*
次_{つぎ}の信号を左にまがってください。	Tsugi no shingō o hidari ni magatte kudasai.	*Please i) _____ _____ at the next j) _____.*

2 What do the commands end in? What does this term mean?

3 What particle do you use after the direction words 右 **migi** and 左 **hidari** (*to the left/right*)?

4 What particle do you use after *first* and *next*?

YOUR TURN How would you say the following in Japanese?

a Go straight ahead.
b Turn left at the crossroads.
c Cross at the pedestrian crossing.
d Turn right at the first traffic lights.
e Cross the footbridge then* turn left at the corner.

* Note: Use the て form and save ください **kudasai** until the end.

> **LANGUAGE TIP**
> If you want to give more than one direction in a sentence, you save ください **kudasai** until the end.

6.8 MAKING AND RESPONDING TO SUGGESTIONS

In Conversation 2 Roger asked Miki:

どこに行きましょうか。	**Doko ni ikimashō ka.**	*Where shall we go (to)?*

You can also use the verb ending ませんか **masen ka** to ask *would you like to? (won't you?)*.

If you want to suggest a particular time, venue or activity, you can use the phrase どうですか **dō desu ka** (*how about?*) with the particle は **wa** to express this:

明日はどうですか。	**Ashita wa dō desu ka.**	*How about tomorrow?*

To accept, say:

いいですね。	**Ii desu ne.**	*That'll be great.*

To refuse politely, say:

ざんねんですが、ゴルフはちょっと …

Zannen desu ga, gorufu (ashita/eigakan) wa chotto …

It's a shame but golf (tomorrow/the cinema) is a bit …

> **YOUR TURN** How would you ask the following?
> a (At) what time shall we go? (use 何時に **nanji ni** for *at what time*)
> b (At) what time shall we meet? (会います **aimasu** means *to meet*)
> c Where shall we meet (at)? (use どこで **doko de** for *where at*)
> d What shall we do?
> e Would you like to eat at a restaurant?
> f Would you like to go to the cinema?
> g How about the cinema?
> h How about golf?

> **LANGUAGE TIP**
> This way of refusing gives an insight into the Japanese psyche because you don't openly turn someone down – you imply that you don't want to or can't make it by trailing off at the end of the sentence.

6.9 PAST TENSE

The past tense (*did, didn't*) is very simple in Japanese. You simply change ます **masu** to ました **mashita** to say *did* and to ませんでした **masen deshita** to say *didn't*.

> **YOUR TURN 1** What would you put in the gaps in the following table?

ate	食べました	**tabemashita**	*didn't eat*	食べませんでした	**tabemasen deshita**
drank	飲みました	**nomimashita**	*didn't drink*	飲みません a) _____	**nomimasen a) _____**
listened	聞き b) _____	**kiki b) _____**	*didn't listen*	聞きませんでした	**kikimasen deshita**
saw	見 c) _____	**mi c) _____**	*didn't see*	見ませんでした	**mimasen deshita**
met	会いました	**aimashita**	*didn't meet*	会い d) _____ _____	**ai d) _____ _____**

> **2** How would you say the following in Japanese?
> a I ate breakfast.
> b I didn't drink any coffee.
> c We met at seven o'clock at the restaurant.

6.10 SAYING *I WANT TO*

To say 'I want to' you use the stem of the verb – the verb without ます masu. For example:

聞きます kikimasu (listen) → 聞き kiki

YOUR TURN 1 Make the stems of these verbs:

Stem	English	Japanese
a) _____	*drink*	飲みます nomimasu
b) _____	*go*	行きます ikimasu
c) _____	*eat*	食べます tabemasu

To say *I want to* you add たいです **tai desu** to the stem. For example:

| ビールを飲みたいです。 | **Bīru o nomitai desu.** | *I want to drink beer.* |
| 日本に行きたいです。 | **Nihon ni ikitai desu.** | *I want to go to Japan.* |

Sometimes the particle が **ga** is used in place of the particle を **o** but both are correct.

YOUR TURN 2 How would you say the following in Japanese?

a I want to go to France next week.

b I want to listen to the news at home.

c I want to buy a Japanese camera.

d I want to drink sake with my neighbour.

6.11 DAYS OF THE WEEK

 In Japanese each day is named after elements of the natural world. Looking at the table, what is the common ending for all days of the week?

English	Japanese	Meaning	Kanji
Sunday	**nichiyōbi**	*sun (day)*	日
Monday	**getsuyōbi**	*moon*	月
Tuesday	**kayōbi**	*fire*	火
Wednesday	**suiyōbi**	*water*	水
Thursday	**mokuyōbi**	*tree*	木
Friday	**kinyōbi**	*gold*	金
Saturday	**doyōbi**	*earth*	土

6.12 TELLING THE TIME (*FIVE PAST, FIVE TO*)

To say *five past*, *ten past* and so on requires some practice but it is logical. First, you need to know these words:

<ruby>五分<rt>ごふん</rt></ruby>	**gofun**	*five minutes*
<ruby>十分<rt>じゅっぷん</rt></ruby>	**juppun**	*ten minutes*

In Japanese, you give the hour first and then the minutes.

1.05	=	一時五分	ichiji gofun	*(one o'clock and five minutes)*
1.10	=	一時十分	ichiji juppun	*(one o'clock and ten minutes)*

To say *15 minutes* you say 15 (十五 **jūgo**) and add ふん **fun** to the end.

To say *20 minutes* you say 20 (二十 **nijū**) and add ぷん **pun** to the end (the sound 'squashes' to にじゅっぷん **nijuppun**).

YOUR TURN 1 What times are shown on these clocks?

a   b   c   d

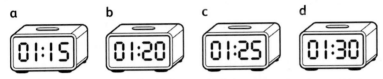

2 Can you complete this rule? When telling the time, all multiples of five end in _____, all multiples of ten end in _____.

As well as saying *30 minutes past* (三十分 **sanjuppun**) you can also say *half past* using <ruby>半<rt>はん</rt></ruby> **han**:

一時半 **ichiji han** = 一時三十分 **ichiji sanjuppun** = *1.30 (half past one)*

To say *five to*, *ten to* the hour and so on you keep the same order but add the additional word 前 **mae**. You have already learned that this means *in front of* or *before* so, in the context of time, it adds the meaning *before the hour* or simply *to*:

二時二十五分前 **niji nijū gofun mae** = *1.35 (twenty-five to two)*

You can also say *1.35* as in *one (o'clock) thirty-five (minutes)*: 一時三十五分 **ichiji sanjū gofun**. (For this, you don't need 前 **mae**.) You can practise telling the time with the audio and table in the Appendices.

6.13 DISTINGUISHING BETWEEN MORNING AND AFTERNOON

To distinguish between morning and afternoon (a.m. and p.m.) you can use 朝 **asa** and <ruby>午後<rt>ごご</rt></ruby> **gogo** or the more formal equivalent of a.m. which is <ruby>午前<rt>ごぜん</rt></ruby> **gozen**. You say the morning or afternoon word before the time:

午前 (朝) 一時半 **gozen (asa) ichiji han** = *1.30 a.m.*
午後一時半 **gogo ichiji han** = *1.30 p.m.*

6.14 *HERE, THERE* AND *OVER THERE*

The words ここ **koko** (*here*), そこ **soko** (*there*) and あそこ **asoko** (*over there*) form a 'family' with the word for *where*: どこ **doko**.

Use these words and この近く **kono chikaku** (*near here*) to explain where places are:
映画館はあそこにあります。 **Eigakan wa <u>asoko ni</u> arimasu.** *The cinema is <u>over there</u>.*

YOUR TURN How would you say the following in Japanese?

a The restaurant is there.
b The company is here.
c The school is near here.
d The post office is over there.
e The art gallery is there.

 Speaking

Look at the map. Your friend (marked X) is standing at the end of the main street. Give him directions and the precise locations for the five places numbered on the map. Start by saying the question he would ask you. You can check your answers in the Answer key but these are only sample answers; yours may be different but equally correct. The first one is done for you.

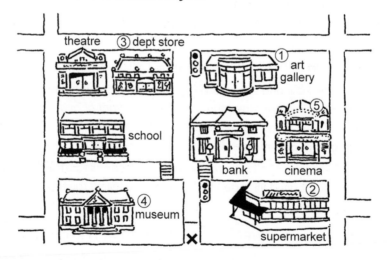

1 すみません、美術館はどこにありますか。
まっすぐ行って、横断歩道を渡ってください。美術館は銀行の後ろにあります。

Sumimasen, bijutsukan wa doko ni arimasu ka.
Massugu itte, ōdan hodō o watatte kudasai. Bijutsukan wa ginkō no ushiro ni arimasu.

Listening

1 06.08 **Select the correct words from the box and complete the sentences a–j by putting the number of each word in the brackets, then work out the English meanings. Listen to the audio to check your answers.**

a レストランは（＿）に（＿）　　Resutoran wa (__) ni (__).

b あの信号（＿）右に（＿）、まっすぐ行ってください。
　　Ano shingō (__) migi ni (__), massugu itte kudasai.

c 私の（＿）は学校（＿）そばにあります。
　　Watashi no (__) wa gakkō (__) soba ni arimasu.

d 私の（＿）はかばんの（＿）にあります。
　　Watashi no (__) wa kaban no (__) ni arimasu.

e 郵便局の（＿）に（＿）がありますか。
　　Yūbinkyoku no (__) ni (__) ga arimasu ka.

f 歩道橋を（＿）、かどを（＿）にまがってください。
　　Hodōkyō o (__), kado o (__) ni magatte kudasai.

g 映画館に（＿）か。　　Eigakan ni (__) ka.

h 七時（＿）レストラン（＿）会いました。
　　Shichiji (__) resutoran (__) aimashita.

i コーヒーを（＿）。　　Kōhī o (__).

j 近所の人（＿）お酒を（＿）です。
　　Kinjo no hito (__) osake o (__) desu.

1	向かい側　mukaigawa		10	飲みたい　nomitai
2	を　o		11	そこ　soko
3	あります　arimasu		12	行きません　ikimasen
4	に　ni		13	名刺　meishi
5	左　hidari		14	渡って　watatte
6	で　de		15	家　uchi
7	飲みませんでした　nomimasen deshita		16	の　no
8	と　to		17	何　nani
9	まがって　magatte		18	中　naka

2 06.09 **Listen to the conversation between Rie and her friend Miki Sugihara. Where do they decide to go and what time do they decide to meet? The script and translation are in the Answer key.**

3 06.10 **Listen to the audio and match the clocks with the times you hear.**

1   2   3

4   5   6

When you have finished this activity try saying the times out loud then check against the audio.

Writing

Complete these sentences using one of the following: ます、ません、ました、ませんでした、たいです (**masu, masen, mashita, masen deshita** and **tai desu**).

a 夕べテレビを見_____。

Yūbe terebi o mi _____.
(Last night I watched TV.)

b 来週ボーリングに行き_____。

Raishū bōringu ni iki _____.
(Next week I want to go bowling.)

c 朝いつも六時に起き_____。

Asa itsumo rokuji ni oki _____.
(I always get up at six o'clock in the morning.)

d お酒を全然飲み_____。

Osake o zenzen* nomi _____.
(I never drink sake.)

e 先週テレビを全然見_____。

Senshū terebi o zenzen mi _____.
(I didn't watch TV at all last week.)

f 来週アメリカに行き_____。

Raishū Amerika ni iki _____.
(I am not going to America next week.)

g りえさんと会い_____。

Rie-san to ai _____.
(I want to meet up with Rie.)

h 来年車を買い_____。

Rainen kuruma o kai _____.
(Next year I want to buy a car.)

* Note: 全然 **zenzen** means *never* and is used with the negative of the verb.

How to read the final 16 **hiragana** symbols

START READING

 06.11 Here are the **16 hiragana** symbols with their pronunciation underneath. Listen to the audio as you read the symbols and say each sound out loud. Try to copy the pronunciation correctly.

ま	み	む	め	も
ma	mi	mu	me	mo
や	ゆ	よ		
ya	yu	yo		
ら	り	る	れ	ろ
ra	ri	ru	re	ro
わ	を			
wa	(w)o			
ん	(n)			

> **LANGUAGE TIP**
> The **wo/o** symbol を is used only as a particle and not as a part of a word. You use お (**o**) in words. を is used to mark the object of a sentence: **osake o nomimasu** (*I drink rice wine*). It is sometimes represented by the letters **wo** to distinguish it from the other **o** sound.

HOW TO REMEMBER **HIRAGANA** SYMBOLS

Here are some more ideas for mnemonics to help you remember the new symbols.

ま (**ma**) mammon, the god of wealth

む (**mu**) a 'moo' cow

や (**ya**) shouts the cowboy as he throws his lasso

よ (**yo**) practising yoga

ら (**ra**) is half a rabbit

を (**o**) Australian sat by a lake

Here are some other ideas that might work for you:

み	(**mi**)	looks like number 4 'me when I was 4'
め	(**me**)	a messy knot – ends showing
も	(**mo**)	she has a modern hairstyle (looks like し **shi** with two hair clips)
ゆ	(**yu**)	looks like an unusual fish
り	(**ri**)	the flow of a river
る	(**ru**)	the loop is a ruby whereas ろ (**ro**) has no ruby because there's been a robbery
れ	(**re**)	can you see a reindeer?
わ	(**wa**)	a baby's wide-open mouth crying 'waaaah'
ん	(**n**)	like a simplified version of え (**e**), which put together almost spell 'the end'!

OTHER IDEAS TO HELP YOU REMEMBER

Add the new **hiragana** to your flashcards. Mix them in with the other 30 symbols (you now have a complete set of the 46 basic symbols) and keep testing yourself. Then try this game. Spread all the cards out, **hiragana** side up. Can you pick out the symbols that spell the following words (most of which you have learned in this or previous units)? Say the words out loud as you pick them up:

あかい *red*	うしろ *behind*
あおい *blue*	まえ *in front*
しろい *white*	となり *next to*
くろい *black*	なか *inside*
おかあさん *mother*	よこ *beside*
おとうさん *father*	ちかく *near*
むすこ *son*	ここ *this place*
むすめ *daughter*	そこ *that place*
うえ *above*	あそこ *that place over*
した *below*	どこ *there where*

> **LANGUAGE TIP**
> You may find it helpful when reading rows of words or sentences if you place a ruler or piece of card under the row you are reading so that you are not distracted by the rows below. You'll find it easier to keep your place too.

Add the final 16 **hiragana** symbols to your table. It should now look like this:

わ	ら	や	ま	は	な	た	さ	か	あ
	り		み	ひ	に	ち	し	き	い
	る	ゆ	む	ふ	ぬ	つ	す	く	う
	れ		め	へ	ね	て	せ	け	え
を	ろ	よ	も	ほ	の	と	そ	こ	お
ん									

The symbol ん (**n**) is traditionally put in its own row but don't worry if you don't have room for this.

SIMILAR-LOOKING HIRAGANA

Here are some more **hiragana** symbols which look similar and some clues to help you tell them apart.

い, り	い (**i**) the left stroke is slightly longer than the right whereas in り (**ri**) the right stroke is much longer than the left.
ほ, ま	The top horizontal line in ほ (**ho**) rests on top of the vertical line whereas in ま (**ma**) both horizontal lines cut through.
ぬ, め	Both ぬ (**nu**) and め (**me**) have two 'vertical' lines at the top but ぬ (**nu**) has a loop (the 'noodles') whereas め (**me**) has none.
す, む	す (**su**) curves to the left; む (**mu**) curves to the right and has an extra 'dash'.
る, ろ	You've been given the story of 'the ruby and the robbery' for this but also remember that る (**ru**) has a loop and ろ (**ro**) looks like number 3.
ね, れ, わ	ね (**ne**) has a loop, れ (**re**) curves out at the end, わ (**wa**) curves in.

Different fonts make these symbols look slightly different:
れ (**re** れ), わ (**wa** わ), も (**mo** も), む (**mu** む), ら (**ra** ら), り (**ri** り), や (**ya** や).

Reading

1 06.12 **Here are some hiragana words containing the new hiragana symbols. Try reading them out loud both with and without the help of the audio.**

a むら village
b よる evening
c ゆめ dream
d ゆり lily
e やま mountain
f もも peach
g もり forest
h みみ ear
i もん gate
j われわれ we
k わん bowl
l まる circle

2 06.13 **Can you read the following hiragana words which contain combinations of all the 46 basic hiragana symbols? You can also listen to the words on the audio.**

a ほん book
b かいもの shopping
c わたし I
d なまえ name
e おはよう good morning
f すみません excuse me
g おやすみ なさい goodnight
h のみます drink
i します do
j かきます write
k かいます buy
l ききます listen
m かえります return
n おきます get up
o ねます go to bed
p みます look
q よみます read
r はなします talk
s つくります make
t はたらきます work

3 06.14 Try reading some simple sentences that include objects, time expressions, ます and ました (**masu/mashita**) verbs and the particle を (**o**). You can either listen to the audio as you read the sentences or read the sentences first then listen. Can you work out the English meaning?

a とけい を かいました。
b はなし を ききました。
c はやく おきました。
d おそく ねました。
e ほん を よみました。
f まいにち はたらきます。
g おそく うち に かえりました。
h あした はは と かいもの を します。
i わたし の なまえ を かきました。
j よる たいてい おさけ を のみます。

4 Here, in random order, are all **46 hiragana** symbols. Can you read them all? **Speak out loud:**

a なん り ひ あ き る そ も わ に ふ
b ぬ へ う こ ま ろ し を お ほ と ゆ
c や た れ ね つ さ み は す い か
d の て ら く む よ け え め せ ち

? Test yourself

1 How do you say the following in Japanese?

   a The post office is opposite the bank.

   b The bank is next to the supermarket.

   c The supermarket is behind the school.

   d The school is near the museum.

   e The teacher is in the school.

   f My business card is inside my bag.

2 Match the English days of the week to the Japanese. What number and letter goes in the brackets next to the English meanings?

Sunday ( ), ( )

Monday ( ), ( )

Tuesday ( ), ( )

Wednesday ( ), ( )

Thursday ( ), ( )

Friday ( ), ( )

Saturday ( ), ( )

曜日 = ようび

1 火曜日		**a** kayōbi
2 木曜日		**b** mokuyōbi
3 日曜日		**c** nichiyōbi
4 土曜日		**d** doyōbi
5 水曜日		**e** suiyōbi
6 月曜日		**f** getsuyōbi
7 金曜日		**g** kinyōbi

SELF CHECK

I CAN...

○ …give the location of places, items and people.

○ …give and follow directions.

○ …arrange to meet someone.

○ …speak in the past (*I did, I didn't*).

○ …make, accept and refuse suggestions.

○ …talk about what I want to do.

○ …say the days of week.

○ …tell the time.

○ …talk about hobbies and leisure activities.

○ …recognize 46 **hiragana** symbols.

7 あの人は有名ですよ！
<ruby>ひと<rt></rt></ruby> <ruby>ゆうめい<rt></rt></ruby>
Ano hito wa yūmei desu yo!
That person is famous, you know!

In this unit you will learn how to:
▶ *use adjectives (describing words).*
▶ *describe people.*
▶ *give an opinion and express your hopes.*
▶ *talk about illness.*

CEFR: *(A2) Can tell a story or describe something in a simple list of points.*
(B1) Can connect phrases in a simple way in order to describe experiences and events, dreams, hopes and ambitions.

 <ruby>にほんさんけい<rt></rt></ruby>
日本三景 Nihon Sankei *Japan's most scenic places*

日本三景 **Nihon Sankei** (*Japan's three most scenic places*) were decided upon several centuries ago and all 日本人 **Nihonjin** (*Japanese people*) know about them and will endeavour to visit them in their lifetime.

松島 **Matsushima** near 仙台 **Sendai** in the 日本の北東 **Nihon no hokutō** (*north-east of Japan*) is a bay filled with rocky islets and small islands covered in 松 **matsu** (*pine trees*) which can be viewed by 船 **fune** (*boat*).

天橋立 **Amanohashidate** in the 南西 **Nansei** (*south-west*) is a long natural sandbar stretching across the 海 **umi** (*sea*). The name means 'bridge of heaven' and, when viewed upside down, is supposed to appear to float between earth and heaven.

宮島 **Miyajima** in the 南東 **Nantō** (*south-east*) is a sacred 島 **shima** (*island*) which has an iconic red 鳥居 **torii** (*gate*) at its entrance and an ancient 神社 **jinja** (*Shinto shrine*) where many traditional ceremonies are held, including 結婚 **kekkon** (*weddings*) and 能 **Noh** (*Noh plays*).

It is part of Japanese tradition to group the best sightseeing places – 一番美しい庭園 **ichiban utsukushii teien** (*the most beautiful gardens*), 一番いい祭り **ichiban ii matsuri** (*the best festivals*), 一番いいお寺 **ichiban ii otera** (*the top temples*), and so on.

 1 **What is the Japanese for** *south*?
2 **What is the Japanese for** *number one* **that can be placed before adjectives to make them** *the most*?

Vocabulary builder

 07.01 Listen to the new vocabulary and practise saying it out loud.

DESCRIBING CHARACTERISTICS

有名（な）	yūmei (na)	*famous*
美しい	utsukushii	*beautiful*
明るい	akarui	*bright, cheerful*
やさしい	yasashii	*kind, gentle*
おとなしい	otonashii	*quiet, shy*
恥ずかしい	hazukashii	*embarrassed, ashamed, shy*
いい	ii	*good, nice*
恥ずかしがり（な）	hazukashigari (na)	*seems shy*
とても上手（な）	totemo jōzu (na)	*very good at*
真面目（な）	majime (na)	*serious, conscientious*
広い	hiroi	*spacious, big* (of places)
にぎやか（な）	nigiyaka (na)	*lively, busy*
きれい（な）	kirei (na)	*beautiful; clean*
恥ずかしがりじゃない	hazukashigari ja nai	*seems not shy*
大きい	ōkii	*big (objects)*
小さい	chiisai	*small*

DESCRIBING APPEARANCE

背	se	*height*
高い	takai	*tall*
低い	hikui	*short*
ふつう	futsū	*average*
目	me	*eyes*
鼻	hana	*nose*
顔	kao	*face*
長い	nagai	*long/narrow*
四角い	shikakui	*square*
丸い	marui	*round*
髪	kami	*hair*
目の色	me no iro	*eye colour*
青い	aoi	*blue*
黒い	kuroi	*black/dark brown*
茶色	chairo	*brown*
髪の色	kami no iro	*hair colour*
金髪	kinpatsu	*blond(e)*
短い	mijikai	*short*
かたぐらい	kata gurai	*mid-length*

7 Ano hito wa yūmei desu yo! **That person is famous, you know!**   91

TALKING ABOUT ILLNESSES

どうしたんですか。	Dō shita n desu ka.	*What's wrong?*
のどが _____ です。	Nodo ga _____ desu.	*My throat is sore.*
かたが _____ です。	Kata ga _____ desu.	*My shoulders ache.*
せなかが _____ です。	Senaka ga _____ desu.	*I've got backache.*
おなかが _____ です。	Onaka ga _____ desu.	*I've got stomach ache.*
気分が悪いです。	Kibun ga warui desu.	*I feel bad/ill.*
かぜをひいてしまいました。	Kaze o hiiteshimaimashita.	*I've caught a cold.*
かぜ	kaze	*a cold*
二日酔い	futsuka yoi	*hangover*
頭	atama	*head*
痛い	itai	*hurts*

NEW EXPRESSIONS

デート	dēto	*date*
どうでしたか。	Dō deshita ka.	*How was it?*
少し	sukoshi	*a little*
そんなに	sonna ni	*(not) especially* (+ negative)
（だ）と思います	(da) to omoimasu	*I think that*
また	mata	*again*
（し）たいと思います	(shi)tai to omoimasu	*I hope to (do)*
所	tokoro	*place*
部屋	heya	*room, bedroom*
あまり	amari	*not very* (+ negative)
だ	da	*is* (informal of **desu**)
好き（な）	suki	*like*

Make sure you lengthen the first sound when you say 大きい **ōkii** (*big*). Each sound of the word has one 'beat' and your voice smoothly moves from one to the next: **o-o-ki-i.**

> **LANGUAGE TIP**
> 恥かしがり **Hazukashigari** is linked to 恥かしい **hazukashii** and they carry overlapping meanings of *shy, embarrassed* and *ashamed*. However, when you are making observations about someone else's shyness you use 恥かしがり **hazukashigari** (*seems shy*).

Conversation 1

 07.02 *Miki and Roger discuss their first date with Rie. First Rie catches up with Roger.*

1 How does Roger describe Miki?

Rie	ねえ、ロジャーさん、みきさんとデートはどうでしたか。
Roger	彼女はいい人ですね。少し恥ずかしがりでおとなしい人ですが美しいですね。
Rie	そんなに恥ずかしがりじゃないと思いますよ。また会いたいですか。
Roger	はい、来週一緒にテニスをしたいと思います。
Rie	Nē, Roger-san, Miki san to dēto wa dō deshita ka.
Roger	Kanojo wa ii hito desu ne. Sukoshi hazukashigari de otonashii hito desu ga utsukushii desu ne.
Rie	Sonna ni hazukashigari ja nai to omoimasu yo. Mata aitai desu ka.
Roger	Hai, raishū issho ni tenisu o shitai to omoimasu

2 What part of Roger's description of Miki doesn't Rie agree with?

3 What is Roger hoping to do on their second date?

Conversation 2

 07.03 *Rie gets Miki's side of the story.*

1 How does Miki describe Roger?

Rie	ロジャーさんはいい人ですね。
Miki	そうですね。とても明るくて優しい人だと思います。彼はボーリングもとても上手です。私はスポーツがちょっと...
Rie	また会いたいですか。
Miki	はい、来週　映画館で映画を見たいと思います。
Rie	*(Sounds surprised)* 映画ですか。
Rie	Roger-san wa ii hito desu ne.
Miki	Sō desu ne. Totemo akarukute yasashii hito da to omoimasu. Kare wa bōringu mo totemo jōzu desu. Watashi wa supōtsu ga chotto …
Rie	Mata aitai desu ka.
Miki	Hai, raishū eigakan de eiga o mitai to omoimasu.
Rie	*(Sounds surprised)* Eiga desu ka.

2 Why is Rie surprised at the end?

3 You saw in the Vocabulary builder that と思います to omoimasu means *I think that*. Look back at the passage and work out the following:

   a Where is this phrase placed in a sentence?   **b** How would you say the following?

     1 I think that he is a kind person.   **3** I think that he is a cheerful and kind person.

     2 I think that she is a beautiful person.   **4** I think that she seems (to be) shy.

🔅 Language discovery

7.1 DESCRIBING PEOPLE

The title of this unit shows us how to say *That person is ...* :

あの人は有名です   **Ano hito wa yūmei desu.**   *That person is famous.*

YOUR TURN 1   Using the new vocabulary, how would you say the following in Japanese?

    a   That person is beautiful.

    b   That person is cheerful.

    c   That person is kind.

To link two adjectives to say sentences such as *that person is beautiful and famous* you can't use the word you have already learned for *and* (と **to**) because this is only used between two nouns. Instead, you change the first adjective like this:

美しい   **utsukushii**   *beautiful*   →   美し<u>くて</u>   **utsukushi<u>kute</u>**   *beautiful and*

You take off the final い **i** sound and add to the adjective the *and* word くて **kute**, so the adjective itself has an *and* form rather than using a separate *and* as we do in English:

あの人は美しくて有名です

Ano hito wa utsukushikute yūmei desu.

That person is beautiful and famous.

YOUR TURN 2   How would you say the following in Japanese?

    a   That person is cheerful and kind.

    b   That person is quiet and shy.

    c   That person is gentle and beautiful.

    d   That person is quiet and nice.

7.2 JAPANESE ADJECTIVES (い、な I AND NA)

The symbol な **na** is written in brackets after some adjectives. This is because there are two types of adjective in Japanese, often referred to as い **i** and な **na** adjectives, which follow different rules. We're going to learn one of these rules here but first we need to work out how we know if an adjective is い **i** or な **na**. It's not always obvious but the following points will help you:

▶ The majority of adjectives are い **i** adjectives.

▶ All **i** adjectives end in the **hiragana** い.

▶ Some な **na** adjectives end in い **i** but if this is preceded by an **e** sound then it must be a な **na** adjective (for example, きれい、ゆうめい **kirei, yūmei**).

▶ Adjectives that don't end in い **i** can't be **i** adjectives (for example, まじめ、じょうず **majime, jōzu**).

▶ Some dictionaries list when an adjective is な **na**.

▶ If the word is only made up of **kanji** with no **hiragana** い **i** at the end, it must be a な **na** adjective – you can see this in all dictionaries that include **kanji**.

The rule is that when the noun you are describing follows immediately after a な **na** adjective you must put な **na** at the end of the adjective. Look at these two sentences:

あの人は有名ですよ！   **Ano hito wa yūmei desu yo!**   *That person is famous, you know!*

あれは有名<u>な</u>人ですよ！   **Are wa yūmeina hito desu yo!**   *That is a famous person, you know!*

YOUR TURN Six sentences follow with brackets after the な na adjective. Decide whether な na is needed or not and work out the English meanings.

a みきさんはきれい（ ）人ですね。   Miki-san wa kirei ( ) hito desu ne.

b ロジャーさんはボーリングが上手（ ）ですね
Roger-san wa bōringu ga jōzu ( ) desu ne.

c 東京はにぎやか（ ）ですね。   Tōkyō wa niqiyaka ( ) desu ne.

d ここはにぎやか（ ）ところですね。   Koko wa nigiyaka ( ) tokoro desu ne.

e 本堂たつやさんは真面目（ ）人だと思います。
Hondō Tatsuya-san wa majime ( ) hito da to omoimasu.

f これはきれい（ ）部屋ですね。   Kore wa kirei ( ) heya desu ne.

By contrast, い **i** adjectives remain the same in both types of sentence:

あの人は<u>美しい</u>ですよ！   **Ano hito wa <u>utsukushii</u> desu yo!**

That person is beautiful, you know!

あれは<u>美しい人</u>ですよ！   **Are wa <u>utsukushii</u> hito desu yo.**

That is a beautiful person, you know!

7.3 A NEW SENTENCE STRUCTURE

All the sentences you have encountered so far have followed the basic pattern of:
(noun) (は **wa** adjective) (noun) (です **desu**).

Here are two examples:

みきさんはきれいな人です。   **Miki-san wa kireina hito desu.**

Miki is a beautiful person.

この部屋は広いです。   **Kono heya wa hiroi desu.**

This room is spacious.

Take a look at the following sentence structure – how does it differ?

ロジャーさんはボーリングが上手です。   **Roger-san wa bōringu ga jōzu desu.**

Roger is good at bowling.

母は頭が痛いです。   **Haha wa atama ga itai desu.**

My mother's head hurts.

Here the sentence pattern is:
(noun 1) (は **wa**) (noun 2) (が **ga**) (adjective) (です **desu**).

In this type of sentence, we are learning more information about the overall subject which is noun 1 and so this noun takes は **wa**. You can sometimes think of は **wa** as meaning *as for*. So the sentence about Roger could mean: *As for Roger, his bowling is skilful.*

The particle が **ga** is used after noun 2 and relates directly to the adjective: *the bowling is skilful, the head hurts.*

YOUR TURN Using this new sentence structure, can you work out how to say the following in Japanese?

a This museum is a busy place.

b Tokyo is very busy, isn't it!

c This is a spacious and clean room. (*this is* = **kore wa**)

d My mother has big eyes. (*as for my mother, the eyes are big*)

e My eyes hurt. (*as for me, the eyes hurt*)

f Roger is tall with big eyes. (*as for Roger, height tall and eyes big*)

g Naoe is good at origami. (*as for Naoe, her origami is skilful*)

h Miki is bad at bowling. (*as for Miki, her bowling is poor*)

7.4 DESCRIBING PHYSICAL APPEARANCE

The Vocabulary builder gives a list of useful words for describing people but there are some points to note when describing physical attributes:

▶ In Japanese, you talk about people's heights as *high/tall* or *low/short* rather than *big* or *small*.

▶ 短い **mijikai** (*short*) refers to length, not height.

▶ Noses are not big in Japanese but *high* (高い **takai**) or *wide* (大きい **ōkii**).

▶ Very dark eyes are referred to as *black* (黒い **kuroi**) rather than *brown* (茶色 **chairo**).

▶ Average length hair is shoulder length (かたぐらい **kata gurai**).

Now you're going to put this together. Use the pattern you've just learned:

(noun 1) (は **wa**) (noun 2) (が **ga**) (adjective) (です **desu**).

(person) (は **wa**) (body part) (が **ga**) (description) (です **desu**).

You can leave out noun 1 when it is clear who is being talked about.

Here's an example:

	私は	背が	低いです
I am short. →	**(Watashi wa)**	**se ga**	**hikui desu.**
	(noun 1)	(noun 2)	(adjective)
	(person)	(body part)	(description)

If you want to make longer sentences, you can use くて **kute** (*and*) with い **i** adjectives only to link together two descriptions as follows:

（私は）背が低くて、髪が茶色です。

I am short with brown hair. → **(Watashi wa) se ga hikukute, kami ga chairo desu.**

YOUR TURN 07.04 How would you say the following in Japanese? Listen to the audio to check your answers.

a I am tall.

b I am tall with blue eyes.

c I am tall with blue eyes and blond(e) hair.

d My mother has a round face.

e My mother has a round face and a high nose.

f My mother has a round face, a high nose and brown eyes.

g She has long, black hair. (Clue: you don't need to repeat the word for *hair*.)

7.5 LINKING ADJECTIVES WITH *AND*

You have already used the connector くて **kute** in 7.1. It can only be used for い **i** adjectives and to use it you drop the final い **i** and add くて **kute**.

For な **na** adjectives you use another *and* word: で **de**. It takes the place of です **desu** as follows:

有名で美しい人です   yūmei **de** utsukushii hito desu
a famous and beautiful person

きれいで広い部屋です   kirei **de** hiroi heya desu
a clean and spacious room

YOUR TURN How would you say the following in Japanese?
- **a** (He is) a serious and quiet person.
- **b** Tokyo is lively and big (spacious).

You can also use が **ga** (*but*) when giving contrasting descriptions. In this case, use です **desu** both before が **ga** and at the end of the sentence.

Look back at the conversation and find out how Roger described Miki as a serious person but beautiful.

If you use が **ga** (*but*) in this way, then the second item being described (and sometimes the first item, too) takes the particle は **wa** (to emphasize contrast) rather than が **ga**:
スポーツが下手ですが折り紙は上手です。
Supōtsu ga heta desu ga origami wa jōzu desu.
I'm poor at sports but I'm good at origami.

7.6 GIVING AN OPINION

You have already used the expression と思います **to omoimasu** to say *I think that* with **i** ending adjectives. Here are the rules for both types of adjective:

▶ い **i** adjectives (including たいです **tai desu** *I want to*) replace です **desu** with と思います **to omoimasu**:
広いです → 広いと思います   hiroi desu → hiroi to omoimasu

▶ な **na** adjectives (and nouns) replace です **desu** with its informal form だ **da** then add と思います **to omoimasu**:
きれいです → きれいだと思います   kirei desu → kirei da to omoimasu

YOUR TURN How would you say the following in Japanese?
- **a** I think that he is famous.
- **b** I think that it is a big (spacious) place.
- **c** I think that she is shy.

7.7 EXPRESSING HOPES

You have learned that by adding たいです **tai desu** to the stem of the verb you can say *I want to do*. By adding たいと思います **tai to omoimasu**, you can say *I hope to*.

YOUR TURN **How would you say the following in Japanese?**

a I hope to go to Japan next year.

b I hope to eat sushi in Japan.

c And I hope to see Mount Fuji (富士山 **Fujisan**).

7.8 HOW TO MAKE THE NEGATIVE FORM OF い I ADJECTIVES

To form the negative of い **i** adjectives you take off い **i** and add くないです **kunai desu** (*it is not*):

大きいです → 大きくないです   **ōkii desu → ōkikunai desu**   *it isn't big*

There is one adjective which changes slightly:

いいです → よくないです   **ii desu** (*good*) → **yokunai desu**   *it isn't good*

Also note → よくて **yokute** *good and …*

7.9 NEGATIVES WITH **NA** ADJECTIVES

Look back to the first conversation to see how Rie-san said of Miki *I don't think she's especially shy.*

The negative of な **na** adjectives and nouns follows the same rule as in English – です **desu** (*is*) changes to the negative (*is not*). (Look back at the table in Unit 1 to remind yourself of negatives.)

YOUR TURN **Using formal or informal, can you change these positive statements into negative ones?**

a きれいです。Kirei desu.　　　　　She is beautiful./It is clean.
　　　　　　　　　　　　　　　　　　(She's not beautiful./It's not clean.)

b 有名な人です。Yūmeina hito desu.　He is a famous person.
　　　　　　　　　　　　　　　　　　(He is not a famous person.)

7.10 TALKING ABOUT ILLNESS

In 7.4 you used the pattern (body part) (が **ga**) (description) (です **desu**) to make descriptions. Using this same structure with the description word 痛い **itai** (*hurts*), can you work out how to say the following? (Use the Vocabulary builder for the body parts.)

YOUR TURN **How would you say the following in Japanese?**

a My eyes hurt/are sore.

b I have a headache.

> **LANGUAGE TIP**
>
> The Japanese phrase for *I've caught a cold* might look rather daunting at first. Try breaking it down like this:
>
> ひーいーて　　**hi-i-te**
> ひーいーて　　しーまーい　　**hi-i-te shi-ma-i**
> ひーいーて　　しーまーい　　まーした　　**hi-i-te shi-ma-i ma-sh(i)-ta**

Listening

 1 07.05 **Listen as Robert complains to Miki and Rie of not feeling well then answer the questions.**

    a List the five symptoms Robert is suffering from.

    b What conclusion does Miki come to?

    c What alternative conclusion does Rie come to?

 2 07.06 **Listen to these sentences and see if you can pick out the missing adjectives, then work out the meanings in English.**

    a 彼女はとても ＿＿＿＿ ですが少し ＿＿＿＿ です。

       Kanojo wa totemo ＿＿＿＿ desu ga sukoshi ＿＿＿＿ desu.

    b 東京は ＿＿＿＿ ＿＿＿＿ ところです。   Tokyo wa ＿＿＿＿ ＿＿＿＿ tokoro desu.

    c 私の部屋はあまり ＿＿＿＿ ではありません。

       Watashi no heya wa amari ＿＿＿＿ dewa arimasen.

    d みきさんはそんなに ＿＿＿＿ じゃないと思います。

       Miki-san wa sonna ni ＿＿＿＿ ja nai to omoimasu.

    e ロジャーさんは ＿＿＿＿ 人だと思います。

       Roger-san wa ＿＿＿＿ hito da to omoimasu.

Reading 1

 07.07 **Before Miki met Roger she wrote this description of herself for a computer dating agency. Read it through, check your understanding, then listen to the audio and repeat it to practise pronunciation.**

私はすぎはらみきです。背がふつうでかみが黒くて長いです。目が黒くて丸いです。顔も丸いですが鼻が四角いです。私はおとなしいですがやさしいと思います。映画が好きですがスポーツは好きじゃありません。

Watashi wa Sugihara Miki desu. Se ga futsū de kami ga kurokute nagai desu. Me ga kurokute marui desu. Kao mo marui desu ga hana wa shikakui desu. Watashi wa otonashii desu ga yasashii to omoimasu. Eiga ga suki desu ga supōtsu wa suki ja arimasen.

📝 Writing

1 Use Miki's computer dating description as your model and write one to describe yourself. Try to write it in Japanese script and, once you have written it, learn it off by heart and say it out loud in a confident manner!

2 How well have you understood the rules for making the negative and connectors of **na** and **i** adjectives? A table of five adjectives follows. See if you can convert them correctly to provide the English meaning.

Adjective	English	Negative	Connector
a おとなしい otonashii			
b まじめ majime			
c 有名 yūmei			
d 明るい akarui			
e いい ii			

How to alter **hiragana** symbols to make new sounds

In this section you will learn how to use the **hiragana** you have already learned to make new sounds.

RULE 1: CHANGING THE SOUNDS OF SINGLE **HIRAGANA** SYMBOLS

You are going to learn how to change the sounds of some **hiragana** symbols by adding the marks ゛ (**tenten**) and ゜ (**maru**). First, review these particular symbols before you learn the new rules:

か	き	く	け	こ
ka	ki	ku	ke	ko
さ	し	す	せ	そ
sa	shi	su	se	so
た	ち	つ	て	と
ta	chi	tsu	te	to
は	ひ	ふ	へ	ほ
ha	hi	fu	he	ho

By adding the **tenten** mark, these symbols change their sounds as follows:

1 **k** sounds become **g** sounds (hard *g* as in *get*)

か	き	く	け	こ	→	が	ぎ	ぐ	げ	ご
ka	ki	ku	ke	ko		ga	gi	gu	ge	go

2 **s** sounds → **z** sounds

さ	し	す	せ	そ	→	ざ	じ	ず	ぜ	ぞ
sa	shi	su	se	so		za	ji*	zu	ze	zo

*じ is pronounced **ji** (not **zi**)

3 **t** sounds become **d** sounds

た	ち	つ	て	と	→	だ	ぢ	づ	で	ど
ta	chi	tsu	te	to		da	(ji	zu)*	de	do

*ぢ (**ji**) and づ (**zu**) are not normally used because they create the same sounds as じ (**ji**) and ず (**zu**) (See 2.)

4 **h** sounds become **b** sounds

は	ひ	ふ	へ	ほ	→	ば	び	ぶ	べ	ぼ
ha	hi	fu	he	ho		ba	bi	bu	be	bo

5 In addition, **h** sounds become **p** sounds when a small circle ° (**maru**) is added:

は	ひ	ふ	へ	ほ	→	ぱ	ぴ	ぷ	ぺ	ぽ
ha	hi	fu	he	ho		pa	pi	pu	pe	po

These five rules cover all the sound changes for single **hiragana** symbols. Practise reading them while listening to the audio from the Pronunciation guide then try the following reading activities to help you practise and learn these rules.

 READING 2

1 Can you read the sequences of symbols that follow? Speak out loud.

a が ざ だ ば ぱ   d ざ じ ず ぜ ぞ
b が ぎ ぐ げ ご   e げ ぜ で べ ぺ
c ご ぞ ど ぼ ぽ   f び ぶ ぴ ぷ

2 Here are the days of the week written in **hiragana**. Say them out loud and translate them into English. Check your answers in Unit 6.

にちようび   もくようび
げつようび   きんようび
かようび   どようび
すいようび

3 Here are some words you learned in Units 1–6 which have **tenten** symbols. Can you read them? What do they mean in English?

a かぞく   e にほんご   i でんわ
b しんぶん   f あさごはん   j しごと
c ぎんこう   g ばんごはん   k ときどき
d ご   h たまご   l ぜんぜん

RULE 2: CONTRACTED SOUNDS

 07.08 These new sounds are made by combining the **hiragana** symbols that end in an **i** sound (き, し, ち, に, ひ, み, り) with a small version of や, ゆ or よ. Each of these new sounds is pronounced as a single syllable or 'beat'. Look at the following, listen to the audio and practise saying the sounds.

き →	きゃ (kya)	きゅ (kyu)	きょ (kyo)
し →	しゃ (sha)	しゅ (shu)	しょ (sho)
ち →	ちゃ (cha)	ちゅ (chu)	ちょ (cho)
に →	にゃ (nya)	にゅ (nyu)	にょ (nyo)
ひ →	ひゃ (hya)	ひゅ (hyu)	ひょ (hyo)
み →	みゃ (mya)	みゅ (myu)	みょ (myo)
り →	りゃ (rya)	りゅ (ryu)	りょ (ryo)

> **PRONOUNCIATION TIP**
> When saying a word, try to move smoothly from one sound to the next – it shouldn't sound disjointed. Be especially careful of this when (**u**) follows a sound.

 READING 3

Here are some words from Units 1–5 that contain these contracted sounds. Can you read them? What do they mean in English?

a しゃちょう

b かいしゃ

c じむしょ

d しゅふ

e しょくじ

f きょうだい

g りょこう

h ちゅうごく

i とうきょう

j きょうと

k でんしゃ

l ゆうびんきょく

m べんきょう

n ひゃく

o らいしゅう

RULE 3: CONTRACTED SOUNDS WITH TENTEN AND MARU

Do you remember the rules you learned for **hiragana** symbols that change their sound (Rule 1)? These rules also apply to the contracted sounds (Rule 2) beginning with **k**, **s** and **b**. Can you work out how to say these sounds? Cover up the **rōmaji** given on the right and see if you can say each sound out loud then uncover and see if you were right (remember: each sound is one syllable/beat).

ぎゃ ぎゅ ぎょ	gya, gyu, gyo
じゃ じゅ じょ	ja, ju, jo
びゃ びゅ びょ	bya, byu, byo
ぴゃ ぴゅ ぴょ	pya, pyu, pyo

📖 **READING 4**

Here, in sequences of random order, is a selection of changed and contracted sound <u>hiragana</u> that you have learned in this unit. Can you read them all?

a が きゃ ぎゃ

b じ しゃ じゃ ちゃ

c ひょ びょ ぴょ

d で ぎ ざ ぶ ぺ

e ぎゅ じゅ びゅ ぴゅ

f ちょ にょ ひょ みょ りょ

g りゃ みゅ ひゅ ぴゅ

h ぎょ じょ びょ ぴょ

i ず ぐ ぶ りゅ

j ぱ ぴ ぷ ぺ ぽ

🔳 Test yourself

1 How would you say the following in Japanese?

   a I don't think she's especially shy.

   b Tokyo is lively and big (spacious).

   c I am tall with blue eyes and blond(e) hair.

   d My mother is tall and has big eyes.

   e I think he's a very cheerful and kind person.

   f That person is serious but kind.

   g I am poor at sports but I am good at origami.

2 Match the Japanese phrases with the English meanings.

   a かたが痛いです kata ga itai desu

   b かぜをひいてしまいました kaze o hiiteshimaimashita

   c おなかが痛いです onaka ga itai desu

   d 気分が悪いです kibun ga warui desu

   e 背中が痛いです senaka ga itai desu

   f どうしたんですか dō shita n desu ka

   g のどが痛いです nodo ga itai desu

   1 What's wrong?

   2 My throat is sore.

   3 My shoulders ache.

   4 I've got backache.

   5 I've got stomach ache.

   6 I feel ill.

   7 I've caught a cold.

SELF CHECK

	I CAN...
⭕	...use adjectives.
⭕	...describe people.
⭕	...give an opinion and express my hopes.
⭕	...talk about illness.
⭕	...alter **hiragana** symbols to make new sounds.

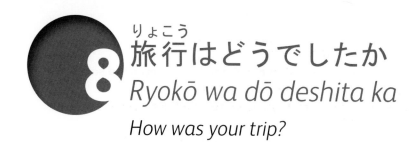

8 旅行はどうでしたか
りょこう

Ryokō wa dō deshita ka

How was your trip?

In this unit you will learn how to:
▸ *describe past events.*
▸ *talk about the weather and listen to weather reports.*
▸ *talk about transport and travel.*

CEFR: *(A2) Can follow changes of topic and factual TV news items, and form an idea of the main content. Can get simple information about travel, use of public transport, give directions and buy tickets. (B1) Can deliver short, rehearsed announcements on a topic pertinent to everyday occurrences.*

🔘 天気と季節 **Tenki to kisetsu** *Weather*
てんき きせつ

天気 **Tenki** is an important subject in Japan – people are more likely to make comments about 天気 **tenki** when they meet up than ask casually after someone's health. A useful phrase to remember for good days is いい天気ですね **Ii tenki desu ne!** (*It's nice weather, isn't it!*).

The following pictures show types of 天気 **tenki** in Japanese.

When talking about 天気 **tenki** you can either use です **desu** (*it is/it will be*) where 天気 **tenki** is definite, or when making a prediction the Japanese use でしょう **deshō** (*it probably will be*). So you might hear 雨です **ame desu** (*it is raining*) or 雪でしょう **yuki deshō** (*it probably will be snowing*). Three other useful words when talking about 天気 **tenki** are のち **nochi** (*later*), 時々 **tokidoki** (*sometimes*) and 一日 **ichinichi** (*all day*).
あめ ゆき いちにち

1 How would you say the following in Japanese?
   a It is foggy.
   b It will probably be sunny.
   c It is cloudy.
   d It will probably rain.

2 Now you are going to work out how to say these weather conditions. All are predictions (use でしょう deshō):
   a Rainy, later fine.
   b Cloudy, sometimes snow.
   c Fine all day. (order: all day fine)
   d Dull, sometimes rain.

Vocabulary builder

 1 08.01 Listen to the new vocabulary and practise saying it out loud.

USEFUL ADJECTIVES FOR DESCRIBING EVENTS

楽しい	tanoshii	*enjoyable, pleasant*
面白い	omoshiroi	*interesting, funny, fun*
いい（よい）	ii (yoi)	*good, nice*
すばらしい	subarashii	*wonderful, great*
つまらない	tsumaranai	*boring*
ふゆかい（な）	fuyukai (na)	*unpleasant, disagreeable*
いや（な）	iya (na)	*awful*
面白かった	omoshirokatta	*it was interesting*
面白くなかった	omoshirokunakatta	*it wasn't interesting*
あたたかくなかった	atatakakunakatta	*it wasn't warm*
楽しくなかった	tanoshikunakatta	*it wasn't enjoyable*
遠すぎました	tōsugimashita	*it was too far*

TRAVEL WORDS AND NEW EXPRESSIONS

旅行（します）	ryokō (shimasu)	*travel, trip (do)*
出張（します）	shutchō (shimasu)	*business trip (do)*
新幹線で	shinkansen de	*by bullet train (**de** = by)*
バス	basu	*bus*
車	kuruma	*car*
大阪行きの切符を二枚ください	Ōsaka-yuki no kippu o nimai kudasai	*Two tickets to Osaka, please.*
片道ですか。往復ですか	Katamichi desu ka. Ōfuku desu ka	*Is it one way or return?*
もうすぐ	mō sugu	*soon (**sugu** = at once)*
まだです	mada desu	*not yet*
（に）なります	(ni) narimasu	*become, get, will be*
だんだん	dandan	*gradually*
行き	-yuki	*bound for*
切符	kippu	*ticket*
まで	made	*until, to*
同僚	dōryō	*colleague*
予報	yohō	*forecast*

SEASONS

四季 (しき) shiki　*the four seasons*

春 (はる) haru　*spring*　　秋 (あき) aki　*autumn/fall*

夏 (なつ) natsu　*summer*　　冬 (ふゆ) fuyu　*winter*

> **LANGUAGE TIP**
> For いいです **ii desu**
> (*good*) use よい **yoi** and
> change it into the past.

 2 08.02 Look at *it was interesting* in the vocabulary list. Can you work out the rule for changing い **i** adjectives into the past tense?

 3 Now look at the vocabulary list and say the past tense of the first five adjectives then listen to the audio to check your answers.

4 Now listen to the audio, say all the new words out loud and focus on good pronunciation.

Conversation

 08.03 *Hondo Tatsuya-san has become friendly with Ian Ferguson, a New Zealander, through work. He meets up with Ian at a bar following a business trip to Osaka.*

1 What does Tatsuya-san think of Osaka?

Tatsuya	先週大阪に出張しました。面白くなかったです。
Ian	そうですか。大阪に行きたいです。面白くない所ですか。
Tatsuya	大阪はすばらしい所ですが仕事はつまらなかったです。
Ian	どうやって行きましたか。
Tatsuya	大阪まで新幹線で行きました。片道の切符を買いました。同僚の車で帰りました。それも楽しくなかったです。遠すぎました。
Ian	お天気はどうでしたか。
Tatsuya	もうすぐ春になりますがそんなにあたたかくなかったです。木曜日は一日雪でした。ふゆかいでした。
Ian	東京の天気の予報を聞きましたか。
Tatsuya	いいえ、まだです。
Ian	明日は寒くなります。雨のち雪でしょう。
Tatsuya	いやですね！
Tatsuya	Senshū Ōsaka ni shutchō shimashita. Omoshirokunakatta desu.
Ian	Sō desu ka. Ōsaka ni ikitai desu. Omoshirokunai tokoro desu ka.
Tatsuya	Ōsaka wa subarashii tokoro desu ga shigoto wa tsumaranakatta desu.
Ian	Dō yatte ikimashita ka.
Tatsuya	Ōsaka made shinkansen de ikimashita. Katamichi no kippu o kaimashita. Dōryō no kuruma de kaerimashita. Sore mo tanoshikunakatta desu. Tōsugimashita.
Ian	O-tenki wa dō deshita ka.
Tatsuya	Mō sugu haru ni narimasu ga sonna ni atatakakunakatta desu. Mokuyōbi wa ichinichi yuki deshita. Fuyukai deshita.
Ian	Tōkyō no tenki yohō o kikimashita ka.
Tatsuya	Iie, mada desu.
Ian	Ashita wa samuku narimasu. Ame nochi yuki deshō.
Tatsuya	Iya desu ne!

2 How did he get there, how did he return and how was the return journey?

3 What was the weather like?

4 What is the weather forecast for Tokyo?

5 Can you answer these questions in Japanese?

    a 出張は面白かったですか。   Shutchō wa omoshirokatta desu ka.

    b たつやさんは大阪まで往復の切符を買いましたか。

        Tatsuya-san wa Ōsaka made ōfuku no kippu o kaimashita ka.

    c 木曜日の天気はどうでしたか。   Mokuyōbi no tenki wa dō deshita ka.

    d 明日はあたたかくなりますか。   Ashita wa atatakaku narimasu ka.

💡 Language discovery

8.1 PAST TENSE, SAYING *IT WAS*

You learned how to link two adjectives in Unit 7 by using the connector くて **kute** (for **i** adjectives) and で **de** (for **na** adjectives). This remains the same when talking about past events with only the final adjective of the sentence in the past tense:

楽しくて面白かったです   **tanoshikute omoshirokatta desu**   *it was enjoyable and fun*

For **na** adjectives, change です **desu** (*is*) to でした **deshita** (*was*):

きれいです → きれいでした   **kirei desu → kirei deshita**   *it was clean/she was beautiful*

YOUR TURN Using the new vocabulary, how would you say the following in Japanese?

a It was interesting and enjoyable.

b It was interesting and good.

c It was wonderful and fun.

d It was nice and enjoyable.

e It was disagreeable.

f He was famous.

8.2 PAST TENSE, SAYING *IT WASN'T* WITH I ADJECTIVES

Look at the Vocabulary builder and find *it wasn't interesting, it wasn't warm.* Can you work out the rule for changing **i** adjectives into the past negative?

The rule is:

    1 Take the present negative: 面白くないです **omoshirokunai desu**

    2 Drop the final い **i** and add the past かった **katta**: 面白くな<u>かった</u>です
       omoshirokuna<u>katta</u> desu

So you are using かった **katta** to put the negative into the past.

Or you can think of it this way: drop い **i** and add くなかった **kunakatta**:

面白いです → 面白<u>くなかった</u>です   **omoshiroi desu → omoshiro<u>kunakatta</u> desu**

YOUR TURN Change the following adjectives into their past negative and give the English meaning.
a 楽しいです   tanoshii desu
b いいです   ii desu (note: be careful)
c すばらしです   subarashii desu
d つまらないです   tsumaranai desu

8.3 PAST TENSE, SAYING *IT WASN'T* WITH **NA** ADJECTIVES

For **na** adjectives you need to change です **desu** into its past negative. Look at the following table.

am, is, are	was not, were not (formal)	was not, were not (informal)	was not, were not (casual)
です	ではありませんでした	じゃありませんでした	じゃなかったです
desu	dewa arimasen deshita	ja arimasen deshita	ja nakatta desu

Example: 有名です → 有名では（じゃ）ありませんでした
yūmei desu → yūmei dewa (ja) arimasen deshita

> **LEARNING TIP**
> じゃ **Ja** is simply a more informal ('squashed') version of では **dewa** so you can use either to form the past. Even more informal is じゃなかったです **ja nakatta desu** – you will hear this a lot in everyday Japanese speech and can use it yourself outside formal/polite situations.

YOUR TURN Say these sentences in Japanese:
a She wasn't beautiful.
b He wasn't serious.
c It wasn't disagreeable.

8.4 SUMMARY OF TENSES

You have now been introduced to four main **masu** and **desu** tenses. Here they are summarized in a table. Can you fill in the gaps?

English	Present (*is*) future (*will be*)	Past (*was*)	Negative present (*isn't*) negative future (*won't be*)	Past negative (*wasn't*)
eat	食べます tabemasu	食べました tabemashita	a _____	食べませんでした tabemasen deshita
big	大きいです ōkii desu	b _____	大きくないです ōkikunai desu	大きくなかったです ōkikunakatta desu
famous	有名です yūmei desu	有名でした yūmei deshita	c _____	有名じゃ（では）ありませんでした yūmei ja (dewa) arimasen deshita
is	です desu	でした deshita	d _____	e _____

8.5 DESCRIBING ACTIONS (ADVERBS)

The function of adverbs is to describe or give more information about the verb, for example: *he talks quickly*, *she writes beautifully*.

In Japanese, as in English, adjectives can be turned into adverbs. You have already come across some adverbs in previous units:

早く　**hayaku**　*early* (also: 速く **hayaku** is pronounced the same but means *quickly, fast*)
遅く　**osoku**　*late*
近く　**chikaku**　*nearby*
よく　**yoku**　*often* (also: *well*)

For **i** adjectives you drop い **i** and add く **ku**:

面白い → 面白く　**omoshiroi → omoshiroku**　*interestingly*

For **na** adjectives, you add に **ni** after the adjective:

上手 → 上手に　**jōzu → jōzu ni**　*skilfully*

YOUR TURN Read these Japanese sentences and see if you can work out their English meanings. The adverbs are underlined.

a みきさんは上手に漢字を書きます　Miki-san wa *jōzu ni* kanji o kakimasu.
b ロバートさんはよく日本語を話します　Robāto-san wa *yoku* nihongo o hanashimasu.
c 本堂さんは真面目に仕事をします　Hondō-san wa *majime ni* shigoto o shimasu.
d なおえさんはきれいに掃除をします　Naoe-san wa *kirei ni* sōji o shimasu.
e ケイティさんはやさしく英語を話します。　Katie-san wa *yasashiku* eigo o hanashimasu.

8.6 なります NARIMASU *TO BECOME*

The verb なります **narimasu** means *to become, to be, to get* in English. For example:

もうすぐ夏になります　　　**Mō sugu natsu ni narimasu.**
　　　　　　　　　　　　　Soon it will be summer.

明日六才になります　　　　**Ashita rokusai ni narimasu.**
　　　　　　　　　　　　　Tomorrow I will be(come) six years old.

なります **Narimasu** can be used with adverbs to talk about things becoming hot, cold, happy, etc. You use the past tense to say things *have become*. Here are examples of its use:

だんだんあつくなります　　　**Dandan atsuku narimasu.**
　　　　　　　　　　　　　　It gradually gets hotter.

この部屋はきれいになりました　**Kono heya wa kirei ni narimashita.**
　　　　　　　　　　　　　　This room has become cleaner.

8.7 DESCRIBING THE SEASONS

We can use this phrase to talk about the seasons:

もうすぐ (season) になります　**mō sugu** (season) **ni narimasu**　*soon it will be (season)*

We can also use adverbs followed by になります **ni narimasu** to describe the weather.

 Can you work out the Japanese adverbs that can be used to describe the weather from the following adjectives?

Adjective	Adverb	English
あつい　atsui	a _____	*hot*
寒い　samui	b _____	*cold*
あたたかい　atatakai	c _____	*warm*
涼しい　suzushii	d _____	*cool/fresh*

YOUR TURN Look at the examples then work out the meaning of the sentences.

Examples: もうすぐ春になります。　　　**Mō sugu haru ni narimasu.**
Soon it will be spring.

だんだんあたたかくなります。　**Dandan atatakaku narimasu.**
It will gradually get warm(er).

a もうすぐ夏になります。だんだんあつくなります。
Mō sugu natsu ni narimasu. Dandan atsuku narimasu.
b もうすぐ冬になります。だんだん寒くなります。
Mō sugu fuyu ni narimasu. Dandan samuku narimasu.
c もうすぐ秋になります。だんだん涼しくなります。
Mō sugu aki ni narimasu. Dandan suzushiku narimasu.

8.8 TRANSPORT AND TRAVELLING

When you want to talk about the type of transport you go by you need the particle **de** after the mode of transport. Look at these examples:

新幹線で	**shinkansen de**	*by bullet train*
電車で	**densha de**	*by train*
新幹線で行きました。	**Shinkansen de ikimashita.**	*I went by bullet train.*
大阪に新幹線で行きました。	**Ōsaka ni shinkansen de ikimashita.**	*I went by bullet train to Osaka.*
新幹線で大阪に行きました。	**Shinkansen de Ōsaka ni ikimashita.**	*I went by bullet train to Osaka.*

To ask *how did you go (there)?* you say どうやって行きましたか **dō yatte ikimashita ka.**

YOUR TURN How do you say the following sentences in Japanese?

a I went by bus.
b I went to town (町 **machi**) by bus.
c I went to my mum's house by car.
d I went to New York (ニューヨーク **Nyū Yōku**) by train.

> **LEARNING TIP**
> The last two examples above show that the meaning is the same whether you say *to Osaka* first or *by bullet train* first. The important thing is to use the particles correctly. The order is less important but always say the verb at the end.

Listening

08.04 **You are going to listen to a weather forecast. Looking at the table, can you pick out for each city the type of weather, temperature and any additional information where given (e.g. *it will be hot*)? The word for 'degree' is ど do and this is said after the number: 十度 jū do = 10˚.**

City	Weather	Temperature	Additional
a Sapporo			
b Sendai			
c Tōkyō			
d Ōsaka			
e Fukuoka			
f Okinawa			

Reading and writing

1 **The following Japanese sentences are incomplete. Complete them by adding the correct tense ending (the tense is indicated in brackets, see the table in 8.4 to remind yourself of these). Then translate them into English.**

a この映画は面白くてよかった ＿＿＿＿＿。
えいが　　　おもしろ

Kono eiga wa omoshirokute yokatta ＿＿＿＿＿. (past)

b 先週の出張はつまらなくてふゆかい ＿＿＿＿＿。
せんしゅう　しゅっちょう

Senshū no shutchō wa tsumaranakute fuyukai ＿＿＿＿＿. (past)

c 明日の天気は曇りのち雨 ＿＿＿＿＿。
あした　　　　　くも　　あめ

Ashita no tenki wa kumori nochi ame ＿＿＿＿＿. (future/probability)

d 明日三十二才になり ＿＿＿＿＿。 Ashita sanjū nīsai ni nari ＿＿＿＿＿. (future)
さい

e この部屋はきれいになり ＿＿＿＿＿。 Kono heya wa kirei ni nari ＿＿＿＿＿. (past)
へ や

f 私はあまり新聞を読み ＿＿＿＿＿。
しんぶん　よ

Watashi wa amari shinbun o yomi ＿＿＿＿＿. (negative)

g 近所の人は目が大き ＿＿＿＿＿ (and) 背が高 ＿＿＿＿＿。
きんじょ

Kinjo no hito wa me ga ōki ＿＿＿＿＿ (link, *and*) se ga taka ＿＿＿＿＿. (negative)

h 旅行は全然楽し ＿＿＿＿＿。 Ryokō wa zenzen tanoshi ＿＿＿＿＿. (past negative)
りょこう　ぜんぜんたの

i あなたの部屋はきれい ＿＿＿＿＿。 Anata no heya wa kirei ＿＿＿＿＿. (negative)
へ や

j 夕べ頭が痛 ＿＿＿＿＿。 何も食べ ＿＿＿＿＿。
ゆう　あたま　いた

Yūbe atama ga ita ＿＿＿＿＿. (past) Nani mo tabe ＿＿＿＿＿. (past negative)

2 08.05 **Listen to the audio while reading the text as Ian explains briefly about the weather and seasons in New Zealand. There is a list of new words below the text.**

ニュージーランドは季節が四つあります。春は九月から十一月までです。天気は晴れ時々雨です。だんだんあたたかくなります。夏は十二月から二月までです。だんだんあつくなります。秋は三月からです。天気は晴れ、風、雨 … 冬は六月からです。とても寒いです。雪がいっぱい降ります。

Nyū Jīrando wa kisetsu ga yottsu arimasu. Haru wa kugatsu kara jūichigatsu made desu. Tenki wa hare tokidoki ame desu. Dandan atatakaku narimasu. Natsu wa jūnigatsu kara nigatsu made desu. Dandan atsuku narimasu. Aki wa sangatsu kara desu. Tenki wa hare, kaze, ame … Fuyu wa rokugatsu kara desu. Totemo samui desu. Yuki ga ippai furimasu.

ニュージーランド	**Nyū Jīrando**	*New Zealand*
いっぱい	**ippai**	*plenty, full, a lot*
から、まで	**kara … made**	*from . . . to* (placed after the noun)
降ります	**furimasu**	*falls* (rain, snow)

Using Ian's description as a model, write out a similar speech that describes the seasons in your own country. (Or, if you are a New Zealander, choose a country in the northern hemisphere.) Use as much of the vocabulary and as many of the structures for months, seasons and weather as you can and try to give your speech some variety.

Extending your skills in **hiragana**

In this section you will learn how sounds are lengthened (two beats), how the small つ (**tsu**) is used to create a pause in a word, how to write particles in Japanese and how to read sentences.

RULE 1: LENGTHENED SOUNDS

 08.06 **Here are some words you have already learned in Units 1–8, written in hiragana. These words all contain う (u). Listen to how they are pronounced and repeat each word out loud.**

きょうだい	siblings	きゅうしゅう	Kyushu
べんきょう	study	とうきょう	Tokyo
ゆうびんきょく	post office	らいしゅう	next week
ぎんこう	bank	りょこう	travel

You learned in the Pronunciation guide that these long syllables (double length) are written with a macron over the vowel to indicate that it is a long sound. When written in hiragana, most commonly う (u) is used but you will also come across: あ (a), い (i), え (e) and お (o) used to lengthen sounds. Read and listen to how you say these words:

おおきい	big	おにいさん	older brother
おねえさん	older sister	おかあさん	mother

RULE 2: USING っ (TSU) TO CREATE A SHORT PAUSE

 08.07 You also learned about double consonants in the Pronunciation guide – words such as: **ju<u>ss</u>ai** (*ten years old*); **ki<u>tt</u>e** (*stamp*); **ga<u>kk</u>ō** (*school*); **ki<u>ss</u>aten** (*coffee shop*); **shu<u>tc</u>hō** (*business trip*) and **ki<u>pp</u>u** (*ticket*).

Here is how these words are written in **hiragana**:

じゅっさい **ju<u>ss</u>ai**　　きって **ki<u>tt</u>e**　　　　　がっこう **ga<u>kk</u>ō**
きっさてん **ki<u>ss</u>aten**　　しゅっちょう **shu<u>tc</u>hō**　　きっぷ **ki<u>pp</u>u**

Notice that the pause (glottal stop) is represented by a small っ (**tsu**).

Listen and read as the words are spoken on the audio.

RULE 3: WRITING PARTICLES IN **HIRAGANA**

An important function of **hiragana** is to represent the grammar parts of Japanese sentences. The various particles you have learned (**o**, **ga**, **de**, **ni**, **wa**, **e**) are all written in **hiragana**.

o = を (you have already met this)　　**ni** = に
ga = が　　　　　　　　　　　　　　　**wa** = は
de = で　　　　　　　　　　　　　　　**e** = へ

They are all as you might expect except:

▶ particle **wa** (は), which is normally pronounced **ha** when part of a word but as **wa** when a particle
▶ particle **e** (へ), which is normally pronounced **he** when part of a word but as **e** when a particle.

RULE 4: PUNCTUATION MARKS

Here is a short selection of Japanese punctuation marks:

full stop = 。
comma = 、
speech marks = 「 」

In addition, rules about spaces between words are different in Japanese – for example, it is all right for words to split over two lines and the particle normally follows a word without a space in between. However, to help you learn to read, the words have been spaced out in these **hiragana** learning sections so that you can easily identify words and particles.

📖 Reading

08.08 Now that you have learned all the main rules for reading **hiragana** you are going to read some sentences and work out what they mean. All of these are taken from Units 1–8 and are also on the audio so that you can listen as you read if you wish to.

Units 1 and 2

    a かない の なまえ は りえです。
    b かぞく は ごにん です。
    c むすめ は じゅっさい です。

Unit 3 and 4

    d かぞく と あさごはん を たべます。
    e あさ そうじ を します。
    f きんじょ の ひと と にほんご を はなします。

Unit 5

    g この しんぶん は いくら ですか。
    h にかい に なにも ありません。
    i あの じむしょ に おとうさん が いますか。

Unit 6

    j まっすぐ いって ください。
    k しんごう を みぎ に まがって ください。

Unit 7

    l とうきょう は ひろくて にぎやかな ところ です。
    m わたし の へや は あまり きれい で は ありません。

Unit 8

    n りょこう は おもしろくて たのしかった です。
    o おおさか ゆき の きっぷ を にまい ください。

FINAL WORDS ON READING

You have now learned the tools for reading **hiragana** and there is plenty of opportunity in this course to practise your reading skills. From Unit 10 the Japanese text will be written in Japanese script only, with the **rōmaji** versions of the conversations located at the end of the course for support. To build your confidence, look back at the **hiragana** versions of all the conversations in Units 1–8 and practise reading them using the audio to support you.

? Test yourself

1 You have learned a lot about particles (は、が、を、で、に、も、の、から、まで、と) (**wa, ga, o, de, ni, mo, no, kara, made, to**). The following sentences are all about the characters and events you have learned about in this book. Can you work out which particles should go into the brackets?

a なおえさん（　）朝早く朝ごはん（　）食べます。
   Naoe-san ( ) asa hayaku asagohan ( ) tabemasu.

b みきさん（　）ボーリング（　）あまり上手ではありません。
   Miki-san ( ) bōringu ( ) amari jōzu dewa arimasen.

c 本堂さん（　）同僚（　）車（　）東京（　）帰りました。
   Hondō-san ( ) dōryō ( ) kuruma ( ) Tōkyō ( ) kaerimashita.

d 六時（　）ボーリング場（　）会いましょう。 Rokuji ( ) bōringujō ( ) aimashō.

e りえさん（　）みきさん（　）映画館（　）行きました。
   Rie-san ( ) Miki-san ( ) eigakan ( ) ikimashita.

f 本堂さん（　）毎日朝早く（　）夜遅く（　）仕事（　）します。
   Hondō-san ( ) mainichi asa hayaku ( ) yoru osoku ( ) shigoto ( ) shimasu.

g みきさん（　）ボーリグ（　）テニス（　）下手です。 Miki-san ( ) bōringu ( ) tenisu ( ) heta desu.

h ロバートさん（　）背（　）ふつうで、目（　）青いです。
   Robāto-san ( ) se ( ) futsū de, me ( ) aoi desu.

i ニュー東京ホテル（　）美術館（　）後ろ（　）あります。
   Nyū Tokyō hoteru ( ) bijutsukan ( ) ushiro ( ) arimasu.

j 大阪（　）すばらしい所です（　）仕事（　）つまらなかったです。
   Ōsaka ( ) subarashii tokoro desu ( ) shigoto ( ) tsumaranakatta desu.

2 Work out the English meanings of these sentences.

a 旅行は面白くて楽しかったです。 Ryokō wa omoshirokute tanoshikatta desu.

b 映画は面白かったですがちょっと長かったです。
   Eiga wa omoshirokatta desu ga chotto nagakatta desu.

c この本はつまらなくて、ふゆかいでした。 Kono hon wa tsumaranakute fuyukai deshita.

d 先週大阪に出張しました。面白くなかったです。
   Senshū Ōsaka ni shutchō shimashita. Omoshirokunakatta desu.

e 本堂さんは新幹線で大阪に行きました。 Hondō-san wa shinkansen de Ōsaka ni ikimashita.

f もうすぐ夏になります。だんだんあつくなります。
   Mō sugu natsu ni narimasu. Dandan atsuku narimasu.

g 明日の天気は曇りのち雨でしょう。 Ashita no tenki wa kumori nochi ame deshō.

h 大阪行きの切符を二枚ください。 Ōsaka-yuki no kippu o nimai kudasai.

SELF CHECK

I CAN...
...describe past events.
...talk about the weather and listen to weather reports.
...talk about transport and travel.

9
うちゅうひこうし
宇宙飛行士になりたいです
Uchūhikōshi ni naritai desu!

I want to be an astronaut!

In this unit you will learn how to:
▸ *talk about likes, dislikes and desires.*
▸ *say what you are good and bad at.*
▸ *use the verb stem to say more.*
▸ *use work-related phrases.*

CEFR: *(B1) Can understand the main points of clear standard input on familiar matters regularly encountered in work, school and leisure. Uses reasonably accurate repertoire of frequently used 'routines' and patterns associated with more predictable situations. Can explain what he likes or dislikes.*

しょくば　　　　　　にほんご
職場における日本語 shokuba ni okeru nihongo
Japanese language in the workplace

The politeness that runs through the Japanese language is also part of 職業生活 **shokugyō seikatsu** (*working life*). 女性 **Josei** (*Women*), who traditionally have held the lower-paid roles such as **OL** pronounced **Ōeru** (*office lady*, someone who does more menial office tasks, makes the tea, etc.), tend to use the politest and humblest levels of language. As a general rule, Japanese workers use 尊敬語 **sonkeigo** (*respectful Japanese*) when addressing their bosses and 先輩 **senpai** (*superiors*) and 丁寧語 **teineigo** (*neutral polite*) or informal levels to their equals and 後輩 **kōhai** (*inferiors*). When talking to 外国人 **gaikokujin** (*foreigners*) working with 日本の会社 **Nihon no kaisha** (*Japanese companies*) you should keep to 丁寧語 **teineigo** (*neutral polite Japanese*, **masu/desu**) so that you don't sound disrespectful regardless of whether you are 男性 **dansei** (*male*) or 女性 **josei**. As you become more familiar with the people you work with then you can begin using more informal language but be led by your peers in this. Even if a 先輩 **senpai** speaks to you very informally, you should still show respect to them by using 丁寧語 **teineigo** – this is the normal order of things.

However, it would seem that Japanese is changing in response to the new demands and expectations of an increasingly global society to such an extent that some Japanese companies are having to teach 若者 **wakamono** (*young people*) how to use 尊敬語 **sonkeigo** and 丁寧語 **teineigo** in the 職場 **shokuba** (*workplace*). Until recent times this would have been unthinkable.

Look through the passage again. Work out the English meanings of the following words and put these Japanese words into 'pairs'.

a 先輩
b 会社
c 丁寧語
d 女性

e 職場
f 後輩
g 男性
h 尊敬語

Vocabulary builder

1 09.01 Listen to the new vocabulary and practise saying it out loud.

JOBS AND OCCUPATIONS

になりたいです	ni naritai desu	*I want to be a …*
仕事	shigoto	*work*
子供のころ	kodomo no koro	*when (I was) a child*
映画スター	eiga sutā	*film star*
俳優	haiyū	*actor*
脳外科医	nō gekai	*brain surgeon*
歌手	kashu	*singer*
消防士	shōbōshi	*firefighter*
ロケット科学者	roketto kagakusha	*rocket scientist*
看護師	kangoshi	*nurse, medical carer*
会社員	kaishāin	*company employee*
銀行員	ginkōin	*bank worker*
社長	shachō	*company president, director*
医者	isha	*doctor*
作家	sakka	*writer*
カメラマン	kameraman	*photographer*
警察官	keisatsukan	*policeman*
弁護士	bengoshi	*lawyer*
宇宙飛行士	uchūhikōshi	*astronaut*

USEFUL PHRASES IN THE WORKPLACE

もしもし	moshi moshi	*hello* (on the telephone – in all situations)
失礼します	shitsurei shimasu	*excuse me for interrupting* (e.g. when entering an office or meeting room, at end of phone call)
失礼しました	shitsurei shimashita	*excuse me* (used when leaving a room)
お先に	osaki ni	*I'm leaving before you* (when leaving work at end of the day – an acknowledgement that other people are still hard at work!)
ご苦労様です・でした	gokurō-sama desu/ deshita	*thanks for your hard work* (said by those left behind when you leave or to thank someone for working for you)
お疲れ様です・でした	otsukaresama desu/ deshita	*similar to the above, used between equals and people 'below' you*
よろしくおねがいします	yoroshiku onegaishimasu	*I'm indebted to you* (said in anticipation of someone helping you/doing you a favour/ when future collaboration is anticipated)
ありがとうございます	arigatō gozaimasu	*thank you very much*
ありがとうございました	arigatō gozaimashita	*thank you very much for something you have done for me*
すみません	sumimasen	*excuse me, sorry*
少々お待ちください	shō shō omachi kudasai	*please wait a minute* (very polite)

NEW EXPRESSIONS

(person) はいらっしゃいますか	(person) wa irasshaimasu ka	*is (person) there?* (respectful)
本堂ですが ...	Hondō desu ga ...	*this is Hondo (speaking)* (used on the phone)
お元気ですか	ōgenki desu ka	*how are you?* (used if you haven't spoken to the person for a while)
おかげさまで	okagesama de	*I'm fine thank you* (said in response)
やってみましょう	yattemimashō	*let's try/I'll give it a try*
僕	boku	*the same as **watashi*** (used by men)
し方	shikata	*how to do/play*
教えます	oshiemasu	*teach*
アパート	apāto	*apartment*
迎え（迎えます）	mukae (mukaemasu)	*pick up (to meet, receive, collect (someone))*

2 **Using the jobs and occupations vocabulary you are going to talk about possible childhood dreams of future jobs. Can you say for each occupation listed: *When I was a child I wanted to be a ...* ?**

   a You need to put なりたい **naritai** (*want to be*) into the past (*wanted to be*). Can you work out how to do that? Clue: なりたい **naritai** works like **i** adjectives.

   b Follow this pattern and speak out loud: 子供のころ、(job title) に (past tense of なりたい) です。**Kodomo no koro, (job title) ni (past tense of naritai) desu.** *When I was a child I wanted to be (job title).*

3 What are the meanings of 毎日 **mainichi** and 朝 **asa**? So can you work out what 毎朝 **maiasa** means?

4 Listen again to the audio and practise saying the new vocabulary with correct pronunciation.

Conversation

 09.02 *Mr Hondo is phoning Robert at work to invite him to play golf at the weekend.*

1 What is Robert's response when Mr Hondo invites him to play golf? (two parts)

Hondō-san	もしもし、ロバートフランクスさんはいらっしゃいますか。
Female voice	はい、少々お待ちください。
(Pause)	
Robert	もしもし？
Hondō-san	ロバートさん、こんにちは。本堂ですが …
Robert	ああ、本堂さん、お元気ですか。
Hondō-san	おかげさまで。あの、ロバートさん、今週の日曜日に一緒にゴルフをしませんか。
Robert	ゴルフですか。僕はあまり上手ではありませんがやってみましょう！
Hondō-san	じゃあ、僕はゴルフのし方を教えます。
Robert	いいですね。よろしくおねがいします。ゴルフ場はどこですか。
Hondō-san	僕の車で行きましょう。十二時にロバートさんのアパートへ迎えに行きます。
Robert	十二時ですね。わかりました。
Hondō-san	じゃあ、日曜日に。しつれいします。
Hondō-san	Moshi moshi, Robāto Furankusu-san wa irasshaimasu ka.
Female voice	Hai, shōshō ōmachi kudasai.
(Pause)	
Robert	Moshi moshi?
Hondō-san	Robātō-san, konnichiwa. Hondō desu ga …
Robert	Ā, Hondō-san, ōgenki desu ka.
Hondō-san	Okagesama de. Ano, Robātōsan, konshū no nichiyōbi ni issho ni gorufu o shimasen ka.
Robert	Gorufu desu ka. Boku wa amari jōzu dewa arimasen ga yattemimashō!
Hondō-san	Jā, boku wa gorufu no shikata o oshiemasu.
Robert	Ii desu ne. Yoroshiku onegaishimasu. Gorufu jō wa doko desu ka.
Hondō-san	Boku no kuruma de ikimashō. Jūniji ni Robāto-san no apāto e mukae ni ikimasu.
Robert	Jūniji desu ne. Wakarimashita.
Hondō-san	Jā, nichiyōbi ni. Shitsurei shimasu.

2 What two things does Mr Hondo offer to do for Robert?

3 When and at what time will they set off to play golf?

4 Are these statements true (まる **maru**) or false (ばつ **batsu**)?

a 本堂さんはロバートさんにゴルフの見方を教えます。
   Hondō-san wa Robāto-san ni gorufu no mikata o oshiemasu.

b 日曜日に一緒にゴルフをします。Nichiyōbi ni isshō ni gorufu o shimasu.

c 本堂さんはゴルフ場へ迎えに行きます。Hondō-san wa gorufu jō e mukae ni ikimasu.

5 Write your answers to these questions in Japanese:

a 何時に迎えに行きますか。Nanji ni mukae ni ikimasu ka.

b バスでゴルフ場に行きますか。Basu de gorufu jō ni ikimasu ka.

c ロバートさんはゴルフが上手ですか。Robāto-san wa gorufu ga jōzu desu ka.

6 Now listen to the audio several times then use your pause button to practise repeating lines of dialogue to help you improve your pronunciation.

Language discovery

9.1 THE FOUR TENSES OF *I WANT TO*

You learned how to say *I want to* in Unit 6. The endings of the different tenses of **tai desu** follow the same rules as for **i** adjectives.

 Look at the following table, work out the pattern and fill in the gaps.

Present	Past	Present negative	Past negative
たいです **tai desu**	たかったです **takatta desu**	たくないです **takunai desu**	たくなかったです **takunakatta desu**
I want to eat	*I wanted to eat*	*I don't want to eat*	*I didn't want to eat*
a) 食べたい＿＿＿ 　　**tabetai** ＿＿＿	**b)** たべた＿＿＿です 　　**tabeta** ＿＿＿ **desu**	**c)** ＿＿＿です 　　＿＿＿ **desu**	**d)** たべ＿＿＿です 　　**tabe** ＿＿＿ **desu**

As with verbs, sometimes the particle は **wa** is used instead of を **o** (or が **ga**). Particularly if you don't mention the subject of the sentence, **wa** sounds more natural in negative sentences.

Look at these examples:

ロバートさんは寿司を食べたくないです。 **Robāto-san wa sushi o tabetakunai desu.**
Robert doesn't want to eat sushi.

寿司は食べたくないです。 **Sushi wa tabetakunai desu.**
He doesn't want to eat sushi.

YOUR TURN How would you say the following in Japanese? Remember that you don't need to say the word for *I*.

a I want to eat.

b I want to eat a banana.

c I don't want to eat toast.

d I don't want to drink coffee.

e I didn't want to drink rice wine.

f Last night I didn't want to drink beer.

9.2 SAYING YOU ARE *GOOD* OR *BAD AT* SOMETHING

In previous units you have met the words 上手 **jōzu** (*good at*) and 下手 **heta** (*bad at*).
For example, Miki said:

私はボーリングが下手です。 **Watashi wa bōringu ga heta desu.** *I am bad at bowling.*

Notice the structure: (person) は (activity) が上手・下手です (person) **wa** (activity) **ga jōzu/heta desu.**

Look now at how Robert says to Mr Hondo *I'm not very good at golf.*

He uses ではありません **dewa arimasen** (also **ja arimasen**, **ja nai desu**) instead of です **desu**.

Jōzu and **heta** are used to talk about skills and practical activities that you are good at or bad at, for example sports, crafts, arts – 'hands-on' activities. If you want to talk about your strong (or weak) points or your talents (including academic or professional skills), you use とくい **tokui** (*good at*) and にがて **nigate** (*poor at*). The structure remains the same: (person) **wa** (subject) **ga tokui/nigate desu.**

Here is a list of skills ordered by more practical skills or sports and more academic skills. However, there can be overlap – for example, speaking Japanese or playing baseball can be both a practical skill and your strong point:

上手・下手 **JŌZU/HETA**			とくい・にがて **TOKUI/NIGATE**		
ボーリング	**bōringu**	*bowling*	英語	**eigo**	*English*
スポーツ	**supōtsu**	*sports*	勉強	**benkyō**	*studying/learning*
ギター	**gitā**	*guitar*	日本語	**nihongo**	*Japanese*
サッカー	**sakkā**	*football*	数学	**sūgaku**	*maths*
ゴルフ	**gorufu**	*golf*	音楽	**ongaku**	*music*
買い物	**kaimono**	*shopping*			
コンピューター	**kompyūtā**	*computer*			
美術	**bijutsu**	*art*			
野球	**yakyū**	*baseball*			
料理	**ryōri**	*cooking*			

YOUR TURN Write five sentences about your own skills and good and weak points using these words – don't worry if the limited vocabulary prevents you from being truthful:

Example: 私は買い物がとても上手です！ **Watashi wa kaimono ga totemo jōzu desu!** *I'm very good at shopping!*

> **LANGUAGE TIP**
> In situations where you want to be modest, use とくい **tokui** rather than 上手 **jōzu**. Japanese people tend not to show off about their own abilities and to use 下手・にがて **heta / nigate** with the negative – *I am not bad at . . .* – more than 上手・とくい **jōzu / tokui**.

9.3 LIKES, DISLIKES AND HATES

Using the **na** adjectives 好き **suki** (*like*) and 嫌い **kirai** (*hate*) you can also use the structure from 9.2 to talk about likes and dislikes. What would go in the gaps?

Person _____ noun _____ 好き・嫌い _____

Person _____ noun _____ **suki/kirai** _____

Take note: 嫌い **kirai** is a strong word – don't use it about people. In any case, it's better to say you don't like something very much using あまり好きじゃありません **amari suki ja arimasen** (*doesn't like very much*).

And if you really like something, use とても好きです **totemo suki desu**.

YOUR TURN How would you say the following in Japanese?

a Miki doesn't like sports very much.
b Roger really likes tennis.
c Rie likes shopping.
d Ian hates the rain.

9.4 HOW TO USE ながら NAGARA (*WHILE*)

The next four explanations are going to explore ways of using the verb stem (drop ます masu) to say more.

Before you start, check you understand what the verb stem is by saying the stems of the following verbs:

Example: 食べます → 食べ　　　　**tabemasu** (*eat*) → **tabe**

a 買います kaimasu (*buy*)　　　　**f** 見ます mimasu (*watch*)
b 書きます kakimasu (*write*)　　　**g** 行きます ikimasu (*go*)
c 聞きます kikimasu (*listen*)　　　**h** 働きます hatarakimasu (*work*)
d 読みます yomimasu (*read*)　　　**i** します shimasu (*do*)
e 飲みます nomimasu (*drink*)　　　**j** 話します hanashimasu (*talk*)

First, we'll look at ながら **nagara** (*while*).

毎朝なおえさんはコーヒーを飲みながら新聞を読みます
Maiasa Naoē-san wa kōhī o nominagara shinbun o yomimasu.
Every morning Naoe reads the paper <u>while drinking coffee</u>.

The underlined part is where you use the verb stem with **nagara**. The order is: verb stem + **nagara** followed by main verb (**masu/mashita**).

Note that you cannot use ながら **nagara** if you are describing the actions of two different people, only when it is the same person doing both actions.

YOUR TURN How would you say the following in Japanese?

a Katie drinks green tea while listening to the news.

b Naoe talks to Yuki while she makes the meal.

c Robert writes **kanji** while he listens to music.

d Ian reads a book while eating breakfast.

e Mr Hondo eats his lunch while working.

To describe past actions, you simply change the final verb to **mashita**. Try this now with the sentences a–e.

9.5 HOW TO USE 方 KATA (*HOW TO DO SOMETHING*)

This is when you want to say *how* something is done.

Can you find the part in the conversation when Mr Hondo tells Robert that he will teach him how to play golf?

By adding 方 **kata** to the stem you are changing the verb into a noun. If there is a noun in front of the **kata** word, you link the two using the particle の **no**:

ゴルフのし方　　　**gorufu no shikata**　　　*how to play golf* (order: golf how to play)

YOUR TURN How would you say the following in Japanese?

a how to eat sushi

b how to make sushi

c how to write kanji

d how to read Japanese

e how to speak English

Now turn these phrases into full sentences by talking about what Rie taught Katie to do (a–d) then what Katie taught Rie to do (e). The first one has been done for you.

a りえさんはケイティさんに寿司の食べ方を教えました。

Rie-san wa Katie-san ni sushi no tabekata o oshiemashita.

9.6 GO TO A PLACE IN ORDER TO DO SOMETHING

Look back at the conversation and find out how Hondō-san said he would go to Robert's apartment to collect him.

When you use this structure, the place you go to normally takes particle へ **e** (*to* – alternatively you can use に **ni**) and the action you are going to do is in the stem form followed by に行きます **ni ikimasu** (*go in order to*). Look at the examples:

go (in order) to buy　　　　　　　買いに行きます　　　　**kai ni ikimasu**

go to town in order to buy　　　　町へ買いに行きます　　　**machi e kai ni ikimasu**

go to town to buy some CDs　　　町へしＣＤを買いに行きます

　　　　　　　　　　　　　　　　　　machi e shii dii o kai ni ikimasu

I went to town to buy some CDs.　私は町へしＣＤを買いに行きました。

　　　　　　　　　　　　　　　　　　Watashi wa machi e shii dii o kai ni ikimashita.

YOUR TURN How would you say the following in Japanese?

a go (in order) to eat

b go to a restaurant in order to eat

c go to a restaurant in order to eat Japanese food (和食 **washoku**)

d Mr Hondo went to Robert's apartment to collect him.

9.7 EXPRESSING A PERSONAL OPINION USING そうです SŌ DESU

To express a personal opinion based on looking at something or at a situation you use the stem + そうです **sō desu** (*it looks, it appears to be*). You can also use the stem of adjectives with this structure – look at the table:

Verbs – drop ます **masu**	食べます → 食べ tabemasu → tabe
i adjectives – drop final い **i**	面白い → 面白 omoshiroi → omoshiro
na adjectives – don't use な **na**	上手な → 上手 jōzuna → jōzu

面白そうです。   **Omoshirosō desu.**   *It looks interesting.*

上手そうです。   **Jōzusō desu.**   *He looks good at it.*

雨が降りそうです。   **Ame ga furisō desu.**   *It looks like it will rain.*

YOUR TURN How would you say the following in Japanese?

a He looks famous.

b This film looks boring.

c He looks like he's got a headache.

d She looks very beautiful, doesn't she?

e He looks like he speaks Japanese.

9.8 SAYING WHAT YOU LIKE BEST

Look back to Unit 7. What was the word for *most* (e.g. *most beautiful gardens*)?

What do these sentences mean?

a ロジャーさんはスポーツが一番好きです。

Roger-san wa supōtsu ga ichiban suki desu.

b ロジャーさんはボーリングが一番上手です。

Roger-san wa bōringu ga ichiban jōzu desu.

YOUR TURN Now use 下手、好き、嫌い、つまらない、 heta, suki, kirai and tsumaranai to say these things about Miki (you can use each adjective only once).

a Miki likes films the best.

b She is least skilful ('most bad') at sports.

c She hates tennis most of all but …

d Baseball is the most boring.

Listening 1

実は・実際は	jitsu wa/jissai wa	*in fact*
しかたがありません	shikata ga arimasen	*it can't be helped*
将来	shōrai	*in the future*
生活	seikatsu	*lifestyle*

 09.03 Listen as Robert talks about his job and his plans for the future and see if you can answer the questions. You don't have to understand every word – listen for the important information.

a What did Robert dream of being when he was a child?

b What time does he work until every day?

c Does he enjoy his job?

d What would he like to do in the future?

e Which lifestyle does he like best?

Speaking

1 Using Robert's speech as a model, make a speech about yourself by changing the underlined parts. If you don't know a word in Japanese simply substitute the English word for now and don't worry about being entirely truthful – the main purpose of this activity is to get you using the structures in a more personal context:

子供のころ消防士になりたかったですが実際はジャーナリストになりました。毎日夜遅くまで働きますが仕事はとても楽しいです。たびたびうちで食事をしながら仕事をしますがしかたがありません。将来アメリカで働きたいです。アメリカの生活は面白そうですが東京の生活が一番好きです。

Kodomo no koro <u>shōbōshi</u> ni naritakatta desu ga jitsu wa <u>jānarisuto</u> ni narimashita. Mainichi yoru osoku <u>made</u> hatarakimasu ga shigoto wa totemo tanoshii desu. Tabitabi uchi de shokuji o shinagara <u>shigoto o shi</u>masu ga shikata ga arimasen. Shōrai <u>Amerika</u> de hatarakitai desu. <u>Amerika</u> no seikatsu wa omoshirosō desu ga <u>Tōkyō</u> no seikatsu ga ichiban suki desu.

2 Look at the pictures of Katie trying different activities and say whether she is good or bad at it, likes it or doesn't like it, or whether it's her strong or weak point.

Listening 2

 09.04 Listen as Ian talks about his childhood and work out if the following statements are true (まる **maru**) or false (ばつ **batsu**).

a As a child Ian wanted to be a rocket scientist.

b He liked football but hated tennis.

c At school he was very good at maths but useless at Japanese.

d His mother really liked shopping but was no good at cooking.

e His father used to make dinner while watching the football.

Reading and writing

 You have learned how to use the stem of the verb with ながら **nagara** (*while*), 方 **kata** (*how to*), そう **sō** (*it looks like*), たいです **tai desu** (*I want to*) and に行きます **ni ikimasu** (*go to do*). The following sentences have one of these words missing – decide which is needed to make sense of the sentence and write out the English meaning as well.

a 本堂さんはロバートさんにゴルフのし＿＿＿＿を教えます。
Hondō-san wa Robāto-san ni gorufu no shi＿＿＿＿ o oshiemashita.

b なおえさんは朝ご飯を食べ＿＿＿＿テレビを見ます。
Naoe-san wa asagohan o tabe＿＿＿＿ terebi o mimasu.

c 明日ケイティさんと一緒に町へ映画を見 ＿＿＿＿。
Ashita Katie-san to issho ni machi e eiga o mi ＿＿＿＿.

d 映画スターの生活はふゆかい ＿＿＿＿ ですね。
Eiga sutā no seikatsu wa fuyukai＿＿＿＿ desu ne.

e 来年日本へ行き＿＿＿＿。 Rainen Nihon e iki ＿＿＿＿.

f ケーキの作り ＿＿＿＿ がわかりません。 Kēki no tsukuri＿＿＿＿ ga wakarimasen.

g みきさんはその寿司を食べ＿＿＿＿ですね。 Miki-san wa sono sushi o tabe ＿＿＿＿ desu ne.

Introduction to kanji 漢字

INTRODUCTION

In this section you will learn how simple **kanji** developed from pictures, how simple **kanji** are used to form more complex **kanji**, how two or more **kanji** form new words and practise reading **hiragana**.

START READING

You have already looked at these kanji – do you remember their meanings?
日 月 木

Look back to the **kanji** section in Unit 1 for the answers.

Now you are going to look at a further 15 simple pictograph kanji. The pictures they are derived from are numbered a–o. Can you match them with the standardized kanji (1–15) which follow?

a gold   **b** root   **c** wood   **d** forest

e mountain   **f** child   **g** fire   **h** water

i power   **j** ground/earth   **k** woman   **l** rice field

m stone   **n** bamboo   **o** river

1 山   **2** 川   **3** 金   **4** 田   **5** 竹   **6** 火   **7** 本   **8** 林
9 森   **10** 水   **11** 土   **12** 石   **13** 力   **14** 女   **15** 子

Here is an artist's impression of how the pictures developed into standard **kanji**:

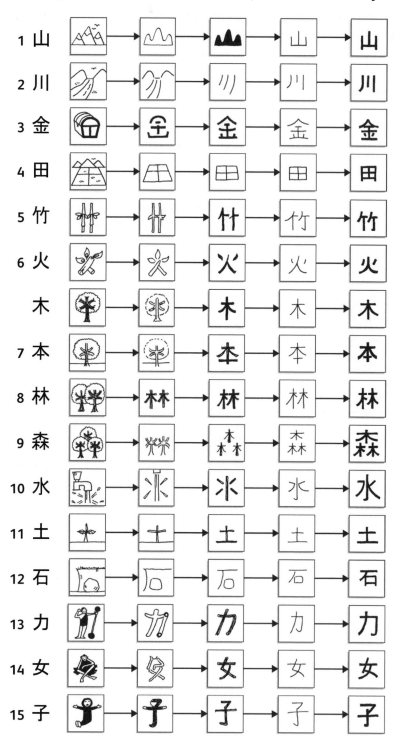

READING 1

How familiar do you feel with the 18 kanji you have learned so far? Can you identify the English meanings without looking at the pictures?

a 山   b 川   c 竹   d 女   e 子   f 森
g 石   h 本   i 日   j 月   k 林   l 火
m 田   n 力   o 土   p 水   q 木   r 金

COMPLEX KANJI

Pictograph and simple **kanji** are used as components of more complex **kanji**. You have already learned three examples of this:

木 + 木 = 林   two trees make a *wood*
木 + 木 + 木 = 森   three trees make a *forest*
木 + 一 = 本   the line through the trunk represents the tree's root or *origin*

Here are some more examples using the **kanji** you have learned so far. The new meanings are in italics:

女 + 子 = 好   woman + child = *love* – a woman's *love* for her child
田 + 力 = 男   a *man* uses his power in the rice field
日 + 月 = 明   the sun and moon out together are *bright*

KANJI COMPOUNDS

Kanji compounds are words made up of two, three or four **kanji**. For example, 日本 means *Japan* (**Nihon**) and is made up of *sun* and *root*. This is because Japan is known as *the land of the rising sun* – it is in the east from where the sun has its root or origin.

READING 2

Here are some more compound kanji words. Can you match them with their English meanings?

a 水力   1 girl
b 水田   2 boy
c 火山   3 water power
d 男子   4 volcano
e 女子   5 paddy field (wet rice growing)

DAYS OF THE WEEK 1

You learned how to say the days of the week in Unit 6. The **kanji** used for writing the days of the week are simple pictorial **kanji** which you have already learned in this reading section. Here they are with gaps for you to work out the meanings:

Kanji	Meaning	Day of week
日	_____	*Sunday*
月	_____	*Monday*
火	_____	*Tuesday*
水	_____	*Wednesday*
木	_____	*Thursday*
金	_____	*Friday*
土	_____	*Saturday*

As well as meaning *sun*, 日 also means *day* because a day is defined by the rising and setting of the sun. When the days of the week are written in full they are written with three **kanji**, the first is one of the seven you have just learned and the second two are the **kanji** for *week* and for *day*. Here is an example:

日曜日 is *Sunday*, made up of *sun*, *week* and *day*

 DAYS OF THE WEEK 2

Match the kanji days of the week with their English meanings and Japanese reading (look back to Unit 6 if you need to review these).

Sunday	**a** 水曜日	**1** nichiyōbi
Monday	**b** 木曜日	**2** kayōbi
Tuesday	**c** 日曜日	**3** doyōbi
Wednesday	**d** 土曜日	**4** getsuyōbi
Thursday	**e** 火曜日	**5** kinyōbi
Friday	**f** 月曜日	**6** mokuyōbi
Saturday	**g** 金曜日	**7** suiyōbi

Translate these sentences into English.

a イアンさんはお酒を飲みたくなかったです。

Ian-san wa osake o nomitakunakatta desu.

b みきさんはビールがあまり好きじゃありません。

Miki-san wa bīru ga amari suki ja arimasen.

c 毎朝なおえさんはコーヒーを飲みながら新聞を読みます。

Maiasa Naoe-san wa kōhī o nominagara shinbun o yomimasu.

d ロジャーさんはみきさんにボーリングのし方を教えました。

Roger-san wa Miki-san ni bōringu no shikata o oshiemashita.

e ケイティさんは町へりえさんに会いに行きました。

Katie-san wa machi e Rie-san ni ai ni ikimashita.

f この映画は面白そうですね。

Kono eiga wa omoshirosō desu ne.

g ロジャーさんはスポーツが一番好きです。

Roger-san wa supōtsu ga ichiban suki desu.

h 本堂ゆきさんは将来医者になりたいです。

Hondō Yuki-san wa shōrai isha ni naritai desu.

i ロバートさんは毎日遅くまで仕事をします。

Robāto-san wa mainichi osoku made shigoto o shimasu.

j 私はケイティさんとレストランへ和食を食べに行きました。

Watashi wa Katie-san to resutoran e washoku o tabe ni ikimashita.

> **TRANSLATION TIPS**
>
> Remember to first find the subject of the sentence (marked by は **wa**).
>
> It often helps to translate 'backwards' – find the verb at the end and move back through the sentence.

	SELF CHECK
	I CAN...
○	...talk about likes, dislikes and desires.
○	...say what I am good and bad at.
○	...use the verb stem to say more.
○	...use work-related phrases.
○	...recognize 21 **kanji** and 12 compound **kanji** words.

Part 2
Extending and manipulating the language

土曜日に十時ごろ起きて…
On Saturdays I get up at about ten …

In this unit you will learn how to:
▶ *use the* **te** *form.*
▶ *talk about daily routine in longer sentences.*
▶ *ask someone to do something.*
▶ *ask, give and refuse permission.*

CEFR: *(B1) Can link a series of shorter, discrete simple elements into a connected, linear sequence of points. Can understand the main point of clear standard speech on familiar matters regularly encountered in work, school, and leisure.*

宿泊 Shukuhaku *Accommodation*

There is a wide variety of 日本の宿泊 **shukuhaku** (*accommodation*) which can offer you a unique Japanese experience.

If staying in a 旅館 **ryokan** or 民宿 **minshuku** (*Japanese inns*), guests have the opportunity to stay in 和室 **washitsu** (*Japanese-style rooms*) where they sleep on a 布団 **futon** laid out on 畳 **tatami** (*woven rush mats*), bathe in communal お風呂 **ofuro** (*baths*) with natural spa water at 温泉 **onsen** (*hot-spring*) resorts and generally receive a very high standard of service. 和食 **washoku** (*Japanese-style meals*) are usually served in your room and provide you with the opportunity to try a wide range of 伝統的なの日本料理 **dentōtekina Nihon ryōri** (*traditional Japanese dishes*).

There is a wide variety of 洋式のホテル **yōshiki no hoteru** (*Western-style hotels*), ranging from the 高い **takai** (*expensive*) and 高級 **kōkyū** (*high-class*) type such as the ホテルニュ ーオータニ **hoteru Nyū Ōtani** (*New Otani Hotel*) in Tokyo, to the inexpensive ビジネス・ホテル **bijinesu hoteru** (*business-style hotel*) aimed at business travellers in need of basic and reasonably priced rooms. One type of business-style hotel is the カプセルホテル **kapuseru hoteru** (*capsule hotel*) so called because the 部屋 **heya** (*rooms*) are about the size of the single bed within them, and contain just a television and light. They are usually located near to 駅 **eki** (*stations*) and are popular with city workers who have missed the last train home and need somewhere cheap to stay the night.

1 Find the words for *Japanese-style meals*, *Japanese-style rooms* and *Western-style hotels*. Can you use the pattern to work out the meanings of these words?

a 洋室　　　　b 洋食　　　　c 和式のホテル

2 If 服 means *clothes*, what do you think these two words mean?

a 和服　　　　b 洋服

Vocabulary builder

10.01 Listen to the new vocabulary and practise saying it out loud. From now on the units are written in Japanese script only with the addition of some **rōmaji** passages in the Answer key. You can also use the audio to support your reading. Can you work out the missing meanings of the verbs in their て form?

VERBS IN THEIR て FORM

食べて	a _____		見せて	d _____
書いて	write		買って	buy
聞いて	listen		読んで	e _____
飲んで	b _____		話して	f _____
見て	c _____		起きて	g _____

NEW VERBS

（メールを）出します	send, submit (an email)
予約（します）	reservation, booking (make)
説明します	explain
開いています	be open
靴をはきます（はいて）	wear shoes（くつ = shoes）
お風呂に入ります（入って）	take a bath
信じられない	I can't believe it!

NEW EXPRESSIONS

ユースホステル	youth hostel		女性	women, female
ルール	rules		食堂	dining room, canteen
日本語でいいですか	is Japanese all right?		部屋	room
…もいいです（か）	you may (may I?) …		でも	but
…はいけません	you may not …		今晩	tonight, this evening
…はだめです	… is not allowed		寝る時間	sleep time
また	again		この階	this floor
昼間	daytime, during the day		べつべつ	separately
男性	men, male			

Conditional... Conversation

10.02 *Katie and Ian are spending the weekend in Nikkō, a famous Shogun shrine in Japan. The rather officious receptionist at the youth hostel is explaining the hostel rules and opening hours.*

1 At what time does the youth hostel close in the morning and when does it reopen?

Receptionist	いらっしゃいませ！
Katie	こんにちは。今日予約をしました。Katie Mears と Ian Ferguson ですが。
Receptionist	はい、わかりました。少しユースホステルのルールを説明します。日本語でいいですか。
Katie	はい、いいです。
Receptionist	このユースホステルは午前十時まで開いています。そしてまた午後四時から開いています。昼間 入ってはいけません。
Katie	夜四時から開いていますね。
Receptionist	はい。そしてユースホステルの中では靴をはいてはいけません。
Ian	*(Looking at his shoes)* ああ、すみません。
Receptionist	それからお風呂のルールです。男性は五時から七時までお風呂に入ってもいいです。女性は七時から九時までです。
Ian	部屋で食べてもいいですか。
Receptionist	食べてはだめです！食堂で食べてください。食堂は九時まで開いています。
Receptionist	そしてテレビの部屋は十時まで開いています。テレビは十時まで見てもいいです。
Ian	十時までですか。でも今晩の映画は十時半までです。十時半まで見てもいいですか。
Receptionist	いけません。テレビの部屋は十時までです。そして、寝る時間は十時半です。
Ian	*(Getting annoyed)* 十時半ですか。それは …
Katie	*(Interrupting)* わかりました。部屋はどこですか。
Receptionist	女性の部屋はこの階です。男性の部屋は二階です。
Ian	部屋は別々ですか。信じられない！
Receptionist	ここはユースホステルですよ！
Katie	*(Quickly)* はい、はい、わかりました。ありがとう。

2 What are the bath time rules?

3 What time is the dining room open until?

4 Why is Ian annoyed about the TV room rules?

5 For what other two reasons is Ian annoyed?

6 The receptionist says this when explaining the bathroom opening times: 女性は
七時から九時までです (*The women are from seven until nine o'clock*). Where do
you place the *from* and *to* words in Japanese?

7 Are these statements true or false?
　a ケイティさんとイアンさんはよやくをしませんでした。
　b 女性のお風呂は七時から九時までです。
　c 昼間十時から四時までユースホステルに入ってはいけません。
　d イアンさんは今晩十時半まで映画を見ます。
　e ケイティさんとイアンさんは今晩部屋で食事をします。

8 Write your answers to these questions in Japanese:
　a テレビの部屋は何時まで開いていますか。
　b 男性の部屋はどこにありますか。
　c 男性のお風呂は何時から何時までですか。
　d ユースホステルでは靴をはいてもいいですか。
　e 寝る時間は何時ですか。

 Language discovery

10.1 VERBS IN THEIR て FORM

10.03 To ask someone to do something for you in Japanese (a polite command) use the て
form of the verb followed by ください (*please*).

YOUR TURN 1 Use the example as your guide and ask someone to please do
something for you using each of the verbs. Listen to the audio to check your
answers.

Example: 食べて *please eat (it)* → 食べてください

please write (it)　　　　　　　　please buy (it)

please listen　　　　　　　　　　please read (it)

please drink (it)　　　　　　　　please speak

please look　　　　　　　　　　please get up

please show me

2 **10.04** Now try saying longer sentences using the example given. Listen to check
your answers.

Example: *eat your breakfast* → 朝ごはんを食べてください

(please) write an essay　　　　　　(please) show me the dining room

(please) listen to the news　　　　　(please) buy me some shoes

(please) drink water　　　　　　　(please) read the rules

(please) look at the room　　　　　(please) speak Japanese

10.2 HOW TO FORM THE て FORM

To understand how verbs work in Japanese, it helps to think of two types of verb, which we shall refer to as Group 1 and Group 2. We will begin with Group 2 verbs because these are more straightforward to manipulate than Group 1 verbs.

Group 2 verbs

Look at the first two examples, work out the rule and try to form the third verb yourself.

出かけます → 出かけて (go out, set off)

食べます → 食べて

起きます → a _____

So the rule is: drop ます and add て.

Group 1 verbs

There are four different rules. To apply these rules you need to look at the stem of the verb (the verb without the ます part). There are examples for each rule then a verb for you to change.

Group 1 verbs, **Rule 1** (き): If the last syllable (sound) is き, change it to い + て.

聞きます (listen) → 聞き → 聞いて

書きます (write) → 書き → b _____

However, if the last syllable is ぎ, change it to い + で:

泳ぎます (swim) → 泳ぎ → 泳いで

Group 1 verbs, **Rule 2** (い、ち、り): If the last syllable is い、ち or り, change it to って.

買います (buy) → 買い → 買って

作ります (make) → 作り → 作って

待ちます (wait) → 待ち → c _____

Group 1 verbs, **Rule 3** (み、び、に): If the last syllable is み、び、に, change it to んで.

飲みます (drink) → 飲み → 飲んで

遊びます (play) → 遊び → 遊んで

死にます (die) → 死に → d _____

Group 1 verbs, **Rule 4** (し): Add て (similar to Group 2 rule).

話します (speak) → 話し → 話して

探します (look for) → e _____

Irregular verbs

There are only three irregular verbs in Japanese! The first two follow the Group 2 rule for て.

します (do) → し → して

来ます (come) → き → きて

行きます (go) → 行って

10.3 MAKING LONGER SENTENCES USING て

Look at the title to this unit then look at the following complete sentence:

土曜日二十時ごろ起きて、ゆっくり朝ごはんを食べます。

On Saturdays I get up at about ten and have a leisurely breakfast.

What do you think is the function of the て form here?

Here are three separate sentences:

十時ごろ起きます。   *I get up at about ten.*

朝ごはんを食べます。   *I eat breakfast.*

買い物に行きます。   *I go shopping.*

And here they are in one long sentence. What does it mean?

十時ごろ起きて、朝ご飯を食べて、買い物に行きます。

Did you work out that the て form is used to say *and* or *then* when making longer sentences?

You can use the て form in this way when the actions you do have an order to them – first you do Action 1, then Action 2, then Action 3 and so on. The final verb in the sequence ends in ます (if present) or ました (if past) and it is this verb which tells you the tense of the whole sentence (present, past, future).

きのう六時に家に帰って、晩ごはんを食べて、テレビを見て、十一時ごろ寝ました。

Yesterday I got home at six, I ate dinner, then I watched TV and I went to bed at about eleven.

 YOUR TURN 10.05 How would you say the following in Japanese? Listen to the audio to check your answers.

a Every day I get up at seven, I eat breakfast and then I clean the house.

b Every day I have lunch at twelve, then I go to work.

c Yesterday I got up late, I drank some coffee then I went into town.

d Tomorrow I will go home at six, have dinner then watch TV.

e On Mondays I study Japanese, then I go to a restaurant to eat lunch.

10.4 食べてから *AFTER I ATE*

You can refine what you want to say a little more by adding から to the end of the て form, giving the meaning *after*.

Look at the example then work out the meaning of the next sentence.

朝ごはんを食べてから、仕事に行きました。　　*After I'd had breakfast I went to work.*

家に帰ってから、新聞を読みます。　　_____.

YOUR TURN How would you say the following in Japanese?

a After I had watched TV, I went to bed.

b After I've had lunch I always listen to the news.

c After I'd phoned my mother I went to my friend's (**tomodachi**) house.

d After reading (after I had read) the newspaper I cleaned the house.

10.5 GIVING AND ASKING FOR PERMISSION

Look back to the conversation and find out how the receptionist said *you may watch the TV until 10 p.m.*

To say *you may do something* (*you are allowed to do something*) attach the phrase もいいです (literally meaning *even that is good*) to the て form of the verb.

YOUR TURN 1　10.06 Convert these verbs into *you may* sentences. The て form is given in brackets. Listen to the audio to check your answers.

Example: *You may drink in here.* (飲んで) → ここで飲んでもいいです

a You may sleep in here. (寝て)

b You may read in here. (読んで)

c You may study in here. (勉強して)

d You may watch TV in here. (見て)

e You may speak Japanese in here. (話して)

f You may listen to music in here. (聞いて)

g You may play in here. (遊んで)

2 Look at the conversation again. How did Ian ask, *May I watch until 10.30?* What do you add to turn *may I* into a question?

3　10.07 How would you say the following in Japanese? The underlined parts are new words, given in the brackets along with the て form:

a May I open the <u>window</u>? (窓を開けて)

b May I <u>close</u> the window? (窓を閉めて)

c May I <u>enter</u> this room? (この部屋に入って)

d May I <u>take a bath</u>? (Also means *enter*.) (お風呂に入って)

> **LANGUAGE TIP**
> Remember to use the verb table at the back of this book to find a list by group of all the verbs used in this course.

10.6 REFUSING PERMISSION

You also use the て form to refuse permission.

Look back at the conversation and find out how the receptionist says *You are not allowed in during the day*.

To refuse permission add はいけません (*not allowed to*) to the て form:

昼間入ってはいけません。 *You are not allowed in during the day.*

YOUR TURN 10.08 How would you say the following in Japanese? New words are given in brackets. Listen to the audio to check your answers.

a You are not allowed to drink in here.
b You are not allowed to open the window.
c You are not allowed to open that door. (その ド<ruby>ア<rt>あ</rt></ruby><ruby>ド<rt>ど</rt></ruby>)
d You are not allowed to enter this room.
e You are not allowed to take a bath.

> **LANGUAGE TIP**
> There is a more informal version of いけません which is だめです. This can sound quite direct and impolite; for example, a teacher might use it with pupils or a parent with their child.

10.7 GIVING TIMES *FROM* AND *TO*

The words から and まで are used when you want to say *from/to* or *open from/to*.
The receptionist says this when explaining the bathroom opening times:

<ruby>女性<rt>じょせい</rt></ruby>は<ruby>七時<rt>しちじ</rt></ruby>から<ruby>九時<rt>くじ</rt></ruby>までです。 *The women are from seven until nine o'clock.*

Look at where these words are placed in the sentence and make sure that you say them after the noun (so the other way round to English):

<ruby>七時<rt>しちじ</rt></ruby>から *from seven o'clock*   <ruby>九時<rt>くじ</rt></ruby>まで *until nine o'clock*

YOUR TURN How would you say the following in Japanese?

Example: *The bank is (open) from nine until three.* → <ruby>銀行<rt>ぎんこう</rt></ruby>は九時から三時までです

a The post office is (open) from nine until five.
b I went from Tokyo to Kyoto.
c I went from Tokyo to Kyoto by bullet train.

Listening

1 10.09 Listen to Katie talk about her daily routine and answer these questions:
    a What does Katie do next after waking up?
    b What does she do after going shopping?
    c Where does she go after going to the supermarket?
    d List three things she does after getting home.

2 Now listen several times more to the audio, using the pause button to listen line by line and repeat. Focus on good pronunciation and speaking confidently. Can you produce a personalized version about yourself?

3 10.10 You are going to listen to a short piece listing what Japanese school students can and cannot do. Match each rule to a picture and do not try to understand every word – the skill you are developing is to pick out the key information.

 4 10.11 Takeshi Ishibashi, a student at Tokyo University and guitarist in a boy band, is describing his daily routine. Listen to the audio and put the sequence of pictures into the right order (1 is done for you).

eating lunch

Now you have done this, boost your reading skills by reading the scripts for Listening 3 and 4 in the Answer key.

✏️ Writing

The following table lists verbs you have not used before. Can you convert them into their correct **te** form using the rules you have learned?

Group 1 verbs	English	te form
もちます	*hold, possess*	a _____
けします	*switch off, rub out*	b _____
うたいます	*sing*	c _____
えらびます	*choose*	d _____
ひきます	*play (an instrument)*	e _____
やすみます	*rest*	f _____
ぬぎます	*take off (clothes)*	g _____
Group 2 verbs	English	te form
きめます	*decide*	h _____
でます	*leave, exit*	i _____
つけます	*switch on, attach*	j _____

🔊 Speaking

Using the verbs from the previous exercise and もいいです（か）、はいけません、ください, **say these sentences out loud.**

a Please hold this camera.

b May I switch on the lights? (でんき)

c Please switch off the lights.

d You are not allowed to sing in here.

e Please choose one (item).

f You may play your guitar (ギター) in this room.

g May I take a rest?

h Please take off your shoes.

i Please decide quickly.

j You are not allowed to go out in the evening.

📖 Reading 1

10.12 Read these sentences, work out their meanings then listen to the audio and repeat them to improve your speed and pronunciation.

a 毎日六時に起きて、朝ご飯を食べて、仕事に行きます。

b 土曜日に九時ごろ起きて、コーヒーを飲んで、町で買い物をします。

c きのう遅くまで仕事をして、会社の人とレストランに行きました。

d 夜晩ごはんを食べて、テレビを見て、遅く寝ます。

e 明日近所の人と買い物に行って、家に帰って、ごろごろします。

More about **kanji** 漢字

INTRODUCTION

In this section you will learn more simple **kanji** developed from pictures, **kanji** used for parts of the body and description, **kanji** radicals and more **kanji** compound words.

START READING

Can you match the following simple pictograph kanji with their standardized kanji?

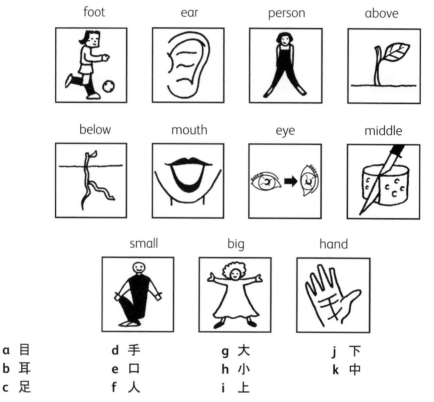

a 目	**d** 手	**g** 大	**j** 下
b 耳	**e** 口	**h** 小	**k** 中
c 足	**f** 人	**i** 上	

Here are some stories to help you remember these new **kanji** (meanings are in italics):

a 目   If you turn this on its side, you can see a square-shaped *eye*.

b 耳   Can you see the folds of skin that make up the *ear*?

c 足   You can see a mouth, an outstretched hand and a big *foot*.

d 手   You may have to work hard to see four fingers and a thumb on this skeletal *hand* but they are there!

e 口   This round *mouth* or *opening* has been simplified into a square.

f 人   This *person* has long legs.

g 大   A person stretching out their arms and legs to be *big*.

h 小   A person squeezing in their arms and legs to be *small*.

i 上   Can you see a plant growing *above* the ground?

j 下   Now can you see its roots *below* the ground?

k 中   A line running through the *middle* of a box.

 READING 2

How familiar do you feel with these kanji? Can you identify their English meanings?

a 大   **c** 小   **e** 中   **g** 口   **i** 人   **k** 手

b 耳   **d** 下   **f** 上   **h** 目   **j** 足

COMPLEX KANJI

Here are some more complex **kanji** made up of elements of simpler ones:

少   This means *few, a little* and uses *small* plus a dash below.

白   This means *white* and uses *sun* plus a speck to represent a ray of sun. (The ancient Chinese saw the sun's colour as white.)

青   This means *blue/green*. You can see *moon* at the bottom, above it a plant is growing in the earth. Plants are *green* and we have the phrase *once in a blue moon*!

黒   This means *black*. You can see *rice field* and *earth* **kanji** and below it is the shortened version of *fire* (火). *Fire* is used to burn the stubble of the rice plant and the colour it burns to is *black*.

KANJI RADICALS

You have already learned that simple **kanji** can become components of more complex ones. One of these components can give a general meaning to the whole **kanji**. This type of component is called the 'radical'. The most common location of a radical is on the left side of a **kanji**. Other locations include on top, below or surrounding. Here are two **kanji** you have learned already:

青   *blue/green*: the radical is *moon* and is below the **kanji** (think of *blue* moon).

黒   *black*: the radical is *fire* (also below) – fire burns things to *black*.

KANJI COMPOUNDS

As you know, **kanji** compounds are words made up of two, three or four **kanji**. Here are two examples from the new **kanji** of this unit:

上手　**jōzu**　This means *good at, skilful* – the above (upper) hand means you are skilled at something.

下手　**heta**　This means *poor/bad at* – and is represented by the below (lower) hand.

READING 3

1 Here are some more compound **kanji** words using **kanji** from this and the previous unit. Can you match them with their English meanings? Some have **hiragana** between them but simply focus on the **kanji** meanings.

a	人口	1	girl
b	日本人	2	boy
c	男の人	3	man (person) power
d	女の人	4	population
e	女の子	5	Japanese person
f	男の子	6	in the public eye
g	人力	7	man
h	人目	8	woman

> **LANGUAGE TIP**
>
> *Population* focuses on 'mouths to feed'; *in the public eye* is literally that – *the people's eyes.*

2 You have now learned 36 single kanji. Can you remember them all? Here they are grouped into themes – can you give their English meanings?

a Position: 上 下 中

b Body parts: 口 耳 目 足 手

c People: 人 女 男 子 力

d Description: 小 大 少 青 黒 白 明 好

e Nature: 山 川 木 森 林 竹 田 日 月 本

f Minerals and elements: 水 火 金 土 石

WRITING

Here in **rōmaji** is Miki's description of herself that she wrote for a computer dating agency. Your challenge is to reproduce it in Japanese script, using **kanji** for the underlined parts. Check your answer with Unit 7 Reading practice.

Watashi wa Sugihara Miki desu. Se ga futsū de kami ga <u>kuro</u>kute nagai desu. <u>Me</u> ga <u>kuro</u>kute marui desu. Kao mo marui desu ga hana wa shikakui desu. Watashi wa otonashii desu ga yasashii to omoimasu. Eiga ga <u>suki</u> desu ga supō tsu wa <u>suki</u> ja arimasen.

？ Test yourself

Fill in the gaps in these sentences by selecting the correct lettered phrase (you can use each word or phrase only once) then write out an English translation.

a ユースホステルの中では靴を _____。

b 学校では靴を _____。

c 男性のお風呂は _____ です。

d たけしさんは _____, 十一時ごろ起きます。

e ケイティさんは朝デパートで _____, レストランで食事をします。

f そして _____ たまにうちを掃除します。

g 昼間ユースホステルに _____。

h 夜晩ごはんを食べてからコンピューターで _____。

i 郵便局は _____ 開いています

j 本堂さんは _____ 新幹線で行きました。

1 入ってはいけません

2 ぬいでください

3 東京から大阪まで

4 買い物をして

5 遅くまで寝て

6 九時から五時まで

7 五時から七時まで

8 家に帰ってから

9 はいてはだめです

10 メールを出します

SELF CHECK

I CAN...

○	...use the **te** form.
○	...talk about daily routine in longer sentences.
○	...ask someone to do something.
○	...ask, give and refuse permission.
○	...recognize 15 new **kanji** and ten more compound words.

いまなに
今何をしていますか

What are you doing at the moment?

In this unit you will learn how to:
▶ *talk about what you are or were doing.*
▶ *describe routines and habitual actions.*
▶ *say* I am trying to.
▶ *talk about what you want.*
▶ *say more about family.*

CEFR: *(A2) Can locate specific information in lists and isolate the information required (e.g. times and dates in a schedule). Can describe plans, arrangements, habits and routines, past activities and personal experiences. (B1) Can exploit a basic repertoire of language and strategies to help keep a conversation or discussion going.*

日本の家族 Nihon no kazoku *The Japanese family*

Respect for others runs through Japanese society and you have already seen ways in which this is reflected in the language. For example, 日本の家族 **Nihon no kazoku** *(the Japanese family)* use 謙譲語 **kenjōgo** *(humble language)* when talking about 家族 **kazoku** *(own family)* and 尊敬語 **sonkeigo** *(respectful language)* when talking about (or to) ご家族 **go-kazoku** *(other families)*.

However, although the Japanese use **kenjōgo** when talking about their own family, when directly addressing members of their own family, they use respect words for older family members and informal 'soft' words to younger family members. Interestingly, within the Japanese family you normally only address 兄弟 **kyōdai** *(brothers and sisters)* by their name if they are younger than you. Otherwise, you address them as お兄さん **onīsan** *(older brother)* or お姉さん **onēsan** *(older sister)*. Husbands and wives will call one another お母さん **okāsan** *(Mum)* and お父さん **otōsan** *(Dad)* in front of the children and あなた **anata** *(you)* in private rather than using first names.

1 The table shows how Japanese family members address each other. What should go in the gaps?

English	Addressing own family	Softer words (used by small children)
Mum	**a** _____	ママ, お母ちゃん
Dad	**b** _____	パパ, お父ちゃん
older brother	**c** _____, あにき	お兄ちゃん、あにき
older sister	**d** _____, あねき	お姉ちゃん、おねき
younger brother	first name	ちゃん e.g. たけしちゃん
younger sister	first name	ちゃん e.g. えりちゃん
Grandma	お祖母さん	お祖母ちゃん
Grandad	お祖父さん	お祖父ちゃん

2 Which ending in particular is used to soften words, especially those used by younger children?

3 Which ending is used to add respect to older family members?

4 What is the common **kanji** used in: a) Mum and Grandma; b) Dad and Grandad?

5 Why do you think the names パパ and ママ are written in **katakana**?

6 Using the table, look at the situation from the Hondo family's point of view and say the correct family terms on behalf of Yuki and Eri.

    a Yuki is 16. How would she address: **1** her mum, **2** her dad, **3** her sister, Eri, **4** her grandfather?

    b Eri is ten. How would she address: **1** her mum, **2** her dad, **3** her sister, Yuki, **4** her grandmother?

Vocabulary builder

 1 11.01 Listen to the new vocabulary and practise saying it out loud. Can you fill in the gaps?

FAMILY

2 Remembering what you have learned about making certain words more respectful, what is the missing word common to the 'other family' terms?

My family	Other family	English
両親 りょうしん	ご両親 りょうしん	*parents*
祖母 そ ぼ	お祖母 _____ ば あ	*grandmother*
祖父 そ ふ	お祖父 _____ じ い	*grandfather*
兄、あにき (boys use) あに	お兄 _____ にい	*older brother*
姉、あねき (boys use) あね	お姉 _____ ねえ	*older sister*
弟 おとうと	弟 _____ おとうと	*younger brother*
妹 いもうと	妹 _____ いもうと	*younger sister*

VERBS AND VERB FORMS

習っています（習います） なら　　　　　なら	*learn*
練習（します） れんしゅう	*practise*
ドライブ（します） ど ら い ぶ	*drive (go for a drive)*
散歩します さんぽ	*go for a walk*
過ごします す	*spend time*
て＋います	*-ing (doing)*
てみましょう（て＋みます）	*have a go at, try*
ほしい（て＋ほしい）	*want to (want you to do)*

NEW EXPRESSIONS

もう	*already (no longer)*
まだ	*not yet (still)*
自分（の）	*oneself (one's own)*
一日	*a (typical) day*
x について	*about (x)*
歩いて	*on foot*
x の後で	*after (x)*
クラブ	*club*
（に）参加（します）	*take part (in)*
（二）回	*times (twice)*
塾	*cram school* (private schools run after school hours to train students to pass exams)
から	*therefore, so (because)*
週末	*weekend*
試合	*tournament, contest*
いつ	*when*
少し	*a little*
だめ	*no good, don't!*

Conversation 1

 11.02 *Robert is interviewing Yuki and Eri as he continues to research his article on Japanese family life.*

1 How do Yuki and Eri get to school?

Robert	ゆきさん、えりちゃん、自分の一日について教えてください。
Yuki	私は毎日歩いて学校に行っています。学校の後でテニスクラブに参加しています。そして毎週二回、塾に行って、数学や英語を勉強しています。七時ごろ、うちに帰って、晩ごはんを食べて、そして遅くまで宿題をします。
Eri	私も歩いて学校に行きます。学校の後でたいてい、家に帰って、母と一緒に晩ごはんを作ります。今ピアノを習っていますから毎日練習をしています。そしてお姉ちゃんと晩ごはんを食べます。毎週二回学校で柔道をしています。十時ごろ寝ます。

2 Briefly describe the daily routine of:

a Yuki

b Eri

Conversation 2

11.03 *Robert finds out about their weekend routine.*

1 What key elements of Yuki and Eri's weekend routine can you pick out?

Robert	週末にたいてい何をしていますか。
Yuki	土曜日の朝、学校でクラブをします。そして午後たいてい友達と町に行って、買い物をします。時々映画を見に行きます。日曜日にたびたび家族と一緒にドライブをします。時々祖父と散歩をします。
Eri	私は土曜日によく、母とお祖父ちゃんと、町に行って、買い物をします。時々学校で柔道の試合に参加します、日曜日はいつも家族と過ごします。
Robert	えりちゃん、いつ宿題をしますか。
Eri	そうですね。毎日少ししていますが今週はまだしていません！
Yuki	えりちゃんは宿題があまり好きじゃないです。
Eri	お姉ちゃんに宿題をしてほしいです。
Yuki	だめですよ！自分でしてみてください。

2 What is the issue about Eri's homework?

3 How does Eri say *I am learning the piano now*?

4 Are these statements true or false?

a ゆきさんは毎日電車で学校に行っています。

b えりちゃんは学校の後でテニスをしています。

c えりちゃんは今ピアノを習っています。

d ゆきさんは今週まだ宿題をしていません。

e えりちゃんは宿題があまり好きじゃありません。

5 Answer these questions in Japanese:

a ゆきさんは学校の後で何をしますか。

b ゆきさんは毎週何回塾に行きますか。

c ゆきさんいつお祖父さんと散歩しますか。

d えりちゃんは学校の後で何をしますか。

e えりちゃんはどこで柔道をしますか。

Language discovery

11.1 A SUMMARY OF THE CONTINUOUS AND SIMPLE FORMS

Look again at the vocabulary list and find the structure which means *-ing, doing*. You use this when you are in the process of doing something:

今朝ごはんを食べ<u>ています</u>。 *At the moment I am eat<u>ing</u> breakfast.*

YOUR TURN 1 11.04 **Using the vocabulary list and the verbs in て form that you already know, how would you say the following in Japanese? Listen to the audio to check your answers.**

    a I am listening to music now.

    b I am listening to the news at the moment.

    c I am watching TV.

    d I am reading a Japanese (language) newspaper.

    e I am having a meal with my family.

2 Can you work out how you would talk about what you were doing (past actions)? Look at the example then try putting the sentences in the previous activity into the past.

朝ごはんを食べ<u>ていました</u>。 *I <u>was</u> eat<u>ing</u> breakfast.*

The simple present and past forms (e.g. 食べます、食べました) are used to talk about what you do or did.

YOUR TURN 3 How do you think you make the present and past negative of the continuous form (*I am not doing, I was not doing*)? Try these sentences:

    a Yuki is not doing her homework.

    b Eri was not watching the TV.

11.2 THE CONTINUOUS FORM MEANING *I AM IN THE PROCESS OF DOING SOMETHING*

The ています form is used to describe something you are in the process of doing, even if you are not actually doing it at the moment, for example learning an instrument, reading a book, watching a TV series. In Conversation 2 Eri says *I am learning the piano now* (she's not literally playing it as she speaks to Robert! It's a process over time).

今とてもいい本を読んでいます。 *I'm reading a really good book currently.*

九月からピアノを習っています。 *I've been learning the piano since September.*

11.3 THE CONTINUOUS FORM TO DESCRIBE HABITUAL ACTIONS

You also use the ています form when talking about things you do on a regular or daily basis, things you are in a habit of doing. There is some overlap here with the simple present form, for example:

毎日家族と晩ごはんを食べます。

毎日家族と晩ごはんを食べています。 *I eat dinner with my family every day.*

YOUR TURN These sentences are from the conversations. What do they mean?

a 私は毎日歩いて学校に行っています。

b 学校の後でテニスクラブに参加しています。

c 毎週二回学校で柔道をしています。

> **LANGUAGE TIP**
>
> Using ています puts an emphasis on the number of times or regularity with which you do an action; in other words, it emphasizes that you are in the habit of doing it. This form is often used with words such as いつも (*always*), 毎日 (*every day*) and たいてい (*usually*), making it absolutely clear that you are talking about habitual or repeated actions.

11.4 THE CONTINUOUS FORM TO DESCRIBE AN ACTION THAT HAS HAPPENED WHERE THE RESULT STILL EXISTS

A clear example of this is the following:

姉は結婚しています。 *My older sister is married.*

In other words, she got married and is still married. Here are some other examples:

私はデジカメを持っています。 *I have got a digital camera.*

近所の人は死んでいます。 *The neighbour has died (is dead).*

ロジャーさん部屋に入っています。 *Roger has entered his room (and is still there).*

This explanation also works for an existing state (*I still am*) which might not have had an initial action:

両親は大阪に住んでいます。

My parents live in Osaka.

東京をよく知っています。

I know Tokyo very well.

> **LANGUAGE TIP**
>
> You will normally find the verbs 住んでいます (*live*), 持っています (*have, possess*), 知っています (*know*) and 死んでします (*die, died*) in the ています form (although not when used to talk about future actions). The ていました form puts it further into the past – *I lived, I knew*.

11.5 VERBS OF MOTION WITH ています

The verbs of motion 行きます (*go*), 来ます (*come*) and 帰ります (*return, go back*) used with ています can have meanings similar to the previous two explanations (habitual actions or *I have done and still am*) depending on context and so it is useful to group them together within a separate explanation. Here are some examples:

Habitual:

いつも六時に家に帰っています。 *I always return home at six o'clock.*

Action and existing state:

両親は日本に行っています。 *My parents have gone to Japan (and are still there).*

友達が来ています。 *A friend has come (and is still here).*

本堂さんは家に帰っています。 *Mr Hondo has gone home (and is there now).*

These verbs never have the meaning of doing now (continuous action).

YOUR TURN **Which is the correct translation of the following sentence, a or b and how would you say the other translation in Japanese?**

今両親は日本に行っています。

a My parents are in Japan now.

b My parents are going to Japan.

> **LANGUAGE TIP**
>
> When the meaning is *I have done and still am* the implication is that the action is temporary – *I am still in Japan at the moment (but I will be returning)*. If the action is permanent, you use ました:
>
> 両親はイギリスに帰りました。　　*My parents have gone back to England (and are staying there).*

11.6 TRYING THINGS FOR THE FIRST TIME

When you use the て form with みます (*see*) it means *try, give something a try* and often refers to things you are trying for the first time. You could even think of it as meaning *I'll do it and see*.

YOUR TURN **1** **What do the following sentences mean?**

a 明日寿司を食べてみます。

b 夕べ酒を飲んでみました。

Notice that you change the みます part when you want to talk about past events. In fact, it is always the みます part you change to say different things.

YOUR TURN **2** **What do these sentences mean?**

a 漢字で書いてみてもいいですか。

b このジャケットを着てみたいです。

11.7 ASKING SOMEONE TO DO SOMETHING FOR YOU

You have learned how to say what you yourself want to do using the verb stem with たいです:

このジャケットを買いたいです。　　　　　*I want to buy this jacket.*

If you want someone else to do something for you then you use the て form with ほしいです (*want*):

宿題をしてほしいです。　　　　　　　　*I want you to do your homework.*

YOUR TURN **1** **Can you find the part in Conversation 2 when Eri says she wants her sister to do her homework for her?**

2 **What does this sentence mean?**

みきさんに日本語を教えてほしいです。

3 **What particle do you use to indicate the person that you want to do the action? In English this particle might translate literally as *for* – *I want for Miki to teach me Japanese.***

You can also use ほしい to talk about things you want. The thing you want is followed by the particle **ga**:

車 がほしいです。 *I want a car.*

YOUR TURN 4 What do the following sentences mean?
a すてきなジャケットがほしいです。
b 何がほしいですか。

> **LANGUAGE TIP**
> The difference between ほしい and たい here is that ほしい is used for things you want whereas たい is used to talk about things you want to do.

11.8 USING まだ (YET, STILL) AND もう (ALREADY, NO LONGER)

You use まだ with the ています form when you want to talk about things you haven't done yet or things you are still in the process of doing. In Conversation 2 Eri says:

今 週はまだしていません。 *I haven't done it (homework) this week yet.*

She could also say:

まだしています。 *I'm still doing it.*

Both examples are describing incomplete actions: the negative (ていません) means *not yet*; the positive (ています) means *still*.

YOUR TURN What do these sentences mean?
a まだ宿題をしています。
b まだ会社に行っていません。

The opposite of まだ is もう (*already, no longer*). It is used when an action is finished. Look at these two examples:

もう朝ごはんを食べました。 *I have already eaten my breakfast.*
もう朝ごはんを食べません。 *I no longer eat breakfast.*

In the first example, the action is complete (*I've already eaten*) so the verb is in the simple past ました. In the second example, the action will no longer be done and so the verb is in the simple negative ません. You can also use ていません when talking about habitual actions you no longer do:

ゆきさんはもうギターを習っていません。 *Yuki no longer learns the guitar.*

You can use まだ and もう when asking and answering questions.
まだ朝ごはんを食べていますか。 *Are you still eating your breakfast?*
いいえ、もう食べました。 *No, I've already eaten it.*
もうビールを飲みましたか。 *Have you already drunk your beer? (Have you finished your beer?)*

いいえ、まだ飲んでいません。 *No, I haven't drunk it yet.*
いいえ、まだです。 *No, not yet.*

Listening

 1 11.05 **Naoe is describing her family as they go about their morning routine. Listen to the audio and answer the questions.**

    a At the moment what are the following people doing: **1** Naoe; **2** Yuki; **3** Eri?

    b What information does she give about her husband and grandfather?

2 11.06 **Pictures 1–10 show Katie doing various activities. Listen to the audio and match the activities you hear with the pictures. Then try saying the activities out loud in complete sentences and listen to the audio to check your answers.**

Speaking

 11.07 **Say the following sentences in Japanese and then listen to the audio to check your answers.**

    a What are you doing now?

    b I am buying a digital camera. (デジカメ)

    c What was Mr Hondo doing?

    d He was making a phone call.

    e I am currently learning flower arrangement. (生け花)

    f I play golf every Sunday. (literally: every week's Sunday)

    g Both Katie and Ian teach English in Japan.

    h My mum lived in Sydney. (シドニー)

    i Katie has returned to America. (for a holiday – temporarily)

    j My parents have gone back to America. (permanently)

    k Robert has come to Japan from England.

Reading 1

1 Complete these sentences by inserting either まだ or もう into the gaps, and then work out the English meanings. The sentences are based on information you know about the main characters in this book. (The **rōmaji** version is available in the Answer key.)

a ロジャーさんは ＿＿＿＿ みきさんとテニスをしていません。

b みきさんは ＿＿＿＿ ロジャーさんとデートをしました。

c 本堂さんは今うちにいません。＿＿＿＿ 会社にいます。

d えりさんは今週 ＿＿＿＿ 宿題をしていません。

e ゆきさんは今週 ＿＿＿＿ 宿題をしました。

f ケイティさんのご両親は ＿＿＿＿ 日本にいます。

g たけしさんは ＿＿＿＿ 仕事をしていません。

h なおえさんの父は ＿＿＿＿ 仕事をしていません。毎日家にいます。

2 Complete each sentence by selecting the appropriate phrase. You can use each phrase only once.

a お姉ちゃんに宿題を ＿＿＿＿ です。

   (I want my sister to do my homework for me.)

b この T シャツを ＿＿＿＿ です。　(I want to try on this T-shirt.)

c 今子供は家で遊んで ＿＿＿＿。

   (At the moment the children are playing in the house.)

d もう東京に住んで ＿＿＿＿。　(I no longer live in Tokyo.)

e 今晩ドイツの料理を食べて ＿＿＿＿。　(Let's try German food tonight.)

f えりちゃんに新聞を ＿＿＿＿ です。　(I want Eri to buy a newspaper for me.)

g 新しい車が ＿＿＿＿ です。　(I want a new car.)

h 去年フランス語を習らって ＿＿＿＿。　(Last year I had a go at learning French.)

1 います
2 かってほしい
3 きてみたい
4 ほしい
5 みましょう
6 みました
7 してほしい
8 いません

Kanji numbers

INTRODUCTION

In this section you will learn the **kanji** for numbers, prices and years, how to read dates and how to read the Japanese calendar. You will also get more practice in reading **hiragana**.

START READING

You have learned the **kanji** for *sun* 日 and *moon* 月. These two **kanji** are also used for dates. 日 represents the days of the month (1st, 2nd, 3rd, etc.) and 月 represents the months of the year (months were traditionally measured by the phases of the moon). Here are some examples:

１日１２日	*1st, 12th*
１月１２月	*January, December*
３月５日	*March 5th*

If you need to remind yourself of the months, look back at Unit 4.

When you write month and date you must write it in that order only – first month then date. If you also include the weekday, this comes third:

２月１８日（月曜日）	*February 18th (Monday)* or *Monday 18th February*
５月２日（日曜日）	*May 2nd (Sunday)* or *Sunday 2nd May*

 READING 2

Here are some important dates in the Japanese calendar. Can you match them to the correct English date?

a　１月１日
b　３月３日
c　５月５日
d　７月７日
e　１２月２３日
f　１２月３１日
g　１１月１５日
h　２月３日
i　４月２９日
j　８月１１日

1　Mountain Day (11th August)
2　7-5-3 (Children's) Festival (15th November)
3　Emperor's birthday (23rd December)
4　Bean-throwing Ceremony (3rd February)
5　Greenery Day (29th April)
6　New Year's Eve
7　New Year's Day
8　Star Festival (7th July)
9　Girls' Day (3rd March)
10　Boys' Day (5th May)

KANJI NUMBERS

The Japanese use both our Arabic system for writing numbers (1, 2, 3, etc.) and also the **kanji** system. These **kanji** are relatively simple; here are the numbers 1–10:

一 二 三 四 五 六 七 八 九 十

Here are some clues to help you remember them.

一 二 三 – these are easy to remember – one line, two lines, three lines.

四 – this is a *four*-sided square.

五 – you can make out the shape of the Arabic number 5 in this – try it!

六 – in Japanese, you say **roku** which sounds like 'rocket' – can you see a rocket taking off in this **kanji**?

七 – turn this **kanji** upside down and you have a Continental number 7

八 – if you turn Arabic number 8 on its side you have the symbol for infinity. Think of 八 as a road leading on to infinity!

九 – can you see the **kanji** for 8 and for 1 in this symbol? 8 + 1 = 9!

十 – the Roman numeral for 10 is X. Tilt 十 to one side to get the same.

 ## READING 3

How well can you remember the kanji numbers 1–10? Match the sequences of kanji numbers with the sequences on the right:

a	二 四 六 八 十	1	1 2 3 4 5
b	三 六 九 六 三	2	2 4 6 8 10
c	一 三 五 七 九	3	10 9 8 7 6
d	十 九 八 七 六	4	3 6 9 6 3
e	一 二 三 四 五	5	1 3 5 7 9

HIGHER NUMBERS

You have already learned to count from 1–99 in the first few units. With this knowledge, it is easy to read higher numbers. Here is a quick reminder of the basic rules:

12 = 10 + 2 = 十二
20 = 2 × 10 = 二十
21 = 2 × 10 + 1 = 二十一
99 = 9 × 10 + 9 = 九十九

 ## READING 4

Here are some sequences of numbers. Can you write them down in Arabic numerals?

a	十一	十二	十三	十四	十五
b	二十	三十	四十	五十	六十
c	九十	九十一	九十二	九十三	九十四
d	三十三	四十四	五十五	六十六	七十七
e	五十九	五十八	五十七	五十六	五十五

READING 5

Here are some dates using kanji numbers. Can you convert them into English dates?

Example: 八月十二日（月曜日）→ Monday 12th August
a 十二月二十五日　　（火曜日）
b 六月十七日　　　　（水曜日）
c 九月三日　　　　　（土曜日）
d 四月二十一日　　　（金曜日）

100S, 1000S AND 10,000S

Look back to Unit 3 if you need to refresh your memory of these numbers. Here are the **kanji**:

百 100 – if you turn this **kanji** on its side, you can see the numerals 1 0 0.
千 1000 – this looks like the **kanji** 十 (10) but with an extra 'load' on top – two more zeros!
万 10,000 – can you see a *T* and an *h* in this **kanji**? *T* for ten and *Th* for thousand – ten thousand!
円 **en** – this is the **kanji** for **yen**, the Japanese currency. Its international symbol is ￥.

 READING 6

Here are some prices. Can you write them in Arabic numerals?

a cup of coffee = 四百円
b plate of **sushi** = 七百円
c T-shirt = 千九百円
d underground ticket = 四百九十円
e **kabuki** theatre ticket = 五千円

THE JAPANESE CALENDAR

The **kanji** for *year* is 年. It contains the left part of bamboo (竹) and behind that a square shape, which we shall interpret as a house. In Japan, bamboo decorations are placed in front of houses at New Year, hence the link with *year*.

The most common way to write years from the Western calendar is like this: ２０１７年.

You may also see this: 二〇一七年.

However, the Japanese also have their own system of numbering the years based on the length of rule of their Emperor. This is the system of 年号 (**nengō**) – *era names*. The present Emperor, Akihito, began his reign in 1989 and this era is called 平成 (**Heisei**), which means *attainment of peace*. To work out the **Heisei** year from the Western calendar year, begin with 1989 as year 1 and count up from there. So 2017 is **Heisei** 29. This is how 2017 is written using this system: 平成二十九年

You can also use Arabic numbers: 平成２９年.

❓ Test yourself

1 What do these sentences mean?

a 今家族と晩ごはんを食べています。

b ギターを習っています。

c 大学で日本語を勉強しています。

d 姉は結婚しています。

e 父は今アメリカに行っています。

f この寿司を食べてみましょう！

g テレビを消してほしいです。

h もう朝ご飯を食べましたか。

i いいえ、まだ食べていません。

2 How would you say the following in Japanese?

a I always eat curry on Saturdays.

b I want to try (drinking) Japanese beer.

c Please try writing it in Japanese.

d I want you to write it in Japanese.

e I want a big car.

f Have you already phoned (to) Mr Hondo? No, not yet.

g Eri hasn't done her homework yet but Yuki is still doing hers.

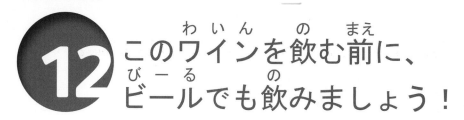

12 この<ruby>ワイン<rt>わ　い　ん</rt></ruby>を<ruby>飲<rt></rt></ruby>む<ruby>前<rt>まえ</rt></ruby>に、
<ruby>ビール<rt>び　ー　る</rt></ruby>でも<ruby>飲<rt>の</rt></ruby>みましょう！

Before we drink this wine, let's drink beer or something!

In this unit you will learn how to:
▸ *make and use the plain form.*
▸ *talk about things you can do and like to do.*
▸ *state intentions, reasons and justifications.*
▸ *say what you are interested in.*

CEFR: *(B1) Can briefly give reasons and explanations for opinions and plans, and actions. Can write simple connected text on topics which are familiar or of personal interest. Has sufficient vocabulary to express self with some circumlocutions on most topics pertinent to everyday life such as family, hobbies and interests, work, travel.*

敬語・非公式日本語 Kengo/hikōshiki Nihongo
Levels of language in Japanese

Every country and every culture uses different types of 言語 **gengo** (*language*) depending on the situation – we say *hi* to a friend or *hello* to be more polite, for example. You will learn about the plain form in this unit which is one of the layers of formal and informal language in 日本語 **Nihongo** (*Japanese*).

日本語 **Nihongo** is interesting because as well as using different 言葉 **kotoba** (*words and phrases*) for particular situations, you also use different 動詞 **dōshi** (*verbs*) or forms of verbs depending on the formality or informality of the situation or the status of the person you are speaking with. As you have learned, Japanese people use 尊敬語 **sonkeigo** (*respectful language*) when speaking to higher-status people and 謙譲語 **kenjōgo** (*humble language*) when referring to themselves and 家族 **kazoku** (*family*) in formal situations. 丁寧語 **Teineigo** (*Neutral polite language using* ます・です **masu/desu**) is used when there is no need to show specific respect to someone and is safe for 外国人 **gaikokujin** (*non-Japanese people*) to use in most situations.

Another interesting point is that there is a gender divide. 日本人の女性 **Nihonjin no josei** (*Japanese women*) use polite, 'softer' language more and 日本人の男性 **Nihonjin no dansei** (*Japanese men*) use 普通形 **futsūkei** (*plain forms*) more.

When 女性 **josei** use plain forms they tend to make them sound less abrupt by using わ **wa** and の **no** at the end of the sentence. わ **Wa** makes a statement either softly assertive or friendly and の **no** is used to ask for or give explanations or for emphasis.

What do these sentences mean and what effect do you think the endings have on them?

a みきさんは恥ずかしがりじゃないわ。

b この映画は面白いの。

Vocabulary builder

 1 12.01 Listen to the new vocabulary and practise saying it out loud.

NEW STRUCTURES AND VERBS

(Note that from now on verbs will be given in plain or dictionary form.)

泳ぐ	swim	つもりです	intend to do
ことができる	can do	（に）興味がある	have an interest (in)
ことが好きです	like doing	ので	therefore, so
x 前に	before doing (x)	から	therefore, so
んです（か）	you see, giving (or asking for) a reason		

NEW EXPRESSIONS

南	south
あのね	hey, erm (friendly)
ひま（な）	free
じゃあ	OK, right, in that case
バドミントン	badminton
ねえ	look (letting someone know something)
ああ、そうですか	oh, really?
でも	but
よ	you know, I tell you（わ before it can make it very feminine)
野球場	baseball stadium
野球	baseball
いろいろ（な）	various
しゃぶしゃぶ	table-top dish of thinly sliced beef cooked quickly in hot water and dipped in sauces
肉	meat
ベジタリアン	vegetarian
魚	fish
大丈夫	fine, all right
寿司屋さん	sushi bar
でも	something like, or something
どうして	why

2 Look at the new structures (underlined) and vocabulary again and see if you can work out the meanings of these sentences:

a えりちゃんはもう<u>泳ぐことができる</u>。

b ロジャーさんは友達とビールを<u>飲むことが好き</u>です。

c 来年南アメリカに<u>行くつもりです</u>。

d 南アメリカに<u>興味があるので</u>行きたいです。

e 日本語を習っていますから日本に来ています。

f <u>どうしたんですか</u>。頭が<u>痛いんです</u>。

Conversation 1

 12.02 *Roger phones Miki to propose a second date.*

1 Why doesn't Miki want to play tennis or badminton?

Miki	もしもし
Roger	もしもし、みきさんですか。ロジャーですが ...
Miki	ロジャーさん、こんにちは！
Roger	こんにちは。あのね、今晩ひまですか。
Miki	今晩ですか、今晩はちょっと ... りえさんと映画を見ます。見る前にレストランで食べるつもりです。
Roger	そうですか。じゃあ、土曜日の晩はどうですか。
Miki	土曜日はいいですよ。何をしましょうか。
Roger	テニスをしましょうか。
Miki	テニスですか。テニスはあまりできません。
Roger	じゃあ、バドミントンはどうですか。
Miki	ねえ、ロジャーさん、すみませんがスポーツをすることがあまり好きじゃないです。
Roger	*(Sounding disappointed)* ああ、そうですか。

2 What is Miki doing with Rie this evening?

3 What evening do they settle on?

Conversation 2

12.03 *The date is fixed.*

1 What does Miki suggest doing and why?

Miki	でもスポーツを見ることは好きですよ！土曜日の晩、野球場で、野球を見に行きましょうか。
Roger	*(Brightening up)* そうしましょう！
Miki	野球場の近くにいろいろなレストランがあります。野球を見る前にしゃぶしゃぶでも食べましょう！
Roger	*(Sounding doubtful)* しゃぶしゃぶは肉ですね。僕はベジタリアンなので肉を食べることができません。
Miki	魚 はどうですか。
Roger	魚 は大丈夫です。食べることができるんです。
Miki	じゃあ、野球の前に寿司屋さんで食べましょう！

2 What does she suggest doing before that?

3 What does Miki say there is near the stadium?

4 What new piece of information have you learned about these people?

  a Miki

  b Roger

5 Are these statements true or false?

  a みきさんはロジャーさんに電話しました。

  b みきさんは今晩ひまじゃありません。

  c ロジャーさんはテニスやバドミントンをしたいです。

  d みきさんは野球が好きじゃありません。

  e ロジャーさんは魚を食べることができません。

6 Write your answers in Japanese (there is more than one way of writing these answers and the answers in the Answer key give one correct version. The rōmaji version is in the Answer key).

  a みきさんは今晩何をするつもりですか。

  b みきさんはどうして野球を見たいですか。

  c ロジャーさんはしゃぶしゃぶを食べることができますか。

  d どうしてですか。

  e どこで食べるつもりですか。

Language discovery

12.1 THE PLAIN OR DICTIONARY FORM OF VERBS

12.04 One of the uses of 辞書形 **jisho katachi** (*the plain* or *dictionary form*) is in informal speech. Listen to ten plain form verbs and work out their English meanings. (Clue: look at the stem of the verb.)

a 食べる   f 買う

b 見る   g 書く

c 教える   h 飲む

d 出る   i 話す

e 聞く   j 行く

Now listen to the audio again and say the verbs out loud as you read them.

 YOUR TURN 1 **12.05** Change these short polite sentences into plain ones using the plain verbs you have used in the previous activity. The first one is done for you as an example. Listen to the audio to check your answers and practise your pronunciation.

Example: 朝ごはんを食べます → 朝ごはんを食べる。

a テレビを見ます。   f メールを書きます。

b 英語を教えます。   g ビールを飲みます。

c 家を出ます。   h 日本語を話します。

d ニュースを聞きます。   i フランスに行きます。

e テレビを買います。

The plain form is fairly easy to work out from its **masu** form (and vice versa). When you look up a new verb in a dictionary it is always in the dictionary (plain present) form so it is useful for you to know how to convert it into the **masu** form.

Here are the rules for changing **masu** into plain form for each group.

Group 1 verbs

Drop ます, change the final **hiragana** from its **i** ending to **u**:

Example: 買います (*buy*) → かい → かう

YOUR TURN 2 Change these verbs into their plain form:

a 書きます (*write*) → かき → _____

b 話します (*speak*) → はなし → _____

c 持ちます (*possess*) → もち → _____

d 泳ぎます (*swim*) → およぎ → _____

e 遊びます (*play*) → あそび → _____

Group 2 verbs

Drop ます, add る.

YOUR TURN 3 Change these verbs into their plain form:

  a 寝ます (go to bed) → ね → _____

  b 起きます (get up) → おき → _____

Irregular verbs

There are three verbs in Japanese that don't always conform to the rules. These are 行きます (*go*), 来ます (*come*) and します (*do*). The plain forms of the second and third are: きます → くる and します → する.

YOUR TURN 4 行きます follows the Group 1 rule. What is its plain form?

You will, in fact, find that 行きます acts like a Group 1 verb, except for the irregular て form (行って).

YOUR TURN 5 Can you work out how to convert verbs back from plain form to masu form? Try these verbs to see if you've got it right then check the rules in the Answer key.

  Group 1:   **a** 話す   **b** 読む   **c** わかる

  Group 2:   **d** 出かける   **e** 出る

12.2 HOW DO I KNOW IF A VERB IS GROUP 1 OR GROUP 2?

Some dictionaries aimed at non-Japanese speakers mark whether a verb is Group 1 or Group 2. However, there are some patterns you can look for to help you decide if a verb is Group 1 or Group 2.

▶ All Group 2 plain form verbs end in **ru** so, if the plain verb doesn't end in **ru** (e.g. **su**, **u**, **ku**, **bu**, **mu**, **nu**, **gu**), then it must be a Group 1 verb.

▶ Many Group 2 verbs have an **e** ending before the **masu** or **ru** (e.g. 食べる、出かける、 ねる、でる). Group 1 verbs never have this so **e** indicates a Group 2 verb.

▶ There are a number of verbs ending in either **ru** (plain form) or **imasu** (polite form) which could be either Group 1 or Group 2 verb (e.g. わかる・わかります (Group 1) and 起きる・起きます (Group 2)). If you know both the plain and **masu** forms, then you can work out which it is following this rule:

  ▷ If it is Group 1, then **ru** becomes **ri** (and vice versa – わかる → わかります).

  ▷ If it is Group 2, then **ru** is dropped or added not changed (起きる → 起きます).

> **LANGUAGE TIP**
> The verb table at the back of this book lists the verbs according to their group so you can use this table to check the verbs used in this course.

12.3 SAYING WHAT HAPPENED BEFORE

Look back at Conversation 1 and find out how Miki said *Before watching we intend to eat at a restaurant.*

Within this sentence is the phrase 見る前に meaning *before watching*. You used 前に in Unit 6 with locations to mean *in front of*. Now you are learning how to use 前に with verbs in the plain form to mean *before doing*.

YOUR TURN 1 What do these phrases mean?

  a 寝る前に
  b 飲む前に

You then continue the sentence with the main verb and it is this verb which decides the tense (past, present/future) of the whole statement. Look at the title of this unit to see an example of this.

YOUR TURN 2 What do these sentences mean?

  a 本堂さんは寝る前にいつも本を読みます。
  b イアンさんはビールお飲む前に晩ごはんを食べました。

You can also use 前に after nouns:

朝ごはんの前に	*before breakfast*
旅行の前に	*before the trip*

12.4 SAYING WHAT YOU CAN DO

Look back at the first question in the Vocabulary builder and remind yourself what this sentence means:

えりちゃんはもう泳ぐことができます。

できます means *can, able to*. It is used directly with nouns to talk about things you can do, particularly sports and practical skills: (person) は (noun) ができます.

YOUR TURN 1 What do these sentences mean?

  a 私 はテニスができます。
  b りえさんは料理ができます。

You can also use it with the dictionary form of verbs to talk about what you can do. To do this you add こと to the verb (this effectively changes the verb into a noun): (person) は (verb) ことができます.

えりちゃんは泳ぐことができます。	*Eri can swim.*
私 は日本語を書くことができません。	*I can't write Japanese.*

YOUR TURN 2 How would you say the following in Japanese?

  a Robert can't drink beer.
  b Rie can speak English.
  c Naoe can speak English <u>a little</u>. (すこし)

12.5 SAYING WHAT YOU LIKE TO DO

You already know 好きです (like) and its negative and past tenses from Unit 9. You can use the dictionary form to say what you like (or don't like) doing: (person) は (verb) ことが好きです.

Example: りえさんは料理をすることが好きです。　　*Rie likes cooking.*

YOUR TURN 1 What does the following sentence mean?
ケイティさんは料理をすることが好きじゃありません。

The structure is very similar to *I can do* except you use 好き in place of できます. In fact, you can replace 好き with other adjectives to add a description to what you do.

YOUR TURN 2 What do these statements mean?
   a 私は日本語を話すことが上手ですが日本語を読むことが下手です。
   b ゆきさんは数学を勉強することがとくいですが英語がにがてです。

12.6 SAYING YOUR PLANS AND INTENTIONS USING つもりです

In Conversation 1 Miki says that she and Rie intend to eat at a restaurant. You will see she uses the dictionary form plus つもりです:

レストランで食べるつもりです。　　*We plan to eat at a restaurant.*

You can ask someone about their plans too:
クリスマスにアメリカに帰るつもりですか。

Are you planning to go back to America for Christmas?

YOUR TURN 12.06 Can you ask some questions using the verbs: 書く (*write*), 飲む (*drink*), 働く (*work*), する (*do*), 見る (*watch*)? **Listen to the audio to check your answers.**
   a Are you planning to write a letter (てがみ) to your mother?
   b Do you intend to drink beer tonight?
   c Do you plan to work until late every day?
   d Are you planning to play golf with Naoe on Sunday?
   e Do you intend to watch the football (サッカー) tonight?

12.7 GIVING REASONS USING から AND ので

When you give a reason for something in English it often involves words such as *because*, *since*, *therefore* or *so*. Look at these examples:

<u>Since</u> I have a headache I am staying at home today.

I am staying at home today <u>because</u> I have a headache.

I have a headache <u>so</u> I am staying at home today.

The reason (or cause) is the headache; the result is I am staying at home.

In Japanese, the sentence order is more rigid. First, you give the reason or cause and then the result. You attach から or ので to the end of the reason like this:

頭が痛いから今日は家にいます。

頭が痛いので今日は家にいます。

Both these sentences mean *I'm staying at home today because I have a headache.*

The order is: the reason (*headache*); attach から or ので; say the result (*staying at home*).

> **LANGUAGE TIP**
>
> Thinking of から and ので as *therefore* or *so* (rather than *because*) helps to get the order right:
>
> 頭が痛いから今日は家にいます。   *I have a headache therefore I'm staying at home today.*

You normally use the plain form of the verb with から and ので (although you can use **masu** verbs with から in more formal situations):

オーストラリアに行くので   *because I will go to Australia*

毎日新聞を読むから   *I read a paper every day therefore*

When using **i** adjectives (including たい (*I want to*)) you don't need です (but can use it in more formal situations):

この本は面白いので   *this book is interesting therefore*

When using **na** adjectives and nouns the rule varies for から and ので.

▶ With ので use adjective or noun plus **na**:

先生なので   *because she is a teacher*

きれいなので   *since she is beautiful*

▶ With から use adjective or noun with the plain form of です – だ (you can also use です in more formal situations):

先生だから   *because she is a teacher*

きれいですから   *since she is beautiful*

You're going to put this into practice now. Can you create and say out loud full sentences as in the example? Give the English meaning too.

	Reason	Connector	Result
Example prompts	病気です	から	会社に行きません
a	日本に行きます	ので	毎日日本語を勉強します
b	先生がやさしいです	から	英語が好きです
c	みきさんはきれいです	ので	ロジャーさんは好きです
d	毎日掃除をします	から	いつもきれいです

Example answer:

病気だから会社に行きません。 *I'm ill so I'm not going to work.*

> **LANGUAGE TIP**
>
> Is there any difference between から and ので?
>
> Generally not: they are two words meaning *because*. However, if you are asking, suggesting, telling or inviting someone to do something it is more common to use から.
>
> You can also use から in answer to the question *why?*. In Japanese this is どうして or なぜ.
>
> どうして部屋を掃除しますか。 *Why are you cleaning your room?*
> 両親が来るからです。 *Because my parents are coming.*

12.8 ASKING FOR OR GIVING JUSTIFICATION (*YOU SEE*)

You use the plain form followed by のです (often shortened to んです) to give an explanation or justification. You use のですか (んですか) to ask for an explanation. It is much softer than から and may not always have a specific meaning in English. Here are some examples:

どうして町に行くのですか。 *Why are going to town?*
友達に会うんです。 *'Cos I'm meeting my friend.*

You could also say:

友達に会うから。 *Because I'm meeting my friend.*
どうして遅く起きるんですか。 *Why do you get up late?*
毎晩遅くまでビールを飲むんです。 *I drink beer until late every night, you see.*

12.9 STATING YOUR INTERESTS USING 興味がある

You use this phrase when talking about what you are interested in. Use the particle に after the thing you have an interest in:

日本のことに興味があります。 *I have an interest in Japanese things.*
スポーツに全然興味がありません。 *I have no interest in sport.*

Listening

 1 12.07 **On their second date, Miki and Roger get on much better and Miki tells him about her plans for next year. Listen to the audio and answer these questions.**

  a Where does Miki want to go next year and why?

  b What two things does she say about Spanish food?

  c What two things is she planning to do tonight?

 2 12.08 **Miki and Roger separately report back to 'matchmaker' Rie about their second date. Listen to them one at a time and select the pictures in order that they happened to fit:**

  a Miki's version of events

  b Roger's version

Speaking

1 12.09 Use the following pictures to talk about sequences of actions using 前^{まえ}に then check your answers and practise with the audio. (Clue: take a shower = シャワー^{しゃわー}を浴^あびる .)

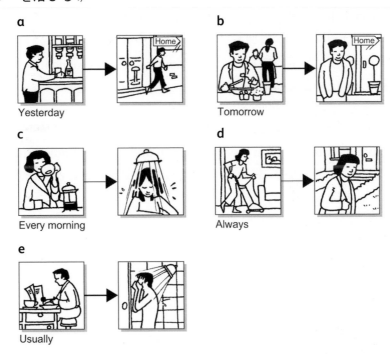

a

Yesterday

b

Tomorrow

c

Every morning

d

Always

e

Usually

2 Using から・ので (*because, therefore*) create Japanese sentences from English prompts as in the example.

	Reason	Connector	Result
Example	I am working late	から	I'm not going to see the film
a	I am no good at sports	ので	I am not a member of the tennis club
b	that restaurant is expensive (たかい)	から	let's eat at home
c	Katie is a skilful teacher	ので	her classes (クラス^{くらす}) are enjoyable

Example:

遅^{おそ}くまで 働^{はたら}くから映画^{えいが}を見ません。

Because I'm working late I'm not going to see the film.

Writing

1 **Give the correct verb and ending to give sense to these sentences. Use the endings:**
ことができます、つもりです、ことが好きです、ことがじょうずです。

a えりさんは _____。(Eri can swim.)

b みきさんはスポーツを _____。(Miki likes watching sports.)

c イアンさんは今晩インド料理を _____。(Ian plans to make Indian food tonight.)

d ケイティさんはインド料理を _____。(Katie enjoys/likes eating Indian food.)

e ロジャーさんはテニスやボーリングを _____。
(Roger is good at playing tennis and bowling.)

f 本堂さんは今晩遅くまで _____。(Mr Hondo can't work late tonight.)

2 **Make complete sentences from the words given and give the English meaning.**
Example: りえ、新聞を読む、好き → りえさんは新聞を読むことが好きです。

a ケイティ、友達と、遊ぶ、好き

b えり、宿題をする、好きじゃありません

c 日本人と会う、面白い

d なおえ、ピアノを弾く、上手

e ロジャー、漢字を書く、とくい

More on kanji

INTRODUCTION

In this section you will learn verb **kanji**, more about **kanji** radicals and more **kanji** compound words.

START READING

The kanji in this section are used with some of the verbs you have been learning. Here are five kanji broken down into components with stories to link them to their meaning. Can you match each story and meaning with the correct kanji?

a 言 **b** 食 **c** 売 **d** 聞 **e** 見

Story 1: Can you see a pile of earth (土) on top of a table (儿)? At the tabletop sale one person was *selling* earth. Meaning: *to sell*

Story 2: Can you see gates (門) and an ear (耳)? The nosey neighbour keeps her ear at the gate (door) to *listen* out for any gossip. Meaning: *to listen, hear*

Story 3: Can you see a mouth (口) with four horizontal lines rising from it? Those are the words that the mouth is *saying*. Meaning: *to say*

Story 4: This **kanji** has a roof (人) on top, white (白) in the middle and a 'squashed' fire (火) below. White symbolizes rice which is being cooked in the home *to eat*. Meaning: *to eat*

Story 5: An eye (目) running around on human legs (儿) is a *looking* machine! Meaning: *to look, see, watch*

Here are the new **kanji** again with their meanings:

言	*to say*		聞	*to listen*
食	*to eat*		見	*to see, watch, look*
売	*to sell*			

KANJI RADICALS

Remember that radicals are components of a **kanji** that can give a very general meaning to the whole **kanji**. Here is a selection with their meanings.

儿　*human legs*

人　*person*, also 'squashed' into a roof on top (食) and a 'leaning T' on the left side (休)

口　*mouth/opening*

土　*earth*

士　*samurai warrior*. Looks like earth but has longer 'arms'.

女　*woman*

彳　*to go*, the 'going person' (see person earlier in the list)

水　*water*. Looks like this on left side シ – three splashes.

心　*heart*. (Can you see two sides of heart?) Used in 'emotion' and 'thought' words.

日　*sun/day/time*

月　*moon* or *flesh* (from 肉 **niku** meaning *meat*)

木　*tree* or *wood* (material)

火　*fire*. Looks like this when written at bottom (e.g. 黒 *black*).

牛　*cow*

貝　*shellfish*. This is an eye on small animal legs.

言　*to say, words*

 READING 1

Here are some new **kanji**. Can you identify their radical? They will either be on the left or at the bottom.

a 休 *rest*

b 物 *thing*

c 買 *buy*

d 吹 *blow*

e 思 *think*

f 海 *sea*

g 畑 *cultivated field*

h 時 *time*

i 行 *go*

j 背 *back, height*

COMPLEX KANJI: MORE VERBS

Here are a further ten verbs which are made up of simpler **kanji** components:

行 *to go*. This has the 'going person' radical on the left.

読 *to read*. You can see *words* on the left (radical) and *to sell* on the right. Words for sale are books for *reading*.

話 *to speak, talk*. *Words* (radical) on the left, *mouth with forked tongue* on right – the tongue is *speaking* words.

買 *to buy*. A horizontal eye looks carefully at the *shellfish* to decide which to *buy*.

休 *to rest, holiday*. A *person resting* under a *tree*.

出 *to exit, go out*. Two sets of *mountains* – find the mountain pass *to exit*.

入 *to enter*. This is a simple **kanji** and a radical in its own right. Be careful not to confuse it with *person* 人.

飲 *to drink*. *Eat* is on the left and can you see a person raising a glass up to *drink* on the right?

書 *to write*. The lower part looks like sun but in fact is from this **kanji** 日 meaning *to utter (say)*. Think of it as a condensed form of 言 with the words about to come out. The upper part was developed from the picture of a brush! Here is a drawing to help you. So *spoken words* are *written* with a *brush*:

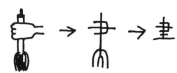

分 *to understand* (also *minute, divide*). This consists of the number 8 (八) and the **kanji** for *sword* (刀). The *sword divides* up time into *minutes*. You might *divide* up a difficult **kanji** into parts to make it easier *to understand*!

 READING 2

You have now been exposed to 15 **kanji** for verbs. How well can you recall them? What do they mean in English?

a 食	d 出	g 話	j 見	m 聞
b 飲	e 入	h 売	k 買	n 行
c 書	f 言	i 読	l 分	o 休

KANJI COMPOUNDS

There are lots of new words that can be created by combining two or three of these new **kanji** words. A useful new **kanji** for creating more words is *thing* – 物. This **kanji** basically turns verbs into nouns. Here are two examples:

食 *eat* → 食べ物 **tabemono** = *food*
飲 *drink* → 飲み物 **nomimono** = *a drink*

READING 3

Here are some more compound **kanji** words using **kanji** from this and the previous unit. Can you match them with their English meaning? Some have **hiragana** elements but simply focus on the **kanji** meanings.

a 入口
b 出口
c 買い物
d 見物
e 売り物
f 読書
g 休日
h 売買
i 飲水
j 買手

1 reading
2 buyer
3 entrance
4 exit
5 drinking water
6 shopping
7 sightseeing
8 items for sale
9 holiday
10 buying and selling

> **READING TIP**
> Be careful not to confuse 入口 (*entrance*) with 人口 (*population*).

 READING 4

You are now going to try to read simple sentences which use some of the **kanji** from this and previous units. Read them out loud and work out the meanings. The reading of the **kanji** is written in **furigana** over the top.

a あさごはん を 食べます。
b ときどき しん聞 を 読みます。
c まい日 ニュース を 聞きます。
d ちちと テレビ を 見ます。
e 明日 日本に 行きます。

f 日本ご を 話しました。
g おも白い 本 を 買いました。
h 土曜日に 買い物を します。
i 日曜日に くるまを 売りました。
j まい日 かんじを 書いてみます。

 READING AND WRITING CHALLENGE

12.07 You have heard Miki talk about her plans for next year in this unit (Listening 1). Using this as your model, you are going to write out your own plans based on the following prompts. Miki's dialogue is printed with various parts underlined. Change these to include the following information:

a You want to go to Japan next year so you are learning Japanese.
b You're not very good at Japanese yet but you are interested in Japanese things.
c You really like Japanese food as well but can't make it.
d You plan to meet a friend in town tomorrow and eat Japanese food at a famous restaurant.

You can listen to the audio again as well to help you read this passage before you change it. Use kanji where you can.

来年 南アメリカ (**a**) に行きたいので今スペイン語 (**a**) を習っています。スペイン語 (**b**) を話すことがまだあまり上手じゃありませんが 南アメリカ人と話すことがとても面白いと思います (**b**)。そしてスペイン (**c**) の料理もとても好きですが作ることができません。今晩 (**d**) 町で友達と会って、おいしい (**d**) レストランでスペイン (**d**) の料理を食べるつもりです。

☑ Test yourself

1 Here is a table of dictionary-form verbs. Your challenge is to convert them into their **masu** form. Many are new verbs – you don't need to remember them, the purpose of the challenge is to practise forming **masu** from verbs you might look up in a dictionary.

Dictionary form	English	masu form
つたえる	*report, tell*	a
いれる	*put in*	b
だす	*take out*	c
おくれる	*be late*	d
がんばる (Group 1)	*try hard*	e
はしる (Group 1)	*run*	f
あるく	*walk*	g
つかう	*use*	h
おく	*put*	i
あらう	*wash*	j

2 What do these sentences mean? (There is a **rōmaji** version in the Answer key.)
a 日本人と話すことが面白いです。
b 病気なので仕事を休んでいます。
c ケイティさんはインド料理が好きだから、それを作るつもりです。
d ロジャーさんは毎日練習をするのでテニスをすることが上手です。
e みきさんは頭が痛いから今コーヒーを飲んでいません。

SELF CHECK

	I CAN...
◯	...make and use the plain form.
◯	...talk about things I can do and like to do.
◯	...state intentions, reasons and justifications.
◯	...say what I'm interested in.
◯	...recognize 15 verb **kanji**, 12 compound **kanji** words and a number of radicals.

13 外国に住んでいたことがあります

がいこく　す

I have lived abroad

In this unit you will learn how to:
▸ *talk in the past using the plain form.*
▸ *talk about your experiences.*
▸ *give advice.*
▸ *say more about routines and actions.*
▸ *make comparisons.*
▸ *quantify your actions.*

CEFR *(A2) Can understand short, simple texts containing the highest-frequency vocabulary, including a portion of shared international vocabulary item. Can write about past events (describe life). (B1) Can describe experiences and events, dreams, hopes and ambitions and briefly give reasons and explanations for opinions and plans.*

Tokyo

東京 **Tōkyō** (*Tokyo*) is both the 首都 **shuto** (*capital city*) of 日本 **Nihon** (*Japan*) and also a metropolitan prefecture. There are over eight million people living in the city of 東京 **Tōkyō** and 28 million people in the metropolitan area. There is no particular city centre to 東京 **Tōkyō** – instead, it is made up of 特別区 **tokubetsu-ku** (*special wards*) and districts all with their own characteristics. The main business areas of 東京 **Tōkyō** are located centrally in the wards of 千代田区 **Chiyoda-ku**, 中央区 **Chūō-ku** and 港区 **Minato-ku**. Within the Chiyoda ward is the national government headquarters known as 議会 **gikai** (*the Diet*) and the emperor's palace. 新宿区 **Shinjuku-ku** has the busiest 駅 **eki** (*railway station*) in the world. To the east, in 東新宿 **Higashi-shinjuku**, is an abundance of bars, nightclubs and shopping centres, and to the west, in 西新宿 **Nishi-shinjuku**, is the largest concentration of skyscrapers in Japan. 渋谷区 **Shibuya-ku** is famous for its fashion and nightlife as well as being the centre of the IT industry. Within this ward is the district of 原宿 **Harajuku**, the centre of youth culture and fashion, 代々木公園 **Yoyogi kōen** (*Yoyogi park*) where the 1964 Olympics were held and the statue of ハチ公 **Hachikō**, the faithful Akita dog, in front of 渋谷駅 **Shibuya eki** (*Shibuya station*). Other famous areas include 秋葉原 **Akihabara**, a major shopping area for computer goods, アニメ **anime** and 漫画 **manga**, 六本木 **Roppongi**, famous for its nightclubs, and 上野公園 Ueno park, home of the 動物園 **dōbutsuen** (*zoo*) and many of Tokyo's 博物館 **hakubutsukan** (*museums*) and 美術館 **bijutsukan** (*art galleries*). There are many important post-war buildings of architectural note including 東京スカイツリ **Tōkyō Sukaitsurī** (*the Tokyo Skytree tower*), the tallest structure in Japan and the tallest free-standing tower in the world (2015), the twin-towered Tokyo Metropolitan Government offices designed by Tange Kenzo, the super dry hall in Asakusa and the Rainbow suspension bridge.

1 How many times does the 漢字 **kanji** 区 appear in the passage and what do you think it means?

2 Look at the 漢字 **kanji** for **Roppongi**. Can you work out its literal meaning?

3 Look at the 漢字 **kanji** for a) museums and art galleries and b) park (as in Yoyogi park) and zoo. Which 漢字 **kanji** do they have in common and what do you think it means?

4 What do the following 漢字 **kanji** mean:

   a 駅

   b 東京

   c 東

   d 西

   e 漫画

Vocabulary builder

 13.01 Listen to the new vocabulary and practise saying it out loud.

NEW VERBS AND STRUCTURES

…とき	*when … (I did)*
…ことがあります	*I have (done) …, I have had the experience of (doing) …*
…ことがありません	*I have never (done) …*
…後(あと)で	*after …*
…ほうがいいです	*you had better, you should*
…教(おし)えたり、旅行(りょこう)したり	*taught and travelled*
…(A) のほうが (B) より	*(A) is … (comparison) than (B)*
忘(わす)れる	*forget*
…しまった（しまう）	*gone and …, completely*
演奏(えんそう)します	*perform*
卒業(そつぎょう)します	*to graduate*
行(い)った	*went (plain past form)*
見(み)た	*saw (plain past form)*
住んでいた	*lived (plain past form)*

NEW EXPRESSIONS

いっぱい	*lots*
外国	*abroad, foreign country*
大学生	*university student*
三年	*three years*
二年間	*two-year period*
夏	*summer*
バンド	*band*
ロックツアー	*rock tour*
ええっと	*er, erm*
名前	*name*
ラブラブボーイズ	*Love Love Boys* (name of Takeshi's band)
あれ！	*hey!, what!*
本当に	*really*
ジャズ	*jazz*
ミックス	*mix*
ポップス	*pop music*
六本木	trendy area of Tokyo
パーティー	*party*

Conversation 1

 13.02 *Miki goes to a university student party and meets Takeshi.*

1 When did Takeshi go to America and where did he go?

Takeshi	みきさんは大学生じゃないですね。
Miki	ええ。三年前に卒業していましたから。そして二年間アメリカで日本語を教えたり、旅行したりしました。
Takeshi	アメリカですか。僕もアメリカに行ったことがあります。去年の夏僕のバンドとロックツアーをしていました。とてもすばらしかったです。
Miki	どこで演奏しましたか。
Takeshi	ええっと、ミネアポリス、ミルウォーキー、シカゴ...
Miki	シカゴですか。バンドの名前は何ですか。
Takeshi	ラブラブボーイズです。

2 When did Miki graduate from university?

3 How many years did Miki spend in America and what did she do there?

Conversation 2

 13.03 *They exchange opinions on music.*

1 When did Miki see Takeshi's band and what did she think of them?

Miki	あれ！見たことがありますよ！シカゴに住んでいたときいろいろな コンサートに行きました。ラブラブボーイズは本当にすばらしかったわ！
Takeshi	見たんですか。信じられない！
Miki	ねえ、あの、ジャズとロックのミックスですね。私はとても好きでした。
Takeshi	ありがとう。ジャズが好きですか。
Miki	はい、ポップスよりジャズのほうが好きです。
Takeshi	僕も好きです。あの、六本木にとてもいいジャズクラブがあります。 このパーティーの後で一緒に行きましょうか。
Miki	パーティーの後でですか。ちょっと遅いわ。
Takeshi	じゃあ、ワインを飲んでしまいましょうか。それから行きましょう。
Miki	いいですね！

2 What music does Miki prefer over pop music?

3 When does Takeshi suggest they go to the jazz club?

4 Are these statements true or false?

   a みきさんは大学生です。

   b たけしさんは去年アメリカで演奏しました。

   c みきさんは三年間アメリカに住んでいました。

   d みきさんはジャズよりポップスのほうが好きです。

   e みきさんはジャズクラブに行きたくないです。

5 Answer these questions in in Japanese:

   a みきさんはどこでたけしさんに会いましたか。

   b たけしさんのバンドの名前は何ですか。

   c みきさんはアメリカで何をしましたか。

   d たけしさんのバンドはどんな音楽のミックスですか。

   e たけしさんはどうして六本木に行きたいですか。

🔘 Language discovery

13.1 INTRODUCTION TO THE PAST PLAIN FORM

All the new structures require the past plain form of the verb in front of them. Look at this example and see if you can work out the rule:

食べて → 食べた   *I ate*

To make the plain past form you change the て ending to た (and the で ending to だ).

買って → 買った   *I bought*
遊んで → 遊んだ   *I socialized*

YOUR TURN 1 Put these て forms into the plain past and give the English meaning too.

a 見て
b 飲んで
c 忘れて
d 演奏して
e 卒業して

YOUR TURN 2 Using the new vocabulary work out the meanings of these sentences:

a 夕べ寿司屋さんで寿司をいっぱい食べた。
b 外国へ行ったことがありません。
c 毎日、晩ごはんを食べた後で、テレビを見ます。
d この水を飲んだほうがいいです。
e パーティーでワインを飲んだり友達と話したりしました。
f 東京のほうがロンドンより大きいです。
g アメリカに住んでいたとき、毎日英語を話した。

13.2 PAST AND PRESENT CONTINUOUS PLAIN FORMS

You can also make past and present continuous plain forms from ています:

食べています → 食べて<u>いる</u> (*am eating*) → 食べて<u>いた</u> (*was eating*)

YOUR TURN Change these ています verbs into their plain present and past forms:
Example: 話しています → 話している (*talking*) → 話していた (*was talking*)

a 飲んでいます
b 書いています
c 住んでいます
d 行っています
e しています

13.3 TALKING ABOUT EXPERIENCES

In Conversation 1 Takeshi says *I have been to America*. Look at how he does this.

You use the past plain form with ことがあります to talk about experiences you have had (or not had – ありません). It translates into English as *I have* or *I haven't* (*I have never*). Look at how it differs from the simple past:

外国に行きました。	*I went abroad.*
外国に行ったことがあります。	*I have been abroad.*
日本に行きませんでした。	*I didn't go to Japan.*
日本に行ったことがありません。	*I haven't been to Japan.*

 YOUR TURN 13.04 How would you say the following in Japanese? Listen to the audio to check your answers.

a I have eaten <u>raw fish</u>. (さしみ)

b I have never seen <u>Mount Fuji</u>. (富士山)

c I have written letters in Japanese.

d I have never read a Japanese newspaper.

e I haven't been to South America.

13.4 SEQUENCES OF EVENTS: SAYING WHAT YOU DID AFTER

In Conversation 2 Takeshi says *after this party*. Look at how he does this.

後で means *after* and is placed after the past plain form of the verb:

コーヒーを飲んだ後で	*after drinking coffee*
家に帰った後で	*after returning home*

Or it is placed after nouns. Here you need to place の in between:

コンサートの後で	*after the concert*
パーティーの後で	*after the party*

> **LANGUAGE TIP**
>
> You have already learned that the て form + から means *after*. There is a slight difference in meaning but in most situations they mean much the same thing. However, てから carries the nuance of *from*, *since* and is often used in situations where you have been doing 'B' since 'A' happened:
>
> 日本に来てから、日本語を勉強しています。
> *Since coming to Japan (A) I have been learning Japanese (B).*
>
> 後で, by way of contrast, is a definite 'after one action finishes the next begins':
>
> 日本に着いた後で、母に手紙を書きました。
> *After I arrived in Japan I wrote a letter to my mum.*

YOUR TURN Link each of these pairs of clauses with 後で to make full sentences:

Example: *took a shower, had breakfast* → シャワーを浴びた後で、朝ご飯を食べました。

a drank beer, slept straightaway

b did homework, went to a party

c went home, phoned (to) a friend

d after the concert, went to a bar

13.5 GIVING ADVICE USING ほうがいいです

You use the plain past with ほうがいいです to say you *should*, you *ought to*, you *had better*. Here are some examples:

この薬を飲んだほうがいいですよ。　　*You ought to take (drink) this medicine* (くすり).

今晩、宿題をしたほうがいいですよ。　*You'd be better off doing your homework tonight.*

The ending よ adds even more assertion to the advice (*you know, I tell you*) but doesn't always need to be translated into English.

You can 'soften' the advice to make it more friendly or tentative by changing です to でしょう which has the meaning *probably*:

この薬を飲んだほうがいいでしょう。　　*You probably ought to take this medicine.*

YOUR TURN Can you give assertive (use よ) advice in the following situations?

a Eri won't eat her vegetables.

b Roger is ill, needs sleep.

c Katie is thirsty, beer or water?

d Mr Hondo still in office, should go home.

e Miki needs to contact a friend; email is best.

Now can you give the same advice in a friendlier manner (use でしょう)?

13.6 SEQUENCES OF EVENTS: RANDOM ORDER

In Conversation 1 Miki says *In America I taught Japanese and I travelled*. Look at how she did this. What do the two verbs end in?

You use what is known as the たり・たり form when you list actions in random order or when you give examples of actions. To form this structure you add り to the た or だ ending and end the sequence with します (present) or しました (past).

土曜日に買い物をしたり、映画を見たり、レストランで食べたりします。
On Saturdays I (do things like) go shopping, watch films and eat at restaurants.

パーティーで、ビールやワインを飲んだりしました。
At the party I drank drinks such as beer and wine.

In some situations the たり・たり form has the meaning *sometimes … sometimes*:

肉を食べたり、魚を食べたりします。　*I sometimes eat meat and I sometimes eat fish.*

What is the difference between the て …て and the たり … たり sequence?

The て form is used for a sequence of actions that have a rigid order: *first I did this, then this, then this.*

たり … たり has no order and the actions given are just examples.

> **YOUR TURN Say this random sequences using たり … たり.**
> **a** On Sundays you chill out, read the paper and send (**dasu**) emails.
> **b** At Christmas (クリスマス) you eat a lot, watch TV, meet up with friends.
> **c** For breakfast, you sometimes drink coffee and sometimes tea (紅茶).

13.7 MAKING COMPARISONS

In Conversation 2 Miki says: *I prefer jazz to pop music*. Find this sentence and think about how this is done in Japanese.

When you make comparisons between two things in English, it is the adjective that changes, usually by adding *-er*: *bigger, smaller, older, happier.*

In Japanese, the adjective does not change. Instead, the 'item' that 'wins' the comparison (*it is bigger, smaller …*) has ほうが attached to it and the 'item' that 'loses' has より (*than*) attached to it. It is important to remember that these are placed after the item they belong to. The structure is:

(A) のほうが (B) より (adjective) です　　*A is …er than B*

or

(B) より (A) のほうが (adjective) です　　*A is …er than B*

So Miki says: ポップスよりジャズのほうが好きです.

You can also use verbs in the plain form to make comparisons like this:

電車で行くほうがバスより早いです。　　*It is quicker to go by train than by bus.*

With verbs you don't need の after ほうが. Also you can miss out the より part and simply say:

本のほうが面白かったです。　　　　　*The book was more interesting.*

YOUR TURN What do these sentences mean?
a 電車のほうがバスより早いです。
b 映画より本のほうが面白かったです。
c 電車で行くほうが早いです。

13.8 SAYING *WHEN* USING とき（時）

In Conversation 2 Miki says *When I lived in Chicago*. Let's look at how she does this.

You place とき when after a plain verb (past or present):

シカゴに住んでいたとき　　　　　　*When I lived in Chicago*

YOUR TURN What do these sentences mean?
a アメリカにいた時、英語を習いました。
b 朝ごはんを食べるとき、いつもテレビを見ます。

You can also use とき with nouns. You need の in between:

学生の時、スペイン語を勉強しました。
When I was a university student I studied Spanish.

13.9 SAYING AN ACTION IS COMPLETELY DONE

Takeshi says to Miki at the end of Conversation 2 *Shall we drink up (completely drink) our wine?* Have a look at this sentence now. How does it work?

The て form with しまう is used when you have either finished something or done something that you can't undo. It can sometimes have negative undertones or a sense of regret such as *I have gone and …, I've totally …*. Here are some examples:

たけしさんは寝てしまった。　　　　*Takeshi fell fast asleep.*
カメラをこわしてしまった。　　　　*I've gone and broken my camera.*
野菜を全部食べてしまいましたか。　　*Have you eaten up all your vegetables?*

YOUR TURN How would you say the following in Japanese using the plain form しまった?
a You've gone and forgotten about your homework.
b You've gone and lost（おとして）your camera.
c You've drunk up all your beer.
d You're totally exhausted（つかれて）.

13.10 USING QUANTITY WORDS WITH VERBS

You've already used the words あまり (*not very*), ぜんぜん (*not at all, never*) and すこし (*a little*) to add more information to a verb (these words are called adverbs).

For example:

コーヒーをぜんぜん飲みません。　　　*I don't drink coffee at all.*

Notice that the quantity word is placed between the particle and the verb. You can, however, also place it before the object:

ぜんぜんコーヒーを飲みません。　　*I never drink coffee.*

> **LANGUAGE TIP**
> In Japanese you use sentence order rather than tone of voice to emphasize something. The important or emphasized information is said towards the end of the sentence.

YOUR TURN 1 Here is a short list of useful quantity words for you to use and refer to. Some you know already. Can you provide the English meanings?

ぜんぜん (+ negative)	**a** _____
あまり (+ negative)	**b** _____
すこし	**c** _____
時々	**d** _____
よく	*often, well*
だいぶ(ん)	*greatly, quite a lot*
たくさん	*a lot*
いっぱい	**e** _____
全部	**f** _____

Look at the difference between たくさん and いっぱい in these examples:

寿司をたくさん食べました。　　　*I ate a lot of sushi.*

寿司をいっぱい食べました。　　　*I ate my fill of sushi.* (implying I was full up)

Use いっぱい to say you are full up or you don't want any more:

すみません、もういっぱいです。　　*Thank you (sorry) but I'm full.*

YOUR TURN 2 How would you say the following in Japanese? Place the quantity word between the particle and the verb:

a I read quite a lot of the Japanese newspaper.

b I sent loads of emails.

c I ate up (use しまった) all the rice.

13.11 PAST TIME EXPRESSIONS

YOUR TURN 1 Here are some useful time expressions for when you're speaking in the past. Can you provide the missing information?)

きのう	**a** _____
けさ	*this morning*
夕べ <small>ゆう</small>	**b** _____
先 週 <small>せんしゅう</small>	*last week*
先月 <small>せんげつ</small>	*last month*
去年 <small>きょねん</small>	*last year*

To say expressions such as *yesterday morning* insert の between the two words like this:
きのうの朝
<small>あさ</small>

YOUR TURN 2 How would you say the following in Japanese?

a last Saturday

b yesterday afternoon

c last March

Listening

1 13.05 **Listen to the audio as people are given advice about various matters, then match the advice given with pictures a–f.**

(The script is in the Answer key.)

2 13.06 **Listen as Takeshi tells his friend Robert about his night and supply the missing information.**

a _____とてもすてきな人に_____。

b みきさんは _____ が _____ _____ 一緒に僕の好きなジャズクラブ _____ _____。
<small>いっしょ ぼく す じゃずくらぶ</small>

c そのクラブでビールを _____、_____、いい音楽を _____ _____。
<small>くらぶ びーる おんがく</small>

d 遅くまでクラブ _____ _____ そして二時ごろうち _____ _____。
<small>おそ くらぶ にじ</small>

e Give a summary in English of what Takeshi says.

Speaking

13.06 Now listen to the audio of Takeshi speaking again, sentence by sentence, and practise saying it out loud, focusing on good pronunciation, then see if you can write it out in Japanese script, using **kanji** where you can.

 Reading 1

Katie describes her busy day today in the passage you will find with Exercise 2 below.

1 **Match the sequence of events with these English summaries and write it out as a sequence of letters (e.g. c, a, and so on).**
    a watch lots of TV and relax this evening
    b sent huge amounts of email
    c p.m., was able to do all Japanese homework
    d spoke with neighbour a lot
    e made lots of phone calls
    f hardly ate any lunch because busy
    g didn't do any cleaning
    h wrote a few letters

2 **Fill in the gaps with the missing quantity words so that they match the English meanings:**

今日メールを a) _____ 出したり、電話を b) _____ したり、手紙を c) _____ 書いたりしました。そして近所の人と d) _____ 話しましたが掃除を e) _____ しませんでした。忙しかったので昼ごはんを f) _____ 食べませんでした。午後日本語の宿題が g) _____ できましたから、今晩テレビ h) _____ 見たり、ごろごろしたりするつもりです。

📝 Writing

Use the following information to make comparisons. You can use と思います instead of です if you feel it is a matter of opinion. You are given the adjective to use as in the example:

Example: 東京、大阪、面白い → 東京のほうが大阪より面白いと思います。

a Roger, Miki, まじめ
b Roger, Miki, スポーツが上手
c Yuki, Eri, 背が高い (taller)
d watching sport, playing sport, 楽しい (enjoyable)
e drinking beer, drinking water いい (good/better)

188

Kanji for weather, family and countries

INTRODUCTION

In this section you will learn **kanji** for weather and seasons, kanji for members of the family and **kanji** used for the names of countries.

WEATHER AND THE SEASONS

You learned about weather and seasons in Unit 8. Here are five kanji broken down into components with stories to link them to their meaning. Can you match each story and meaning with the correct kanji?

a 雨   b 雪   c 晴   d 天   e 秋

Story 1: *Autumn* is the time when the rice stubble (禾) is burnt (火). Meaning: *autumn*
Story 2: *Sun* (日) and *blue* (青) mean *fine weather*. Meaning: *fine, sunny*
Story 3: Drops of rain at the window. Meaning: *rain*
Story 4: Rain falling over a sideways mountain (山) freezes to snow. Meaning: *snow*
Story 5: The number *one* (一) and *big* (大) add up to the *biggest/greatest*. Meaning: *sky, heaven, celestial, weather*

Here are the other three seasons with stories to help you:

春   *spring* (**haru**): Can you see the components *three* (三), *person* (人) and *sun* (日)? Spring arrives in the *third* month (March) and seeing the *sun* again puts a *spring* in a *person's* step!

冬   *winter* (**fuyu**): This radical 夂 means *winter*. The two drops of ice create a chilly feel.

夏   *summer* (**natsu**): The winter radical 夂 is here again but this time it is smothered by *one* (一) and *eye* (目) – the eye of the hot sun!

READING 2

Here are the seasons and weather terms with some compound words which include them. Can you match each word to its English meaning?

a 夏休み
b 冬休み
c 春休み
d 天気
e 天の川
f 雨水
g 雨天
h 雪山
i 雪女
j 雪明り
k 秋分
l 晴天

1 clear skies
2 the Milky Way (heavenly river)
3 snowy mountain
4 summer holidays
5 winter holiday
6 spring holiday
7 Snow Woman (Japanese legend)
8 weather
9 rainy weather
10 snow light
11 fall (autumn) equinox
12 rain water

THE FAMILY

Here are the **kanji** for members of the family:

母 *mother* (**haha**): A mother is drawn as two breasts, showing her role in rearing children.

父 *father* (**chichi**): He has dimples in his cheeks and a long moustache!

兄 *older brother* (**ani**): Easy to remember – a mouth on legs!

姉 *older sister* (**ane**): *Woman* (**女**) on the left and on the right the **kanji** for *city* 市 – can you see someone carrying bags on both arms after shopping in the city? The older sister works in the city!

弟 *younger brother* (**otōto**): A snakelike shape with horns – like a little brother up to mischief.

妹 *younger sister* (**imōto**): Woman on the left and a tree that has not fully grown (shorter upper branch – 未) – a younger sister is not yet a woman.

 ## READING 3

Here are the six family kanji again, this time written with additional hiragana to make them into the 'other family' terms. What do they mean in English?

a お父さん (otōsan)

b お母さん (okāsan)

c 妹さん (imōtosan)

d 弟さん (otōtosan)

e お姉さん (onēsan)

f お兄さん (onīsan)

KANJI COMPOUNDS: COUNTRIES

The names for countries are written in **katakana** because they are 'borrowed' words (so not originally Japanese). For example:

アメリカ	**Amerika**	*America*
ドイツ	**Doitsu**	*Germany*
イギリス	**Igirisu**	*England*

However, there are also **kanji** to represent most countries of the world. For example: *China* is 中国, meaning *middle country* because it is in the centre of Asia.

The **kanji** for *country* is 国 made up of 口 which is a surround showing boundaries and 玉 meaning *jewel* or *king*. Therefore a king rules to the boundaries of his country.

Here is a selection of country names in **kanji**. Generally the **kanji** were chosen not for their meaning but because their pronunciation is close to the sounds (syllables) of a country's name. However, the meaning is given, anyway. These **kanji** words are often used in newspaper articles:

英国 *England* ('excellent' country)

米国 *America* ('rice' country)

独国 *Germany* ('independent' country)

韓国 *Korea* (**kanji** means 'Korea')

豪州 *Australia* ('outstanding province')

新西蘭 *New Zealand* ('new west Holland')

仏国 *France* (means 'France' and also 'the Buddha')

西国 *Spain* (west country)

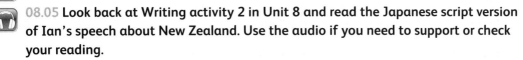

READING 4

You have learned 15 single **kanji** in this unit. Here they are in random order, give their English meanings.

a 弟　　　d 雪　　　g 秋　　　j 天　　　m 兄
b 妹　　　e 晴　　　h 母　　　k 夏　　　n 姉
c 雨　　　f 春　　　i 父　　　l 冬　　　o 国

READING CHALLENGE

08.05 **Look back at Writing activity 2 in Unit 8 and read the Japanese script version of Ian's speech about New Zealand. Use the audio if you need to support or check your reading.**

WRITING CHALLENGE

13.07 You are going to write out the prompts into full sentences using the past plain tense. Underlined words indicate where you can include **kanji**. For verbs, the 'rule of thumb' is that the **kanji** replaces the first **hiragana** and the rest of the verb is written in **hiragana**. In some cases (e.g. **hanashimasu**) the **kanji** replaces the first two **hiragana**. Listen to the audio to check the full sentences and to practise saying them correctly.

Example: kinō, Ōsaka (*yesterday I went to Osaka*) → きのうおおさかに行った。

a   senshū, eiga (last week I <u>saw</u> a film)

b   kesa, <u>7 ji</u> (this morning I got up at seven)

c   yūbe, <u>12 ji</u> (last night I went to bed at about twelve)

d   tomodachi, tegami (I <u>wrote</u> a letter to a friend)

e   tomodachi, ongaku (I <u>listened</u> to music with a friend)

f   yūbe, bīru, ippai (last night I <u>drank</u> lots of beer)

g   <u>Nihongo</u>, manga (I <u>read</u> a Japanese comic book)

h   atarashii, sensei (I <u>talked</u> to the new teacher)

i   heya, Indo ryōri (I made Indian food in my room/lodgings)

j   kinō, haha to chichi, Igirisu (yesterday my <u>mum</u> and <u>dad</u> went back to <u>England</u>)

? Test yourself

How would you say the following in Japanese?

a I have been to South America.

b I haven't heard the Love Love Boys' music.

c I prefer rock music to jazz.

d When I was a student I went to lots of concerts.

e When I lived in Australia I spoke English well.

f I went to bed late last night so I am completely exhausted.

g I think that this camera is better than that camera.

h After talking to Takeshi, Miki phoned (to) Roger.

i At the weekend I sometimes go shopping and sometimes watch a film.

SELF CHECK

	I CAN...
○	...talk in the past using the plain form.
○	...talk about my experiences.
○	...give advice.
○	...say more about routines and actions.
○	...make comparisons.
○	...quantify my actions.
○	...recognize **kanji** words to do with weather, seasons and family.

14 来年アメリカに帰ろうと思います
I'm thinking of going back to America next year

In this unit you will learn how to:
▶ *use the plain form to say* let's do.
▶ *discuss plans and decisions.*
▶ *distinguish between possibilities and probabilities.*
▶ *talk about things you've tried to do.*
▶ *say more about hours, weeks, months and years.*

CEFR: *(B1) Communicates with reasonable accuracy in familiar contexts; generally good control though with noticeable mother tongue influences. Can write personal letters describing experiences and impressions.*

義理 Giri *Social obligation*

日本の社会 **Nihon no shakai** (*Japanese society*) is often described as vertical or hierarchical because in many of the key areas of life such as work and community life, 社会的関係 **shakai-teki kankei** (*social relationships*) are built on respect for 年長者 **nenchōja** (*elders*) and 目上の人 **me ue no hito** (*superiors*). Through this system, people are tied into reciprocal relationships in which 義理 **giri** (*social obligation*) plays an important role. For example, a junior member of staff in a 会社 **kaisha** (*company*) may want to go home to his 家族 **kazoku** (*family*) at the end of a long day but will have to carry out his 義理 **giri** by going drinking with his 上司 **jōshi** (*boss*).

Another aspect of 日本の社会 **Nihon no shakai** is the importance of 友好関係 **yūkō kankei** (*harmonious relations*) and group solidarity. Even if a person's private views differ from the group's, decisions are reached through consensus. 日本人 **Nihonjin** (*Japanese people*) tend not to speak their minds, especially if it might cause conflict. An example is when a visitor has outstayed their welcome. The host might insist that they stay longer – this is their 建前 **tatemae** (*stated reasons or public stance*) – when in fact their 本音 **honne** (*real thoughts or motives*) is to ensure that they leave. Japanese people often use non-verbal communication to convey their true feelings and this can be easily misunderstood by 外国人 **gaikokujin** (*non-Japanese people*).

1 Look at the passage again and see if you find the common **kanji** in the following:
   a superiors and boss   **b** superiors, Japanese people and non-Japanese people.

What do you think these kanji mean?

2 Match these **kanji** to their English meanings:
   a 仕事   **1** family
   b 家族   **2** real thoughts
   c 義理   **3** public stance
   d 本音   **4** work
   e 建前   **5** social obligation

Vocabulary builder

 14.01 Listen to the new vocabulary and practise saying it out loud.

NEW VERBS AND STRUCTURES

雨が降る	*rain falls, it will rain*
洗う	*wash*
転勤する	*transfer (work)*
行う	*hold (an event)*
散歩する	*take a walk*
やめる	*give up*
行こう	*let's/will go*
行こうと思います	*I think I will go*
見つけよう（見つける）	*let's/will find (find)*
… としています（とする）	*attempt to, try to do …*
… だろう (plain form of でしょう)	*will probably …*
かもしれません	*might, may* (not certain) *do …*
んじゃないでしょうか	*probably* (polite)
… ことにしました（ことにする）	*I've decided (decided on) …*
… ことにしている	*make it a rule, be in the habit of …*
… ことになりました	*has been arranged that …*
… ことになっています	*supposed to, the custom is …*

NEW WORDS AND EXPRESSIONS

残念です	*it's a shame, pity*	本当	*really, real*
もうすぐ	*shortly, soon*	おめでとうございます	*congratulations*
中国	*China*	ヨーロッパ	*Europe*
チャンス	*chance*	プール	*swimming pool*
ほかの	*other*	一時間	*one hour*
どう	*how, what*	くらい	*about*
くらい	*about*	新しい	*new*
はっきり	*clearly*	レポート	*report*
私たち	*we*	定食	*set meal*

Conversation 1

Katie meets up with Rie to tell her that she and Ian will shortly be leaving Japan.

1 What did Ian try to do when he found out he was going to be transferred to China?

Katie	残念ですが、イアンはもうすぐ 中国に転勤することになりました。
Rie	中国ですか。いいチャンスですね。
Katie	東京でほかの仕事を見つけようとしましたが 全然ありませんでした。
Rie	ケイティさんはどうしますか。
Katie	そうですね。まだ日本で働きたいですが 私も中国に行こうと思います。
Rie	残念ですね。何年間日本に住んでいましたか。
Katie	イアンは二年間です。私は三年くらいだと思います。
Rie	いつ転勤しますか。
Katie	イアンは来月中国に行くかもしれませんが まだはっきりわかりません。そして、私は八月に行こうと思います。
Rie	中国で何をするつもりですか。
Katie	まだわかりませんが 結婚することにしました。
Rie	本当ですか。おめでとうございます。じゃあ、中国に行く前にパーティーをしましょうね！日本では転勤する前にさようならパーティーを行うことになっていますよ！
Katie	いいですね。さようならと結婚のパーティーをしましょう！

2 What was Katie's reaction to Ian's transfer?

3 What have Katie and Ian decided to do?

4 To what 'custom' does Rie refer?

5 What does Katie think of this?

6 Are these statements true or false?
 a イアンさんは もうすぐ アメリカに転勤します。
 b ケイティさんは 中国に行くつもりはありません。
 c イアンさんは 二年間日本に住んでいます。
 d イアンさんとケイティさんは 来月に 結婚するつもりです。
 e りえさんは さようならパーティーを 行うことにしました。

7 Answer these questions in Japanese:
 a ケイティさんは いつ中国に行くつもりですか。
 b イアンさんは どうして中国に行きますか。
 c りえさんは イアンさんが 中国に行くことについて どう思いますか。
 d イアンさんはいつ転勤しますか。
 e 中国に行く前に 何をするつもりですか。

Language discovery

14.1 SAYING *LET'S DO SOMETHING*

You have already learned the polite way to make suggestions using ましょう and ましょうか (*let's, shall we?*). The plain, more casual form ends in a **yō/ō** form (e.g. よう・こう・そう). Look at the Vocabulary builder and find two examples of this.

For Group 1 verbs, change the dictionary-form **u** ending to its **o** ending + う: 買う → 買おう, 持つ → 持とう

For Group 2 verbs, replace る ending with よう: 食べる → 食べよう

 YOUR TURN 14.03 **Convert these verbs into their yō/ō form, add the English then listen to the audio to check your answers. (The group is given in brackets where you might need it.)**

Dictionary form	yō/ō form	English	Dictionary form	yō/ō form	English
見る (2)	a		休む	f	
聞く	b		話す	g	
書く	c		泳ぐ	h	
会う	d		見せる	i	
行く	e		待つ	j	

14.2 SAYING *I WILL*

The plain **yō/ō** form has another meaning. It is also used to say *I will* (when you are being decisive) or *shall I?* when talking to or about yourself.

僕は来週京都に行こう。 *I will go to Kyoto next week.*

YOUR TURN **What do these two sentences mean?**

a 私は映画を見よう。

b 寝ようか。

This is how you change two irregular verbs: くる (きます) and する (します)

くる → こよう   する → しよう

14.3 SAYING *I THINK I WILL* ...

You use the **yō/ō** form with と思います to say *I think I will* and you use it with と思っています (思っている) to say *I think someone else will* or *I am thinking of doing*.

思っている is used when you talk about other people's intentions because it implies that you can't be sure of another person's thoughts.

 a I am thinking of going to China as well.
 b I think I will go in August.

You have learned two similar structures – たいと思います (Unit 7) and つもりです (Unit 12). Look at the difference in meaning:

南アメリカに行きたいと思います。	*I hope to go to South America.*
南アメリカに行こうと思います。	*I think I will go to South America.*
南アメリカに行くつもりです。	*I plan to go to South America.*

The examples are in descending order of certainty:

つもりです	*definite, a concrete plan*
ようと思います	*statement of intent (not sure it will happen)*
たいと思います	*wish or hope (may or may not happen)*

YOUR TURN 2 **Using yō/ō と思う, how would you say the following in Japanese? Use either polite 思います・思っています form or plain 思う・思っている.**

 a I think I will go to Japan next year.
 b My mother thinks she will go to Europe next year.
 c I think I will buy a new car.
 d Takeshi thinks he will meet with Miki again.

14.4 HOW TO SAY *I TRY/TRIED TO* …

You have already learned how to say give something a try using the て form plus みる (Unit 11). Look at the conversation and find how Katie says *He (Ian) tried to find work in Tokyo but …*

Now look at these two examples:

東京でほかの仕事を見つけ<u>ようとしました</u>。	*He tried to find work in Tokyo (but failed).*
東京でほかの仕事を見つけ<u>てみました</u>。	*He had a go at finding work in Tokyo.*

When you use **yō/ō** plus とする it implies that you have tried and failed or that something is a struggle, whereas when you use the て form plus みる it has a more positive sense.

When you use **yō/ō** plus としている (continuous form) it means you are about to do something:

朝ごはんを食べようとしています。	*I'm about to eat breakfast.*

YOUR TURN **How would you say the following in Japanese?**
 a I'm about to learn the piano.
 b I've tried (and failed) to write that report (レポート).
 c My father tried (and failed) to buy a new jacket.
 d I tried to go to Japan last year (but didn't).

14.5 DEGREES OF PROBABILITY USING でしょう AND かもしれません

In the conversation Katie says *Ian will possibly go to China next month*. Can you find this sentence?

When you use でしょう (or its plain form だろう) preceded by a plain-form verb, you are saying something will probably happen whereas when you use かもしれません (plain form かもしれない) preceded by the plain verb, you are saying that something will possibly happen but it is not certain. Here are some examples:

雨が降るでしょう。	*It will probably rain.*
雨が降るかもしれません。	*It will possibly rain.*
全部食べただろう。	*He probably ate it all.*
全部食べたかもしれない。	*He might have eaten it all.*

If you add the word きっと to a でしょう phrase, then you are even more definite – *I bet that …*:

きっとパーティーに行くでしょう。　　*I bet that he goes to the party.*

When you need to be especially polite or show particular respect to someone, for example your boss, then you can express でしょう in a negative phrase: plain verb form ＋んじゃないでしょうか:

本堂さんはパーティーに行くんじゃないでしょうか。

Is it not probable that Mr Hondo will go to the party? (Mr Hondo will probably go to the party)

> **LANGUAGE TIP**
> The negative is used a lot in Japanese to add uncertainly and therefore respect (as it is sometimes in English: *Wouldn't you like another cup of coffee? Shouldn't you phone your mother?*).

YOUR TURN Look at the sentences a–e and complete them with one of the following:

> 1 きっと ... でしょう
> 2 でしょう
> 3 んじゃないでしょうか
> 4 かもしれません

a 明日会社を休む ___。(I will probably have a day off work tomorrow.)

b イアンさんは気分が悪いから今日家にいる ___。(Ian isn't well so he might stay at home today.)

c 今日は晴れだから明日も ___ 晴れ ___。(Today it is fine so I bet it'll be fine tomorrow.)

d みきさんまたたけしさんと会う ___。(Miki might meet Takeshi again.)

e 社長は本堂さんに電話する ___。(Is it not probable that the director will phone Mr Hondo?)

14.6 TALKING ABOUT DECISIONS AND RULES USING **KOTO NI SURU**

In the conversation Katie says *We have decided to get married*. Find this phrase now and look at the verb form and ending.

You will see plain form する + ことにしました. You can say the following with this structure:

ことにする	*I will decide, I'll go for*
ことにした	*I've decided*

ことにしている is used for decisions you make routinely, in other words, things you do as a rule or habit.

YOUR TURN What do these sentences mean?
a コーヒーにします。
b 明日　会社を休むことにしました。
c ヨーロッパを旅行することにしましょう。
d 毎朝　散歩することにしている。

14.7 TALKING ABOUT DECISIONS, ARRANGEMENTS AND RULES USING ことになる

In the conversation Katie says *It has been decided that Ian will transfer to China soon*. Find this phrase and look at the verb form and ending.

You use ことになる・なった rather than ことにする when you are not in control of the decision – *it has been (will be) decided* or *it has been (will be) arranged*. You can also use ことになった even when you have made a decision if you wish to appear more humble and not to be 'boasting' or over-assertive about your decisions. The Japanese use language in this indirect way to be more polite or more tentative.

ことになっている (continuous form) takes on the meaning of how things are supposed to be done or how they work so is often used with rules and customs.

YOUR TURN What do these sentences mean?
a 明日本堂さんに会うことになりました。
b 家族とイギリスに旅行することになった。
c 日本では　お風呂に入る前に　洗うことになっています。

14.8 SAYING LENGTHS OF TIME USING 間

間 means *period of time*. When you attach it to words such as 時 (*o'clock*), 週 (*week*) and 年 (*year*) it changes these words into lengths of time.

Time word	Length of time	Example	How many?
時 *o'clock*	時間 *hour*	二時間 *two hours*	何時間？
週 *week*	週間 *week*	二週間 *two weeks*	何週間？
月 *month*	ヶ月 *month*	二ヶ月 *two months*	何ヶ月？
年 *year*	年間 *year*	二年間 *two years*	何年（間）

Note that for months add か and don't use 間. For years you can use 年 without 間.

When you want to ask how long it takes you can say:

何時間かかりますか。	*How many hours does it take?*
どのぐらいかかりますか。	*How long does it take?*
どのぐらいですか。	*How long (far) is it?*

Listening

1 14.04 **Eri hasn't been practising on the piano so she is preparing the excuses she will give to her teacher. Listen to the audio and see if you can answer the questions. You'll hear these additional words:**

もんだい（がある）	*problem (have a)*
とつぜん	*unexpectedly*

a Why couldn't she practise on Monday?

b On which day(s) did she have a lot of homework?

c What happened unexpectedly on Thursday?

d What is almost definite about next week?

e How many hours of practice per day is she going to promise to do?

Now listen to the audio again and find out how Eri says the following phrases:

f I tried to practise but …

g It was arranged (for me) to go to a baseball game.

h Next week I will almost definitely be free all week.

2 14.05 **Listen to the audio about journey times and note down the mode of transport and the length of time for these journeys:**

a Tokyo to Hiroshima

b London to Edinburgh

c Seattle to New York

d Tokyo to Sapporo

e Melbourne to Sydney

Speaking

14.06 Using plain speech, how would you suggest the following in Japanese? Listen to the audio to check your answers.

Example: *Shall we watch a film?* 映画を見ようか。

a Shall we listen to the news?

b Shall we write an email?

c Shall we meet in front of the cinema?

d Shall we go to the party now?

e Shall we have a rest?

f Shall we talk in Japanese?

 Reading 1

The sentences that follow require either ことにする or ことになる (in various forms) – you decide!

a 日本でははしでごはんを食べる。(In Japan, you are supposed to eat rice with chopsticks)

b みきさんに電話する。(I decided to call Miki)

c このレポートを本堂さんに出す。(It has been arranged for me to send this report to Mr Hondo)

d 食事を食べる前に手を洗う。(Before eating a meal you're supposed to wash your hands)

e 毎日漢字を少し習う。(I make it a rule to learn a few **kanji** every day)

Reading and writing

14.07 Eri has written her excuses for not having done her homework. Using this as a model, write a letter to your Japanese teacher to explain why you haven't done your homework. Replace the underlined parts with the information provided. Try to write in Japanese script with kanji where possible. Listen to the audio to check your answers.

Eri's excuses:

すみませんが、今週ピアノの<u>練習</u>時間は　あまりありませんでした。練習をしようとしていましたが、<u>いろいろなもんだいが　ありました</u>。月曜日に　<u>家族と野球ゲームに行く</u>ことになりました。そして、<u>火曜日も水曜日も　宿題がたくさんありました</u>。木曜日に、とつぜん私は　<u>柔道の試合に参加する</u>ことになりました。来週は　一週間　きっと、ひまだと思います。だから、毎日一時間ぐらいは練習をしようと思います。

Your excuses:

You didn't do much Japanese study this week. You meant to but you were very busy (いそがしい). On Monday it was arranged that you have a meal with the sales manager (営業部長). Then on Tuesday and Wednesday you worked at the company until late. On Thursday it was unexpectedly decided that you go on a business trip to Nagoya. Next week you're bound to be free so you'll do two hours' study every day!

Introduction to **katakana**

INTRODUCTION

Katakana is used primarily to write non-Japanese words. There are many borrowed words in the Japanese language such as food items, drinks, clothes and electrical goods so **katakana** is very useful and it is very rewarding to be able to read a word and understand its meaning straightaway.

THE FIRST 15 KATAKANA SYMBOLS (A–SO)

 14.08 The **katakana** script has 46 basic symbols and follows all the same rules as **hiragana**. The only difference is that the symbols are different, although some look very similar to their **hiragana** counterparts, much as upper- and lower-case letters represent the same sound in English. Here are the first 15 **katakana** symbols with their pronunciation. Listen to the audio if you need to remind yourself how to pronounce each sound:

ア	イ	ウ	エ	オ
a	i	u	e	o
カ	キ	ク	ケ	コ
ka	ki	ku	ke	ko
サ	シ	ス	セ	ソ
sa	shi	su	se	so

HINTS FOR REMEMBERING KATAKANA SYMBOLS

Some **katakana** look similar to their **hiragana** counterpart and you may find these similarities a useful way to remember them. Here they are with the **katakana** symbol listed first:

ウ う = **u**   **hiragana** is more curvy

エ え = **e**   not immediately similar but closer on examination

オ お = **o**   partially similar when you look closely

カ か = **ka**   **hiragana** is more curvy and extra dash

キ き = **ki**   **hiragana** is more curvy and extra dash/curve

ケ け = **ke**   **hiragana** is separated out into two sides

コ こ = **ko**   **katakana** has joined up into three sides

セ せ = **se**   **hiragana** has extra dash

Try thinking of some mnemonics too – perhaps you can visualize an antelope in ア (**a**), a cupola in ク (**ku**) or a superwoman in ス (**su**)!

SIMILAR-LOOKING KATAKANA

The following **katakana** symbols look quite similar and you may find that this is confusing at times. Here are some clues to help you tell them apart:

ク ケ	(**ku**, **ke**)	the horizontal line in **ke** is longer
サ セ	(**sa**, **se**)	**se** faces the same way as Roman alphabet *e*

READING 2

You are going to try reading some **katakana** words that use the first 15 symbols.

> **READING TIPS**
>
> ▶ Remember that borrowed words are changed to fit Japanese pronunciation so you may need to say the word a few times to work out the meaning.
> ▶ Try shortening **u** and **i** sounds to fit the word back to its original English pronunciation.
> ▶ Do you remember the rules for changing **hiragana** sounds using these marks: ゛ (**tenten**) and ゜ (**maru**)? (see Unit 7). These apply in exactly the same way to **katakana**.
> ▶ Unique to **katakana** is the use of a dash — to indicate the lengthening of the sound. For example: キ = **ki**; キー = **kii** (or **kī**).

Can you match each word to one of the English words?

a	アイス	**1**	kiwi
b	ケーキ	**2**	cake
c	ウイスキー	**3**	cocoa
d	ココア	**4**	quiz
e	スキー	**5**	ski (skiing)
f	クイズ	**6**	gas
g	キウイ	**7**	whisky
h	キス	**8**	kiss
i	アジア	**9**	Asia
j	ガス	**10**	ice

THE MIDDLE 15 KATAKANA SYMBOLS (TA–HO)

14.09 Here are the middle 15 **katakana**. Use the audio to practise reading them as you listen to the pronunciation:

タ	チ	ツ	テ	ト
ta	chi	tsu	te	to
ナ	ニ	ヌ	ネ	ノ
na	ni	nu	ne	no
ハ	ヒ	フ	ヘ	ホ
ha	hi	fu	he	ho

SIMILARITIES WITH HIRAGANA

Again, here are some useful tips for remembering them, with **katakana** symbols listed first:

テ て	both have a 'table top' – **katakana** has a 'plate' on the table!
ナ な	**katakana** is the left half of the **hiragana**
ニ に	**hiragana** has an additional vertical line
フ ふ	**katakana** is created from the middle section of **hiragana**
ヘ へ	very similar, **katakana** version is shorter

IDEAS FOR MNEMONICS

Can you see a *che*erleader in チ (**chi**), a plant on *top* of the ground ト (**to**), the **kanji** for number two ニ (**ni**), a *ne*st in a tree ネ (**ne**), the bridge of a *no*se ノ (**no**), **kanji** number eight – *hachi* ハ (**ha**) and a jolly Father Christmas face – *ho, ho, ho* ホ (**ho**)?

SIMILAR-LOOKING KATAKANA

チ テ (**chi, te**)	the vertical line cuts through in **chi**
シ ツ (**shi, tsu**)	the long stroke in **tsu** has a steeper angle
タ ヌ (**ta, nu**)	think of **nu** as a Continental number 7 (with a line through)
ウ フ (**u, fu**)	**u** has two extra dashes

READING 3

Match the katakana words with their English meaning (a–h use the middle 15 katakana only; i–p use the first 30).

a	ヒーター	1	tuna
b	ツナ	2	data
c	ノート	3	team
d	データ	4	taxi
e	タヒチ	5	necktie
f	パート	6	Germany
g	ドーナツ	7	Tahiti
h	バー	8	high tech
i	タバコ	9	bus
j	タクシー	10	doughnut
k	チーム	11	bar
l	バス	12	heater
m	ドイツ	13	cheesecake
n	チーズケーキ	14	cigarette (tobacco)
o	ハイテク	15	note (book)
p	ネクタイ	16	part (time)

> **LEARNING TIP**
> When working out the meaning, remember that there is no sound for 'ti' or 'tu' in Japanese; **chi** and **tsu** are used instead.

ⓘ Test yourself

The following ten sentences are incomplete. Using the structures you have learned in this unit, can you complete them? (The verb is given in masu form.)

a 新しいカメラを（買います）(I hope to buy a new camera.)

b 来年中国に（行きます）(I think I will go to China next year.)

c 明日友達に（会います）(I intend to meet my friend tomorrow.)

d きのう　友達と（会います）(I tried to meet up with my friend yesterday.)

e イタリア語を（習います）(I have decided to learn Italian.)

f この映画は面白くないので、家へ（帰ります）(This film isn't interesting so he might go home.)

g きっと、明日の野球の試合を（見に行きます）(I bet he goes to see the baseball match tomorrow.)

h 今日　遊びに（来ます）(I think I will come and visit today.)

i 毎日　水をたくさん（飲みます）(As a rule I drink lots of water every day.)

j 来週　仕事を（休みます）(I don't plan to be off work next week.)

SELF CHECK

I CAN...
...use the plain form to say *let's do*
...discuss plans and decisions.
...distinguish between possibilities and probabilities.
...talk about things I've tried to do.
...say more about hours, weeks, months and years.
...recognize and read the first 30 **katakana** symbols.

あの会議室に入らないでください
かいぎしつ　はい
Please don't go into that meeting room

In this unit you will learn how to:
▶ *use the negative* (don't, didn't) *in plain forms.*
▶ *say more with polite and plain forms.*
▶ *say* you must, you don't have to, you shouldn't.
▶ *say* if *and* when *(the conditional).*
▶ *say* while.

CEFR *(B1) Can fluently sustain a straightforward description of one of a variety of subjects of interest, presenting in a linear sequence of points. Can deal with most situations likely to arise while travelling in an area where the language is spoken.*

日本の家について Nihon no ie ni tsuite
About Japanese houses

There is a range of 日本の家 **Nihon no ie** (*Japanese houses*) including アパート **apāto** (*low-rise apartment blocks*) and マンション **manshon** (*high-rise blocks of flats*; literally *mansion*) in the 都市 **toshi** (*cities*), 二階家 **nikaiya** (*two-storey houses*) and 平屋建て **hirayadate** (*single storey*), often wooden or prefabricated, in the 市外 **shigai** (*suburbs*) and smaller cities, and 農家 **nōka** (*farmhouses*) in the いなか **inaka** (*countryside*).

All 日本の家 **Nihon no ie** have a 玄関 **genkan** (*porch*) which separates the 外 **soto** (*outside*) from the 内 **uchi** (*interior*) of the 家 **ie**. It is here that you must remove your 靴 **kutsu** (*shoes*) and step into the スリッパ **suripppa** (*slippers*) that are set out for you. This reinforces the idea of a separation between the 外 **soto** and the 内 **uchi**, and of course, in practical terms, it keeps the 家 **ie** freer from dirt.

Many, but not all, 日本の家 **Nihon no ie** have 部屋 **heya** (*rooms*) with 畳の床 **tatami no yuka** (*tatami floors*). 畳 **Tatami** mats are made from rice straw and rushes woven around a frame. When you enter a 座敷 **zashiki** (*tatami room*) you always take off the スリッパ **suripppa** and leave them in the 廊下 **rōka** (*hallway*). Many houses and restaurants also have a pair of plastic スリッパ **suripppa** or げた **geta** (*wooden clogs*) for use only in the トイレ **toire** (*toilet*).

1 Find the 漢字 **kanji** for *cities* and *suburbs*.
  a What is the common 漢字 **kanji** and what do you think it means?
  b Where have you seen the second 漢字 **kanji** in *suburbs* before?
  c What do you think is the literal meaning of the word *suburbs*?

2 In this passage the word *house* is given as 家 **ie**. What other word for *house* have you learned and what do you think the difference is?

Vocabulary builder

 15.01 Listen to the new vocabulary and practise saying it out loud.

NEW VERBS AND STRUCTURES

食べないで	*without eating*
書かないでほしい	*I want you not to write*
しなければなりません	*(you) must do*
しなくてもいいです	*you don't have to do*
吸わないほうがいいです	*it's better not to smoke, you shouldn't smoke*
ないうちに	*while not (before)*
間に	*while, during*
もし	*if*
行ったら	*if I go*
出席（する）	*attend*
タバコを吸う	*smoke cigarettes*
連絡（する）	*(make) contact*
遊びに行って（行く）	*go and visit*
遊びに来て（来る）	*come and visit*
心配（する）	*worry*

NEW EXPRESSIONS

会議室	*meeting room*
会議	*meeting*
そんなことを言って（言う）	*say those sorts of thing*
ぜひ	*be sure to*
楽しみにしています	*I'm looking forward to it*
急に	*suddenly*
言い訳	*excuse*
あなたのこと	*you (literally: your things)*
たけしさんのこと	*Takeshi, about Takeshi*
も	*also, as well*
二人	*two (people)*
平気	*it's cool, OK*

Conversation 1

 15.02 Robert and Rie are holding a farewell and pre-wedding party for Katie and Ian before they go to China. All the characters from this course are there. Katie is talking with Tatsuya-san and Eri-chan.

What is Mr Hondo's reaction when Eri asks Katie if she can visit her in China?

Eri	ねえ、ケイティさん、チャンスがあったら、中国へ遊びに行ってもいいですか。
Tatsuya	えりちゃん！だめですよ。そんなことを言ってはいけないですよ。
Katie	大丈夫です。もしチャンスがあったら、ぜひご家族と中国へ遊びに来てください。
Eri	ありがとう！楽しみにしています。
Tatsuya	ねえ、えり、中国に行きたかったら、その前に、毎日 ピアノの練習をしなければなりませんよ！
Eri	*(In a resigned voice)* はい

Conversation 2

 15.03 Ian is talking with Naoe.

1 What is Naoe's advice about the best time to get married?

Naoe	いつ結婚をするつもりですか。
Ian	まだはっきりわかりませんが、できたら中国に行く前に 結婚したいと思います。
Naoe	そうですか。天気があつくないうちに結婚したほうがいいですね。
Ian	しかし急にしたらよくないと思います。
Naoe	イアンさん、言い訳しないでください！

2 What is Naoe's reaction when Ian says it won't do to rush the wedding?

Conversation 3

 15.04 *Robert and Rie realize that Miki is dating both of their friends.*

1 What level of politeness is used in this conversation and why?

Robert	ねえ、みきさん、たけしさんは　あなたのことが　とても好きだと思うよ。
Rie	たけしさん？ラブラブボーイズのたけしさん？ロジャーさんとどうしたの？
Robert	ロジャーさん？ロジャーさんともデートをしたの？
Miki	そうねえ。たけしさんも　ロジャーさんもとても　いい人だと思う。いつも楽しく　過ごしているわ。
Rie	でもロジャーさんは　あなたが本当に好きよ。たけしさんのことを言わなければならない　と思うわ。
Miki	大丈夫よ。夕べ、三人で遊んだから。映画を見たり、おいしいレストランで食べたり、いろいろなバーで飲んだりしたの。とても楽しかった。
Robert	みきさん！二人の人とデートをしないほうがいいよ。
Miki	平気よ。心配しないで。ああ、二人が来た。*(Roger and Takeshi enter the room together.)* ロジャーさん、たけしさん、今晩は！夕べ本当にありがとう！
Rie and Robert	信じられない！

2 What does Rie advise Miki to tell Roger?

3 What does Miki say about Roger and Takeshi?

4 Are these statements true or false?
   a えりちゃんは中国に行きたいです。
   b イアンさんとケイティさんは中国で結婚するつもりです。
   c みきさんはたけしさんのことがあまり好きじゃありません。
   d ロバートさんは二人の人とデートをすることがいいと思っています。
   e みきさんとたけしさんとロジャーさんと三人がいい友達でしょう。

5 Answer these questions in Japanese:
   a えりちゃんはどうして毎日ピアノの練習をしなければなりませんか。
   b イアンさんとケイティさんはいつ結婚したいですか。
   c イアンさんは何がよくないと思っていますか。
   d みきさんは夕べ何をしましたか。
   e どうしてロバートさんとりえさんは「信じられない」といいましたか。

Language discovery

15.1 HOW TO SAY *I DON'T* IN THE PLAIN FORM

In the Vocabulary builder and conversations you will have seen a number of verbs with the ending ない. This is the plain present negative, *I don't*.

For Group 1 verbs: change final **u** ending (or **i** in **masu**/stem form) to **a** ending + **nai**:

書<u>く</u> → 書<u>か</u> → 書<u>かない</u>

（書きます → 書き → 書か → 書かない）

For Group 2 verbs: as usual, this is very straightforward – drop る (or ます), add ない.

For the irregular verbs:

行く → 行かない　　する → しない　　くる → こない

YOUR TURN 1 Change these verbs into their ない form:

a 話す

b 読む

c 聞く

d 遊ぶ

e 見る

f 食べる

g 見せる

There is one exception to this rule. You replace う・い with わ rather than あ because it's easier to say:

買う → 買わない　　（買います → 買わない）

YOUR TURN 2 So how do you say 会います (*to meet*) in the ない form?

You can use this form in plain, casual speech and it can be 'softened' by adding です:

コーヒーは飲まないですよ！　　　　*I don't drink coffee, you know!*

You also use this form with でください to say *please don't*:

食べないでください。　　　　*Please don't eat.*

YOUR TURN 3 15.05 How would you say the following in Japanese? Listen to the audio to check your answers.

a Please don't speak.

b Please don't read.

c Please don't listen.

d Please don't play.

e Please don't look.

f Please don't show (me).

15.2 SAYING *WITHOUT DOING*

As with *please don't*, you use ないで in a sentence to mean *without doing*:

レポートを読まないで、出しました。　　　*I submitted the report without reading it.*

YOUR TURN How would you say the following in Japanese?

a I went home without drinking beer.

b I went to the restaurant without phoning Miki.

15.3 SAYING *I WANT YOU NOT TO* (*I DON'T WANT YOU TO*)

Attach ないで with ほしい (*want*) to make a polite negative request with です at the end:

そんなことを書かないでほしいです。

I want you not to write those sorts of things. (I don't want you to write those sorts of things.)

> YOUR TURN **How would you tell someone you don't want them to do the following things?**
> **a** smoke cigarettes
> **b** go into the meeting room
> **c** drink up (use **shimau**) all the beer

15.4 USING THE PLAIN NEGATIVE FORM IN THE PAST TENSE (*I DIDN'T*)

To make the past plain negative of verbs change ない to なかった (add です to be more polite).

> YOUR TURN **How do you say the following in Japanese?**
> **a** I didn't eat
> **b** I didn't buy

15.5 MAKING THE PLAIN FORMS OF ADJECTIVES

The good news is that this is easy!

▶ You make the plain forms of **i** adjectives by dropping です.
▶ You make the plain form of **na** adjectives by using plain forms of です.
▶ The negative です forms have layers of politeness.

Here are the <u>plain</u> です forms:

だ (*is*)   だった (*was*)
じゃない（です）(*isn't*)   じゃなかったです (*wasn't*)

Here are all the <u>negative</u> です forms in order of politeness.

	Negative (*isn't*)	Past negative (*wasn't*)
Most polite	ではありません	ではありませんでした
Very polite	じゃありません	じゃありませんでした
Middle polite	ではないです	ではなかったです
Polite	じゃないです	じゃなかったです
Plain	じゃない	じゃなかった

15.6 SAYING *I MUST*

To say *must, have to, need to* in Japanese sounds long and complicated but, once you know it as a phrase, it is not difficult.

Remove ない from the ない form.

> **LANGUAGE TIP**
> You will find it safer when speaking Japanese to use either the most polite or the polite forms of the negative.

Add なければ なりません (literally: *if you don't, it won't do – you/I must*).

 YOUR TURN 15.06 **What do these sentences mean?**

a 勉強 しなければ なりません。

b 会社に 行かなければ なりません。

c 薬を 飲まなければ なりません。

d タバコを やめなければ なりません。

e レポートを 書かなければ なりません。

f How would you say these sentences in a more casual way? (Clue: you need to change なりません to the plain form.)

15.7 SAYING *YOU DON'T HAVE TO*

出席しなくてもいいです means *You don't have to attend.*

Look at the underlined part. To say *you don't have to* you take off the final い of ない and add くても いいです. This phrase literally means *even if you don't, it's all right* so has the English meanings of *you don't have to, it's all right if you don't.*

 YOUR TURN 15.07 **What do the following sentences mean?**

a 今週 日本語を勉強 しなくてもいいです。

b そのレポートを 書かなくても いいですよ。

c 日本語を 話さなくてもいいですよ。

d その高いカメラを 買わなくてもいいです。

e 気分が悪いから会社に行かなくてもいいですか。

15.8 SAYING *YOU SHOULDN'T*

You have already learned how to give positive advice (*you should*) using the plain past with ほうがいいです.

To advise someone *not* to do something you still use ほうがいいです but this time with the ない form.

YOUR TURN 1 What do these sentences mean?

   a そのビールを飲まないほうがいいです。

   b そのカメラを買わないほうがいいです。

2 Can you advise someone not to do the following?

   a Meet Roger tonight

   b Take a day off work today

   c Send an email to the boss (社長)

15.9 SAYING *WHILE*

You learned how to say *while* using ながら in Unit 9. You can use this structure only when the same person is doing both actions. If you want to talk about two different people, you can use 間 (に).

イアンさんは中国にいる間に、ケイティさんは仕事を探します。

During the time that Ian is in China, Katie is looking for a job.

> ### LANGUAGE TIP
> The plain verb form before 間 is either ている (present continuous) or いる (*to be*).
> The verb form before 間 is always plain present tense.
> 間 means *throughout the whole time* whereas 間に means *at some point(s) during that time*.
> The person/subject of the 間 part of the sentence takes the particle が not は.
> The same person can do both actions with 間 in which case the particle is は:
> みきさんはアメリカにいる間、旅行をしていました。
> *During the time Miki was in America she did some travelling.*
> 間 can also be used with two nouns to mean *between*:
> 東京と大阪の間に   *between Tokyo and Osaka*

There is also うちに which is used with the ない verb form to mean *while it is not* or *before*.

YOUR TURN Can you give two English translations for this sentence?

雨が降らないうちにゴルフをしました。

You can also use うちに with ている to mean *while*. It tends to be used instead of 間に (or ながら) when there isn't a specific time period:

紅茶があたたかいうちに飲んでください。   *Drink the tea while it's warm.*

> ### LANGUAGE TIP
> Use:
> ▶ ながら for the same person.
> ▶ 間 for two different people/throughout the time.
> ▶ 間に for two different people and during the time.
> ▶ うちに to mean *while*.

15.10 THE CONDITIONAL (*IF/WHEN*)

There are several ways to say *if* in Japanese but we shall focus on the most wide-ranging one (which also happens to be the easiest). You simply add ら to the past plain (positive or negative) of the verb or adjective. For example:

食べた (*ate*)   食べた<u>ら</u> (*if/when I eat*)

食べなかった (*didn't eat*)   食べなかった<u>ら</u> (*if/when I don't eat*)

YOUR TURN 1 Complete the endings of these verbs and adjectives to give the meaning of *if/when*:

a 面白かった (if/when it is/was interesting)

b 面白くなかった (if/when it isn't/wasn't interesting)

c きれいだった (if/when she is/was beautiful)

d 行った (when/if I go/went)

e 好きだった (when/if you like)

You can usually tell if the meaning is *if* or *when* from the context of the sentence. When もし is added to the beginning of the sentence, then it is clearly an *if* sentence. The tense of the sentence (present or past) is decided by the phrase that follows ら. Look at these examples:

日本に行ったら、寿司を食べてみてください。 *If you go to Japan, please try the sushi.*

酒を飲んだら、頭が痛くなりました。   *When I drank the sake, I got a headache.*

YOUR TURN 2 Select a verb or adjective from the box and say the following sentences:

a If I go to Japan, I want to see Mount Fuji.

b If I study well, I will be able to speak Japanese.

c If she is not beautiful, I don't want to date her. (デートをします)

d If you like sumo, please watch tonight's tournament.

e If that film had been interesting, I would have probably watched it all.

面白かったら	勉強したら	行ったら
きれいじゃなかったら	好きだったら	

Listening

たち	makes certain words plural
ために	for
こんなに	such
盛大（な）	splendid
送別会	farewell party
結婚前夜祭	pre-wedding party
開いてくださって	organize (hold) for us
感謝（する）	appreciate
皆さん	everyone
親切（な）	kind
お世話になりました	you have helped us/looked after us
いつか	sometime, one day

 15.08 Ian makes a speech during the party to thank everyone. He uses polite Japanese with a number of specific respectful expressions (these are underlined). Listen to the audio and see if you can answer these questions:

a How does he describe the party?

b What two things does he say they have done while in Japan?

c When are they going to China?

d Why does he say it's a shame they are going?

e What does he ask people to do if they go to China?

今日はケイティと私たちのために　こんなに盛大な送別会と結婚前夜祭を<u>開いてくださって</u>ありがとうございます。とても感謝しています。日本にいる間、たくさんの人たちに会い、たくさんのことを勉強しました。日本の皆さんはとても親切でたいへん<u>お世話になりました</u>。来月中国へ行くことになりましたが　まだしたいことや見たいところがあったので、少し残念です。でも、またいつか、日本に来て、皆さんと会いたいです。いろいろと　ありがとうございました。もし中国に来るチャンスがあったら、ぜひ連絡してください。ありがとうございました。

Speaking

15.09 Listen to the audio in chunks and try to learn the speech off by heart – you may find it very useful if you go to Japan!

You are now going to personalize Ian's speech. Change it to include the following information:

    a Say *thank you* for the farewell party organized for you.

    b Say you will go back (return) to your own country next month.

    c Invite people to contact you if they come to your country.

All other information remains the same. When you have done this you will have your own farewell speech!

More **katakana**

THE FINAL 16 KATAKANA SYMBOLS (MA–N)

 15.10 Here are the final 16 **katakana**. Use the audio to help you if you wish:

マ	ミ	ム	メ	モ
ma	mi	mu	me	mo
ヤ	ユ	ヨ		
ya	yu	yo		
ラ	リ	ル	レ	ロ
ra	ri	ru	re	ro
ワ	ヲ			
wa	(w)o			
ン				
(n)				

The symbol for **(w)o** has only a grammatical function, normally written in **hiragana**. It used to be used for writing telegrams so it is rarely used nowadays.

SIMILARITIES WITH HIRAGANA

Katakana symbols are listed first:

モ も   **hiragana** is more curvy and vertical cuts through

ヤ や   **hiragana** is more curvy with extra dash

リ り   **hiragana** is more curvy

IDEAS FOR MNEMONICS

Can you see drops of rain in the *mist* ミ (**mi**), a *moo*se ム (**mu**), a number 1 – *you* are number 1 ユ (**yu**), a *razor* レ (**re**), a *ru*ined razor ル (**ru**) and a *ro*tation ロ (**ro**)?

SIMILAR-LOOKING KATAKANA

ウ フ ワ (**u, fu, wa**)   we've discussed **u** and **fu**; **wa** has one additional dash

ア マ (**a, ma**)   **ma** is shorter and squatter

ナ メ (**na, me**)   **me** tips to one side and is slimmer

ル レ (**ru, re**)   **ru** has an additional line (the *ru*ined part!)

ソ ン (**so, n**)   the angle on **so** is steeper

Once again, match the **katakana** words with the English meanings. The first eight words use only the final 15 sounds; the others use all 45 sounds (not including ヲ **wo**):

a	レモン	**1**	radio
b	メモ	**2**	melon
c	メロン	**3**	Rome
d	ルール	**4**	London
e	ローマ	**5**	milk
f	ローン	**6**	loan
g	リレー	**7**	marathon
h	メモリー	**8**	memory (computer)
i	アイスクリーム	**9**	rule
j	レンタカー	**10**	relay (race)
k	ロンドン	**11**	chicken
l	マラソン	**12**	ice cream
m	ミルク	**13**	my car
n	マイカー	**14**	rental car
o	ラジオ	**15**	memo
p	チキン	**16**	lemon

> **READING TIPS**
>
> Remember there is no distinction between **l** and **r** in Japanese so if an 'l' sound won't work, try 'r'. For example, *hotel* is pronounced **hoteru**. You will find it really helps to change **ru** into 'l' as a general rule.
>
> Also, there is no 'th' sound in Japanese – **s** sounds are used instead.

CONTRACTED SOUNDS

In Unit 7 you learned about contracted sounds for **hiragana** symbols. Exactly the same rules apply to **katakana**. For example:

キ (**ki**)	キャ (**kya**)	キュ (**kyu**)	キョ (**kyo**)
ギ (**gi**)	ギャ (**gya**)	ギュ (**gyu**)	ギョ (**gyo**)
シ (**shi**)	シャ (**sha**)	シュ (**shu**)	ショ (**sho**)
ジ (**ji**)	ジャ (**ja**)	ジュ (**ju**)	ジョ (**jo**)

Look back to Unit 7 to remind yourself of these rules.

READING 2

You have learned many borrowed words throughout this course. There follows a selection grouped by theme. Can you read them and match them with the English words?

Sport

a スポーツ

b ボーリング

c テニス

d プール

1 tennis

2 sport

3 bowling

4 swimming pool

Food and drink

e コーヒー

f トースト

g メニュー

5 toast

6 menu

7 coffee

Countries

h アメリカ

i イギリス

j イタリア

k オーストラリア

l ニュージーランド

8 Italy

9 England

10 America

11 New Zealand

12 Australia

Technology

m テレビ

n ニュース

o カメラ

p コンピューター

13 TV

14 computer

15 camera

16 news

Places

q レストラン

r ユースホステル

s スーパー

t デパート

17 department store

18 supermarket

19 youth hostel

20 restaurant

? Test yourself

What do these sentences mean?

a あの会議室に入らないでください。

b その映画は面白くなかったと思います。

c 朝ごはんを食べないで、会社に行きました。

d そのレポートを書かないでほしいです。

e 本堂さんに電話しなければなりません。

f 会議に出席しなくてもいいです。

g タバコをすわないほうがいいです。

h 雨が降らないうちに、ゴルフをしました。

i イアンさんが料理をしている間、ケイティさんは本を読んでいました。

j もし中国に来たら、連絡してください。

SELF CHECK

	I CAN...
◯	...use the negative (*don't, didn't*) in plain forms.
◯	...say more with polite and plain forms.
◯	...say *you must, you don't have to, you shouldn't*.
◯	...say *if* and *when*.
◯	...say *while*.
◯	...recognize and read all **katakana** symbols.

Answer key

UNIT 1

Culture point: a Kenichi-kun; **b** Suzuki-sensei; **c** Hana-chan *or* Hana-san

Conversation: 1 He comments on his job and position – company sales manager;
2 Surname then first name; **3** Watashi no meishi desu.

Key sentences: 2 a I am a journalist; **b** My wife's name is Rie; **c** My family is five people
(there are five in my family); **d** My son is six years old; **e** My daughter is ten years old;
3 a kazoku wa roku nin desu; **b** Musume wa go sai desu; **c** Musuko wa jānarisuto desu;
d Watashi wa shufu desu

1.1 Your turn: a Watashi wa jānarisuto desu; **b** Musume wa kaisha no eigyō buchō desu;
c Watashi wa jussai dewa arimasen.

1.2 a さん; **b** san; **c** go; **d** go; **Your turn: a** musukosan; **b** goshujin; **c** haha

1.3 Your turn: a Kocchi wa kazoku desu; **b** Kocchi wa chichi desu; **c** Kochira wa
Suzuki sensei desu.

1. 4 Your turn: a add **gozaimasu/nasai**; **b** English, 'bye bye' (goodbye)

1. 5 です (**desu**) covers these forms of the English verb: *am, is, are*; **Your turn: a** There are
five people in my family; **b** This is not the teacher Suzuki; **c** She's not my wife

1.6 Your turn: a roku sai; **b** nana nin; **c** musuko wa yon sai desu

Listening and speaking: 1 a 4; **b** 16; **c** 10; **d** housewife

Speaking: 1 ohayō gozaimasu; konnichi wa; sumimasen; ja mata ne; sayōnara; konbanwa;
oyasumi nasai; **2 a** Hajimemashite, name desu. (Dōzo) yoroshiku (onegaishimasu).
b Arigatō gozaimasu. Watashi no (meishi) desu. (Dōzo) **c** Ā, Suzuki san wa kaisha no eigyō
buchō desu ne. **d** Oisogashi deshō ne.

Speaking 3: (Hondō san no) gokazoku wa yo nin desu. Goshujin no Hondō Tatsuya san to
musumesan no Yuki san to Eri chan desu. Yuki san wa jūroku sai desu. Soshite, Eri chan wa
jussai desu. Goshujin wa eigyō būchō san desu. Okusan wa shufu desu.

Reading 1: a Suzuki Naomi; sales manager; **b** Her husband; **c** 3; **d** 10 and 12; **e** her son

Reading 2: a 5; **b** 1; **c** 6; **d** 3; **e** 2; **f** 4

Test yourself: 1 a ohayō; **b** oyasumi nasai; **c** kocchi wa kanai/shujin/kazoku desu;
d Hajimemashite, (*your name*) to mōshimasu. Dōzo yoroshiku onegaishimasu; **e** Watashi
wa jānarisuto desu; **f** Watashi wa shufu dewa arimasen.

UNIT 2

Culture point: 1 a meishi, *business card*; **b** namae, *name*; **c** rōdōsha, *working people*;
d shokuba, *workplace*; **e** sonkei, *respect*; **2 a** Watashi no shokuba desu; **b** Nihon no meishi
desu; **c** Watashi no namae desu.

Conversation 1: 1 Kanai no Naoe desu, my wife Naoe; **2** surname then first name.

Conversation 2: 1 his daughters; **2** ten; **3** Japan Now; **4** yōkoso; **5 a** 1; **b** 2

Key sentences: 1 a Is Robert an American? (*or:* Are you, Robert, an American?); **b** No, he is not an American (*or:* No, I am not an American.); **c** This is the company president, Mr Takahashi; **d** This is French wine; **e** Is that (over there) the Tokyo Bank?; **2 a** Robāto-san wa furansujin desu ka; **b** Are wa Nihon no wain desu ka; **c** Iie, Nihon no wain dewa arimasen.

2.1 Your turn: 1 a It's Rie's; **b** It's French; **2 a** my daughter, Yuki; **b** my wife, Rie; **3 a** Amerika no ginkō アメリカの銀行_{ぎんこう}; **b** watashi no wain 私_{わたし} のワイン; **c** Nihon no desu 日本_{にほん}のです

2.2 a England; **b** Itaria, Italy; **c** New Zealand; **d** Supein, Spain; **e** Portugal; **f** Mekishiko, Mexico; **g** Brazil; **h** Doitsu, Germany; **i** Argentina; **j** Ōsutoraria, Australia

2.3 Your turn: 2 a Amerikajin; **b** Doitsujin; **c** Ōsutorariajin; **d** Igirisujin; **e** Itariajin

2.4 Your turn: a Furansugo; **b** Chūgokugo; **c** Porutogarugo; **d** Kankokugo; **e** Supeingo

2.6 Your turn: a Kono meishi wa watashi no desu; **b** Sore wa Robāto-san no desu; **c** Sono wain wa Itaria no desu; **d** Are wa Supein no desu.

Speaking: a Amerika no アメリカの; **b** Furansugo no フランス語_ごの; **c** Nihon no 日本_{にほん}の; **d** Eigo no 英語_{えいご}の; **e** Chūgokujin no 中国人_{ちゅうごくじん}の; **f** Kankokujin no/kankokugo no (*could be either*) 韓国人_{かんこくじん}の・韓国語_{かんこくご}の

Writing: country name + **jin** at end for nationality, **go** for language except America: Beikokujin (Amerikajin), eigo

Reading 1: a Kono; **b** Ano; **c** Sono; **d** Kocchi; **e** kochira; **f** are

Reading 2: 1 hiragana; **2** kanji; **3** katakana

Test yourself: 1 a Kore wa watashi no hon desu; **b** Sore wa Furansu no wain desu; **c** Ano uisukī wa Nihon no dewa arimasen; **d** Musume no Yuki wa Nihonjin desu; **e** Are wa Kankoku no ginkō desu; **f** Watashi no eigo no sensei wa Amerikajin desu; **2 a** desu; **b** dewa arimasen; **c** dewa arimasen; **d** desu; **e** dewa arimasen; **f** desu; **g** desu

UNIT 3

Culture point: 1 gohan, rice, meal; **2** morning rice, midday rice, evening rice

Conversation: 1 with her family; **2 a** 4; **b** 5; **c** 6; **d** 3; **e** 2; **f** 1; **3 a** watch the TV news; **b** talk to her neighbour; **c** early

3.2 Your turn: 1 a rice; **b** coffee; **c** TV; **d** Japanese; **2 a** kōhī o nomimasu; **b** terebi o mimasu; **c** sōji o shimasu; **d** Nihongo o hanshimasu

Key sentences: 1 a Kazoku to asagohan o tabemasu; **b** Tokidoki terebi o mimasu; **c** Itsumo kōhī o nomimasu; **d** Kinjo no hito to Nihongo o hanashimasu; **e** Asa sōji o shimasu; **2 a** I get up at six o'clock; **b** For breakfast, I have toast and eggs; **c** I don't eat rice; **d** I eat lunch at work (the company)

3.3 Your turn: a Hirugohan o tabemasu; **b** Tokidoki shinbun o yomimasu; **c** Itsumo nyūsu o kikimasu; **d** E o kakimasu; **e** Hirugohan o tsukurimasu; **f** Hayaku nemasu; **g** Terebi o kaimasu; **h** Haha wa asa sōji o shimasu

3.5 Your turn: a Kanojo wa hayaku nemasu; **b** Karera wa hayaku okimasu; **c** Watashitachi wa itsumo issho ni bangohan o tabemasu; **d** Kare wa terebi o mimasu; **e** Anata(tachi) wa kōhī o nomimasu ka

3.6 Your turn: after the word it marks

3.7 Your turn: a Asa itsumo shinbun to kōhī o kaimasu; **b** Tokidoki kyōdai to terebi o mimasu; **c** Itsumo haha to shujin to bangohan o tsukurimasu

3.8: a do the cleaning; **b** make a phone call; **c** play football; **d** play golf; **e** have a meal

3.9 Your turn: a ichiji ni; **b** goji ni; **c** jūji ni

3.10: a every day; **b** every week; **c** every month; **d** every year; **e** this week; **f** this month; **g** this year; **h** next week; **i** next month; **j** next year

3.11 Your turn: a Mainichi jimusho de kōhī o nomimasu; **b** Tama ni sūpā de shinbun o kaimasu; **c** Musume wa maishū depāto de kaimono o shimasu; **d** Kyō kazoku to resutoran de tabemasu *or* Kyō resutoran de kazoku to tabemasu

3.13: Your turn: a jūshi **b** jūroku **c** jūnana *or* jūshichi **d** jūkyū

Listening: 1 a breakfast; **b** drink; **c** neighbour; **d** do the shopping; **e** restaurant; **f** supermarket; **g** occasionally; **h** work; **2 a** 1) 7 a.m.; 2) from seven in the evening; **b** coffee; **c** shop at the department store; **d** goes to the supermarket; **e** makes dinner

Writing: 1 a Hirugohan ni tamago to tōsuto o tabemasu. Soshite kōhī o nomimasu; **b** Mainichi rokuji ni okimasu. Sorekara asagohan o tsukurimasu; **c** Ashita kinjo no hito to gorufu o shimasu; **d** Gogo taitei shinbun o yomimasu. Tokidoki nyūsu o mimasu; **e** Itsumo jū ji ni uchi ni kaerimasu. Tama ni kazoku to bangohan o tabemasu. **3 a** で; と; を de;to;o **b** で; と; を *or* で; は; を de;to;o *or* de;wa;o **c** に; と; に ni;to;ni **d** に; で; を ni;de;o **e** で; を de;o

Reading: a 6; **b** 8; **c** 9; **d** 2; **e** 3; **f** 1; **g** 4; **h** 10; **i** 7; **j** 5

Test yourself: 1 a 3, **b** 6, **c** 5, **d** 2, **e** 7, **f** 1, **g** 4; **2 a** wa; **b** ni; **c** to; **d** ni; **e** de

UNIT 4

Culture point: 1 a Tokidoki Nihon no resutoran de tabemasu; **b** Tabitabi sushi o tabemasu. Soshite ocha o nomimasu. Tokidoki sashimi o tabemasu; **c** Nihonjin wa tabitabi sakana o tabemasu ga tama ni fugu o tabemasu; **d** Ashita kazoku to yakitori to shōyu o tabemasu. Soshite sake o nomimasu; **2 a** That one please; **b** Welcome (we are ready to serve you); **c** That was delicious; **d** restaurant

Conversation 1: 1 eight o'clock, around ten or 11 o'clock; **2** six o'clock; **3** has dinner at restaurant with people from office; **4 a** 4, **b** 3, **c** 1, **d** 2; **5** tōsuto, kōhī, toast and coffee; **6** plays golf with colleagues sometimes, usually relaxes/chills out with family at home; **8 a** let's eat; **b** let's drink; **c** let's watch TV; **d** let's speak Japanese; **e** let's do the cleaning; **9** Add **ka** to the end; change **masu** to **mashō** (*let's*) and **mashō ka** (*shall we*) as follows: 食べましょう tabemashō; 食べましょうか tabemashō ka; 飲みましょう nomimashō; 飲みましょうか nomimashō ka; 見ましょう mimashō; 見ましょうか mimashō ka; しましょう shimashō; しましょうか shimashō ka

Key sentences: 1 a Let's eat dinner at that restaurant over there!; **b** Tomorrow I will go to France; **c** Shall we go to a restaurant together? **2 Your turn: a** Kono resutoran de hirugohan o tabemashō! **b** Nichiyōbi ni Amerika ni ikimasu; **c** Issho ni uchi de tabemashō ka.

4.1 Your turn: a Ashita jimusho ni (e) ikimasu; **b** Musuko to sūpā ni (e) ikimasu; **c** Tokidoki hayaku uchi ni (e) kaerimasu; **d** Chichi wa asa korejji ni (e) kimasu; **e** Ashita Nihon ni (e) kaerimasu

4.2 Your turn: a gorufu o/wa shimasen; **b** Tsuma wa uchi o sōji shimasen (or Tsuma wa sōji o shimasen) (can also use **Kanai** for *wife*); **c** (Kare wa) shigoto o/wa shimasen (or kare wa hatarakimasen)

4.3 1 a 二月; **b** nigatsu; **c** 三月; **d** sangatsu; **e** 六月; **f** rokugatsu; **g** 十 月; **h** jūgatsu; **i** 十 一 月; **j** jūichigatsu

Speaking: 1 Kazoku to shokuji o/wa shimasen; **2** Kinjo no hito to hanashimasen; **3** Asagohan ni kōhī o/wa nomimasen; **4** Uchi o/wa sōji shimasen; **5** Hayaku shigoto (or kaisha/jimusho) ni ikimasen

Reading 1: 1 a 4; **b** 1; **c** 3; **d** 5; **e** 2; Answers to questions: **a** Jūji, jūichiji goro kaerimasu; **b** Mainichi rokuji ni okimasu; **c** Osoku made hatarakimasu; **d** Tokidoki jimusho no hito to gorufu o shimasu ga taitei kazoku to uchi de gorogoro shimasu; **e** Asagohan ni taitei tōsuto o tabemasu; **2 a** 7; **b** 9; **c** 8; **d** 4; **e** 1; **f** 11; **g** 2; **h** 5; **i** 12; **j** 3; **k** 6; **l** 1 0; **3 a** February, April, October; **b** Sunday

Reading 2: a e; **b** ai; **c** au; **d** ue; **e** kao; **f** aoi; **g** akai; **h** aki; **i** eki; **j** kusa; **k** kesa; **l** koe; **m** sushi; **n** seki; **o** soko; **p** suki; **q** sekai; **r** seiki; **s** ookii; **t** oishii

2 (*some words appear more than once but the answers below show only one of these*)

あ		け	く		う	え
	う	あ	さ		え	
	す	き		せ	か	い
	し			い	そ	こ
お				き		え
	お	せ			あ	い
	え	き			か	お
お	い	し	い		い	

3 ka; shi; u; ku; sa;   ki; so; a; o; ke;   e; su; i; ko; se

Test yourself: 1 a Resutoran de tabemashō ka; **b** Resutoran de tabemashō!; **c** Ano depāto ni ikimashō; **d** Kono sūpā de sushi o kaimashō; **e** Uchi ni kaerimashō ka; **f** Rainen Nihon ni ikimasu; **g** Haha wa sushi wa/o tabemasen; **2** answers given in **masu** form (change **masu** to **masen** to make negative): *drink*, nomimasu; *eat*, tabemasu; *see/watch/look*, mimasu; *listen*, kikimasu; *speak/talk*, hanashimasu; *write*, kakimasu; *read*, yomimasu; *work*, shigoto (o) shimasu; *make*, shimasu; *buy*, kaimasu; *go*, ikimasu; *return*, kaerimasu; *come*, kimasu; *do*, shimasu; *get up*, okimasu; *go to bed*, nemasu; *play golf*, gorufu o shimasu; *chill out*, gorogoro shimasu; *study*, benky ō shimasu; *play football*, sakkā o shimasu; *do the shopping*, kaimono o shimasu; *travel*, ryokō (o) shimasu; *have a meal*, ryōri (o) shimasu; *make a phone call*, denwa (o) shimasu

UNIT 5

Culture point: 1 a gohyaku en; **b** nihyaku en; **c** happyaku en; **d** hassen en

Conversation 1: 1 An English newspaper and Christmas cards, 1000 yen; **2** 400 yen **3** two

Conversation 2: 1 one postcard is 100 yen and one stamp is 75 yen; **2** He buys 3 postcards and 3 stamps; **3** 525 yen; **4 a** Sore wa Igirisu no shinbun desu ka; **b** Kono kurisumasu kādo o ni-mai kudasai; **c** Sumimasen, hagaki o utteimasu ka; **d** Kono hagaki o san-mai to nanajū go-en no kitte mo san-mai kudasai; **5 a** Hagaki ga arimasu ka; **b** Sumimasen, yukata o utteimasu ka; **c** Kono sensu wa ikura desu ka; **d** Sono shinbun o misete kudasai; **e** Kono o-sake o kudasai; **f** Kono tokei to kono kaban o kudasai; **6 a** nanahyaku; **b** yonsen; **c** nihyaku yonjū; **d** nanahyaku gojū; **e** gosen gohyaku; **f** nanasen gohyaku nanajūgo

Key sentences: a How much is this newspaper?; **b** May I have two of these Christmas cards?; **c** Excuse me, do you have any French newspapers?; **d** On the second floor there are TVs, computers etc.; **e** On the second floor there is nothing.

5.1 Your turn: a kutsu hassoku, 8 pairs; **b** ringo rokko, 6 apples; **c** sake gohon, 5 bottles; **d** bīru yonhon, 4 bottles; **e** yukata sanmai, 3 kimono; **f** terebi ichidai, 1 TV; **g** hon jussatsu, 10 books

5.2 Your turn: a kōhī mittsu; **b** kaban tō; **c** keitai denwa futatsu (you can also use ni dai); **d** tokei yottsu; **e** kēki hitotsu

5.3 Your turn: a Kaban o futatsu kudasai; **b** Tokei o itsutsu kudasai; **c** Kōhī o yottsu kudasai; **d** Sake o nihon kudasai; **e** Bīru o roppon kudasai; **f** Ringo o sanko kudasai; **g** Kitte o gomai kudasai; **h** Nōto o sansatsu kudasai

5.4 Your turn: a imasu; **b** arimasu; **c** arimasu

5.5 Your turn: a hon ga arimasu; **b** ringo ga arimasu; **c** kinjo no hito ga imasen

5.6 Your turn: a In the house there is my mother *or* My mother is in the house; **b** On the second floor there are TVs *or* There are TVs on the second floor; **c** Uchi ni kazoku ga imasu; **d** Sangai ni sūpā ga arimasu; **e** Ano jimusho ni Furansujin to Igirisujin no jānarisuto ga imasu

5.7 Your turn: 1 a Ichiji desu; **b** Shichiji ni okimasu; **c** (Nichiyōbi ni) gorufu o shimasu; **2 a** Nikai ni nani ga arimasu ka; **b** Terebi to tokei ga arimasu; **3 a** Jimusho ni dare ga imasu ka; **b** Uchi ni dare ga imasu ka; **c** Sangai ni dare ga imasu ka

5.8 Your turn: 1 a Kono jimusho ni dare ka imasu ka; **b** Ikkai ni nani ka arimasu ka; **c** Uchi ni dare ka imasu ka; **d** Hai, dare ka imasu; **e** Hai, nani ka arimasu; **2** You put **mo** after the question word and change **arimasu/imasu** to **arimasen/imasen**; **3 a** Kono jimusho ni dare mo imasen; **b** Ikkai ni nani mo arimasen; **c** Uchi ni dare mo imasen

5.9 Your turn: 1 a O-hashi wa gohyaku en desu; **b** Shinbun wa sambyaku gojū en desu; **c** Yukata wa yonsen yonhyaku en desu; **d** Ningyō wa rokusen happyaku en desu; **e** Kono kamera wa kyūsen kyūhyaku kyūjū en desu

5.10 Your turn: a sanman gosen, roppyaku en; **b** sanjū goman, rokusen roppyaku en; **c** sanjū goman rokusen roppyaku rokujū roku en

5.11 1 There are TVs, computers and so on, on the second floor; **2** I eat both rice and toast for breakfast; **Your turn: a** ya, nado; **b** mo, mo

Listening 1: Dialogue 1: buying one kilo of apples and two kilos of bananas, apples = 400 yen per kilo, bananas = 600 yen per kilo, total = 1600 yen; **Dialogue 2:** buying one yukata and three folding fans, 4500 yen and 1500 yen, total = 9000 yen; **Dialogue 3:** buying camera, camera at sale price = 24650 yen

(Script: **SA** = shop assistant, **C** = customer:

Dialogue 1: SA Irasshai, irasshaimase; **C** Sumimasen, ano ringo wa ichi kiro ikura desu ka; **SA** Ringo desu ka. Ichi kiro yonhyaku en desu; **C** Jā, ichi kiro onegaishimasu. Soshite banana wa ikura desu ka; **SA** Sore wa ichi kiro roppyaku en desu; **C** Ē to, ni kiro kudasai; **SA** Hai, zembu de sen roppyaku en desu; **C** Dōzo

Dialogue 2: C Sumimasen, ano yukata o misete kudasai; **SA** Kore desu ka. Dōzo. Kore wa rokusen en de gozaimasu; **C** Chotto takai desu ne … ; **SA** Kore wa yonsen gohyaku en de gozaimasu; **C** Ā, sō desu ka. Jā, kore o kudasai; Soshite sensu ga arimasu ka; **SA** Hai, kore wa sen gohyaku en de gozaimasu; **C** Jā, kore o sanbon kudasai; **SA** Kashikomarimashita. Zembu de kyūsen en de gozaimasu;

Dialogue 3: SA Irasshaimase; **C** Sumimasen, kono kamera wa ikura desu ka; **SA** Sore wa sanman en desu; **C** Sō desu ka. Ano sony F310 o utteimasu ka; **SA** Sony F310 … hai, kochira ni arimasu. Kore mo sanman en desu ga kyō no sēru de niman yonsen roppyaku gojū en desu yo; **C** Niman yonsen roppyaku gojū en desu ne. Sore wa ii desu ne. Jā, sono sony no kamera o kudasai)

Listening 2: a ii, **b** i, **c** 2, **d** 1, **e** 3 (Script: **1 A** Sumimasen, ima nanji desu ka; **B** Shichiji desu; **2 A** Okāsan, piano no ressun wa nanji kara desu ka; **B** Yoji kara desu yo. Hayaku!; **3 A** Irasshaimase! **B** Sumimasen, kono ningyō wa ikura desu ka; **A** Sore wa nisen en desu; **4 A** Ano ne … kono apāto no yachin wa ikura desu ka; **B** Ikkagetsu sanman issen en desu; **B** Sanman issen en desu ka. Takai desu ne! **5 A** O-tanjōbi wa nangatsu desu ka; **B** Atashi desu ka. Rokugatsu desu)

Speaking: All end in **kudasai**; **1** yukata o nimai; **2** bīru o sanbon; **3** ningyō o hitotsu; **4** kitte o hachimai; **5** ringo o goko

Writing: 1 a ni, ga, arimasu; **b** ni, ga, imasu; **c** ni, imasen; **d** ni, ga, imasu; **e** ni, ga/wa arimasen; **2 a** だれかいます dare ka imasu; **b** だれもいません dare mo imasen; **c** なにか あります nani ka arimasu; **d** なにもありません nani mo arimasen; **e** だれかいます dare ka imasu; **f** だれかいます dare ka imasu

Reading: 1 a tate; **b** nani; **c** fune; **d** chichi; **e** hitotsu; **f** futatsu; **g** nanatsu; **h** haha; **i** heta; **j** nuno; **k** hone; **l** te; **m** natsu; **n** hana; **o** hito; **2 a** tokei; **b** heso; **c** kata; **d** saifu; **e** ani; **f** ane; **g** otōto (otouto); **h** uchi; **i** kanai; **j** ashita; **k** ohashi; **l** osake; **m** hoho; **n** senaka; **o** taitei; **p** futsū (futsuu); **q** itsutsu; **r** kokonotsu; **s** tō (tou); **t** ikutsu; **3** Odd one out is: **a** し; **b** け; **c** あ; **d** さ; **e** ね; **f** こ; **g** さ; Correct symbol is: **a** さ; **b** は; **c** お; **d** き; **e** ぬ; **f** い; **g** ち;

Reading challenge (read L to R): ta, nu, ka, hi, shi, tsu; u, ho, ku, na, sa, chi; ki, he, so, te, a, fu; o, to, ke, e, ni, su; ha, i, no, ko, ne, se.

Test yourself: 1 a 6; **b** 8; **c** 4; **d** 7; **e** 10; **f** 9; **g** 1; **h** 2; **i** 5; **j** 3

UNIT 6

Culture point: 1 Question: shumi wa nan desu ka. Answer: shumi wa (origami / ikebana / budō) desu; **2** shodō, budō, jūdō, kendō, kyūdō , aikidō; **dō** means *path* or *way*

Conversation 1: 1 The Tokyo art gallery; **2** Gozonji desu ka; **3** At the traffic lights

Conversation 2: 1 Have coffee and cake at a coffee shop; **2** Roger isn't keen – he suggests bowling instead; **3** Thursday at 7.30

Conversation 3: 1 Behind the cinema; **2** In front of the New Tokyo Theatre; **3** Turn right at the traffic lights and go straight ahead; **4** a preposition (in front of, next to …) is said after the place it is attached to (**hoteru no tonari** means *next to the hotel*)

Key sentences a Go straight ahead please; **b** Turn right at the traffic lights please; **c** The art gallery is next to the hotel; **d** Is there a post office near here? **e** In front of the department store, there is a bus stop.

6.1 Your turn: a hoteru no mae; **b** depāto no ushiro; **c** ginkō no mae; **d** bijutsukan no ushiro; **e** resutoran no ushiro

6.2 Your turn: a resutoran no tonari; **b** ginkō no yoko; **c** gakkō no soba; **d** hakubutsukan no ue; **e** depāto no shita; **f** gekijō no naka; **g** yūbinkyoku no mukaigawa

6.3 Your turn: a The bus stop is beside the bank; **b** My house is alongside the school; **c** Rie is in the theatre; **d** Katie is by me

6.6 1 You would leave out **Yūbinkyoku wa** and just say **Ginkō no tonari ni arimasu.**
2 Who is there in front of the bank? **3 Your turn: a** Ginkō no ushiro ni nani ga arimasu ka; **b** Gakkō no soba ni nani ga arimasu ka; **c** Yūbinkyoku no mukaigawa ni dare ga imasu ka

6.7 1 a please; **b** turn; **c** turn; **d** right; **e** please; **f** cross; **g** left; **h** traffic lights; **i** turn left **j** traffic lights; **2** The commands end in ください **kudasai** (*please*) unlike English commands when we just say the verb (*turn, go,* etc.); **3** に ni; **4** You use particle の **no** after saying 'first' and 'next'.

6.7 Your turn: a Massugu itte kudasai; **b** Kōsaten o hidari ni magatte kudasai; **c** Ōdan hodō o watatte kudasai; **d** Hitotsume no shingō o migi ni magatte kudasai; **e** Hodōkyō o watatte, kado o hidari ni magatte kudasai

6.8 Your turn: a Nan ji ni ikimashō ka; **b** Nan ji ni aimashō ka; **c** Doko de aimashō ka; **d** Nani o shimashō ka; **e** Resutoran de tabemasen ka; **f** Eigakan ni ikimasen ka; **g** Eigakan wa dō desu ka; **h** Gorufu wa dō desu ka

6.9 Your turn: 1 a deshita でした; **b** mashita ました; **c** mashita ました; **d** masen deshita ませんでした; **2 a** Asagohan o tabemashita; **b** Kōhī o nomimasen deshita; **c** Shichiji ni resutoran de aimashita

6.10 Your turn: 1 a nomi のみ; **b** iki いき; **c** tabe たべ; **2 a** Raishū Furansu ni ikitai desu; **b** Uchi de nyūsu o kikitai desu; **c** Nihon no kamera o kaitai desu; **d** Kinjo no hito to o-sake o nomitai desu

6.11: yōbi

6.12 Your turn: 1 a ichiji jūgofun; **b** ichiji nijuppun; **c** ichiji nijū gofun; **d** ichiji sanjuppun;
2 fives = **fun**, tens = **pun**

6.14 Your turn: a Resutoran wa soko ni arimasu; **b** Kaisha wa koko ni arimasu; **c** Gakkō wa
kono chikaku ni arimasu; **d** Yūbinkyoku wa asoko ni arimasu; **e** Bijutsukan wa soko ni arimasu

Speaking: 1 Question: Sumimasen, *name of place* wa doko ni arimasu ka/desu ka;
2 Hitotsume no shingō o migi ni magatte, massugu itte kudasai. Sūpā wa eigakan no
mukaigawa ni arimasu; **3** Futatsume no shingō o hidari ni magatte kudasai. Depāto wa
hidarigawa ni arimasu. Gekijō no tonari desu; **4** Tsugi no shingō o hidari ni magatte,
massugu itte kudasai. Hakubutsukan wa gakkō no mukaigawa desu; **5** Tsugi no shingō o
migi ni magatte kudasai. Eigakan wa sūpā no mukaigawa desu

Listening 1: a 11, 3; **b** 2, 9; **c** 15, 16; **d** 13, 18; **e** 1, 17; **f** 14, 5; **g** 12; **h** 4, 6; **i** 7; **j** 8, 10;
Translations: **a** The restaurant is there; **b** Turn right at those traffic lights and go straight
on; **c** My house is alongside the school; **d** My business cards is in my bag; **e** What is there
opposite the post office?; **f** Cross over the footbridge and turn left at the corner; **g** Would you
like to go to the cinema?; **h** We met at the restaurant at seven o'clock; **i** I didn't drink coffee;
j I want to drink sake with my neighbour; **Listening 2** They decide to go to the cinema and
meet at seven.

Listening 2 Script and translation

Miki	Ashita doko ka issho ni ikimasen ka.	Tomorrow shall we go somewhere together?
Rie	Hai, doko ni ikimashō ka.	Yes, where shall we go?
Miki	Eigakan wa dō desu ka.	How about the cinema?
Rie	Ē, eigakan ni ikimashō!	Yes, let's go to the cinema?
Miki	Nan ji ni aimashō ka.	What time shall we meet?
Rie	Shichiji wa dō desu ka.	How about seven o'clock?
Miki	Ii desu ne. Mata ashita!	That'll be great. See you tomorrow.

3 a 5; **b** 2; **c** 1; **d** 6; **e** 3; **f** 4

Writing: a mashita ました; **b** tai desu たいです; **c** masu ます; **d** masen ません; **e** masen
deshita ませんでした; **f** masen ません; **g** tai desu たいです; **h** tai desu たいです

Reading: 1 a mura; **b** yoru; **c** yume; **d** yuri; **e** yama; **f** momo; **g** mori; **h** mimi; **i** mon;
j wareware; **k** wan; **l** maru; **2 a** hon; **b** kaimono; **c** watashi; **d** namae; **e** ohayō (ohayou);
f sumimasen; **g** oyasumi nasai; **h** nomimasu; **i** shimasu; **j** kakimasu; **k** kaimasu; **l** kikimasu;
m kaerimasu; **n** okimasu; **o** nemasu; **p** mimasu; **q** yomimasu; **r** hanashimasu; **s** tsukurimasu;
t hatarakimasu; **3 a** Tokei o kaimashita – I bought a watch; **b** Hanashi o kikimashita –
I listened to the talk/story; **c** Hayaku okimashita – I got up early; **d** Osoku nemashita – I went
to bed late; **e** Hon o yomimashita – I read the book; **f** Mainichi hatarakimasu – I work every
day; **g** Osoku uchi ni kaerimashita – I went home late; **h** Ashita haha to kaimono o shimasu
– I am doing the shopping with my mum tomorrow; **i** Watashi no namae o kakimashita –
I wrote my name; **j** Yoru taitei osake o nomimasu – in the evenings generally I drink rice
wine; **4 a** na n ri hi a ki ru so mo wa ni fu; **b** nu he u ko ma ro shi (w)o o ho to yu; **c** ya ta re ne
tsu sa mi ha su i ka; **d** no te ra ku mu yo ke e me se chi

Test yourself: 1 a Yūbinkyoku wa ginkō no mukaigawa ni arimasu; **b** Ginkō wa sūpā no tonari ni arimasu; **c** Sūpā wa gakkō no ushiro ni arimasu; **d** Gakkō wa hakubutsukan no chikaku ni arimasu; **e** Sensei wa gakkō (no naka) ni imasu; **f** (Watashi no) Meishi wa kaban no naka ni arimasu; **2** Sunday 3c; Monday 6f; Tuesday 1a; Wednesday 5e; Thursday 2b; Friday 7g; Saturday 4d

UNIT 7

Culture point: 1 nan (pronounced 'minami' when used as a single **kanji**); **2** ichiban

Conversation 1: 1 A bit shy and quiet but beautiful; **2** She doesn't think Miki is especially shy; **3** He hopes to play tennis

Conversation 2: 1 He is very cheerful and kind and he is very good at bowling; **2** Miki says they are going to see a movie whereas Roger told Rie he's hoping to play tennis; **3 a** at the end; **b** 1 Yasashii hito da to omoimasu; **2** utsukushii hito da to omoimasu; **3** akarukute yasahii hito da to omoimasu; **4** hazukashigari da to omoimasu

7.1 Your turn: All start with Ano hito wa; **1 a** utsukushii desu; **b** akarui desu; **c** yasashii desu; **2 a** akarukute yasashii desu; **b** otonashikute hazukashigari desu; **c** yasashikute utsukushii desu; **d** otonashikute ii desu

7.2 Your turn: na is needed in a, d, e and f; **a** Miki is a beautiful person, isn't she?; **b** Roger is good at bowling isn't he?; **c** Tokyo is lively isn't it?; **d** This is a lively place isn't it?; **e** I think Tatsuya Hondo is a serious person; **f** This is a clean room isn't it?

7.3 Your turn: a Kono hakubutsukan wa nigiyakana tokoro desu; **b** Tōkyō wa totemo nigiyaka desu ne; **c** Kore wa hirokute kireina heya desu; **d** Haha wa me ga ōkii desu; **e** (Watashi wa) me ga itai desu; **f** Roger-san wa se ga takakute me ga ōkii desu; **g** Naoe-san wa origami ga jōzu desu; **h** Miki-san wa bōringu ga heta desu

7.4 Your turn: a–c start with **watashi wa** then: **a** se ga takai desu; **b** se ga takakute me ga aoi desu; **c** se ga takakute, me ga aokute, kami ga kinpatsu desu; d–f begin with **haha wa** then: **d** kao ga marui desu; **e** kao ga marukute, hana ga takai desu; **f** kao ga marukute, hana ga takakute, me ga chairo desu; **g** Kami ga nagakute, kuroi desu

7.5 Your turn: a (Kare wa) majime de otonashii hito desu; **b** Tōkyō wa nigiyaka de hiroi desu

7.6 Your turn: a (Kare wa) yūmei da to omoimasu; **b** (Sore wa) hiroi tokoro da to omoimasu; **c** (Kanojo wa) hazukashigari da to omoimasu

7.7 Your turn: a Rainen Nihon ni ikitai to omoimasu; **b** Nihon de sushi o tabetai to omoimasu; **c** (Kanojo wa) Soshite Fujisan o mitai to omoimasu

7.9 *I don't think she's especially shy* = sonna ni hazukashigari ja nai to omoimasu

Your turn: a Kirei dewa arimasen/ja nai desu; **b** Yūmeina hito dewa arimasen/ ja nai desu

7.10 Your turn: a Me ga itai desu; **b** Atama ga itai desu.

Listening: 1 a feels bad; headache, stomach ache, sore throat, shoulder ache; **b** It's a cold; **c** He's hungover! **2 a** やさしい；真面目; yasashii; majime; She is very kind but a bit serious; **b** 広くてにぎやかな; hirokute nigiyakana; Tokyo is a big and busy place; **c** きれい; kirei;

My room is not very clean; **d** 恥ずかしがり; hazukashigari; I think that Miki is not especially shy; **e** 明るい; akarui; I think that Roger is a cheerful person.

Reading 1: I am Miki Sugihara. I am average height with long black hair. My eyes are black and round. My face is also round but my nose is square. I think that I am quiet but kind. I like films but I don't like sports.

Writing 2: a and **d** are i adjectives so drop final i and add kunai (negative) and kute (connector); **b** and **c** are **na** adjectives so add **dewa arimasen** (negative) and **de** (connector); **e** is irregular i adjective – ii → yokunai, yokute

Reading 2: a ga za da ba pa; **b** ga gi gu ge go; **c** go zo do bo po; **d** za ji zu ze zo; **e** ge ze de be pe; **f** bi bu pi pu; **3 a** kazoku – family; **b** shinbun – newspaper; **c** ginkō – bank; **d** go – five; **e** Nihongo – Japanese; **f** asagohan – breakfast; **g** bangohan – dinner; **h** tamago – egg; **i** denwa – phone; **j** shigoto – work; **k** tokidoki – sometimes; **l** zenzen – not at all/never

Reading 3: a shachō (shachou) – company director; **b** kaisha – company; **c** jimusho – office; **d** shufu – housewife; **e** shokuji – meal; **f** kyōdai (kyoudai) – siblings; **g** ryokō – travel; **h** Chūgoku – China; **i** tōkyō; **j** kyōto; **k** densha – train; **l** yūbinkyoku – post office; **m** benkyō – study; **n** hyaku – 100; **o** raishū – next week

Reading 4 a ga kya gya; **b** ji sha ja cha; **c** hyo byo pyo; **d** de gi za bu pe; **e** gyu ju byu pyu; **f** cho nyo hyo myo ryo; **g** rya nyu hyu pyu; **i** zu gu bu ryu; **j** pa pi pu pe po

Test yourself: 1 a Sonna ni hazukashigari ja nai to omoimasu; **b** Tōkyō wa nigiyaka de hiroi desu; **c** Watashi wa se ga takakute, me ga aokute, kami ga kinpatsu desu; **d** Haha wa se ga takakute me ga ōkii desu; **e** Totemo akarukute yasashii hito da to omoimasu; **f** Ano hito wa majime desu ga yasashii desu; **g** Supōtsu ga heta desu ga origami wa jōzu desu; **2 a** 3; **b** 7; **c** 5; **d** 6; **e** 4; **f** 1; **g** 2

UNIT 8

Culture point: 1 a Kiri desu; **b** Hare deshō; **c** Kumori desu; **d** Ame deshō; **2 a** Ame nochi hare deshō. **b** Kumori tokidoki yuki deshō. **c** Ichinichi hare deshō. **d** Kumori tokidoki ame deshō.

Vocabulary builder: 2 To make the past tense drop the final い i and add かったです **katta desu**: 面白いです → 面白かったです omoshiroi desu → omoshirokatta desu

Conversation: 1 He thinks it's a great place (just the business trip that was not interesting!); **2** He went by bullet train (he bought a single ticket) and returned in a colleague's car (not enjoyable and too far!); **3** It was not especially warm and it snowed all day Thursday; **4** Tomorrow it will get cold. Rain later snow; **5 a** Iie, omoshirokunakatta desu; **b** Iie, katamichi no kippu o kaimashita; **c** Ichinichi yuki deshita (fuyukai deshita); **d** Iie samuku narimasu

8.1 Your turn: a omoshirokute tanoshikatta desu; **b** omoshirokute yokatta desu; **c** subarashikute tanonshikatta desu; **d** yokute tanoshikatta desu; **e** fuyukai deshita; **f** yūmei deshita

8.2 Your turn: a tanoshikunakatta desu – it wasn't enjoyable; **b** yokunakatta desu – it wasn't good; **c** subarashikunakatta desu – it wasn't wonderful; **d** tsumaranakunakatta desu – it wasn't boring

8.3 Your turn: all end in **dewa** (or **ja**) **arimasen deshita**; **a** kirei; **b** majime; **c** fuyukai

8.4: a tabemasen 食べません; **b** ōkikatta desu 大きかったです; **c** yūmei ja/dewa arimasen 有名じゃ（では）ありません; **d** ja /dewa arimasen /ja nai desu じゃ・ではありません・じゃないです; **e** ja (dewa) arimasen deshita /ja nakatta desu じゃ・ではありませんでした・じゃなかったです

8.5 Your turn: a Miki writes **kanji** skilfully; **b** Robert speaks Japanese often (to say *well* in this context use **jōzu ni**); **c** Mr Hondo does his work seriously/conscientiously; **d** Naoe cleans beautifully/neatly; **e** Katie speaks English kindly/softly/sympathetically

8.7: a atsuku; **b** samuku; **c** atatakaku; **d** suzushiku; **Your turn:** All start with 'Soon it will be': **a** summer. Gradually it will get hot; **b** winter. Gradually it will get cold; **c** autumn/fall. Gradually it will get cooler

8.8 Your turn: a basu de ikimashita; **b** machi ni basu de (or basu de machi ni) ikimashita; **c** haha no uchi ni kuruma de (or reverse order) ikimashita; **d** nyū yōku ni densha de (or reverse order) ikimashita

Listening: a windy sometimes snow, 0 degrees, very cold; **b** cloudy later fine, 5 degrees; **c** cloudy later rain, 10 degrees; **d** rainy all day, 12 degrees; **e** fine sometimes cloudy, 15 degrees; **f** Sunny/fine all day, 22 degrees warm

Script for weather report: Ashita no tenki yohō desu. Mazu hokkaidō no tenki desu. Sapporo wa kaze ga tsuyokute tokidoki yuki deshō. Rei do deshō. Totemo samui deshō. Sendai wa kumori nochi hare desu. Go do deshō. Tōkyō wa kumori nochi ame deshō. Jū do deshō. Ōsaka wa ichinichi ame deshō. Kion wa jūni do deshō. Tsugi wa kyūshū no tenki yōhō desu. Fukuoka wa hare tokidoki kumori deshō. Kion wa jūgo do deshō. Okinawa wa ichinichi hare deshō. Kion wa nijū-ni do deshō. Atatakai desu

Reading and writing: a です desu. This film was interesting and good; **b** でした deshita. Last week's business trip was boring and disagreeable; **c** でしょう deshō. Tomorrow's weather will be cloudy later rain; **d** ます masu. Tomorrow I will be 32; **e** ました mashita. This room has become clean; **f** ません masen. I don't read a newspaper very much; **g** くて、くないです kute, kunai desu. The neighbour has big eyes and isn't tall; **h** くなかったです kunakatta desu. The trip wasn't at all enjoyable; **i** ではありません・じゃないです dewa arimasen/ja nai desu. Your room is not clean; **j** かったです、ませんでした katta desu, masen deshita. Last night I had a headache. I didn't eat anything

Test yourself: 1 a wa o; **b** wa ga; **c** wa no de ni; **d** ni de; **e** wa to ni; **f** wa kara made o; **g** wa mo mo; **h** wa ga ga; **i** wa no ni; **j** wa ga wa; **2 a** The trip was interesting and enjoyable; **b** The film was interesting but a bit long; **c** This book was boring and disagreeable; **d** Last week I did a business trip to Osaka. It wasn't interesting; **e** Mr Hondo went to Osaka by bullet train; **f** Soon it will be summer. It will gradually get hotter; **g** Tomorrow's weather will probably be cloudy, later rain; **h** Please may I have two tickets for Osaka.

UNIT 9

Culture point: a with **f**, superior/inferior; **b** with **e**, company/workplace; **c** with **h**, polite/respectful language; **d** with **g**, woman/man

Vocabulary activity 2: a なりたいです → なりたかったです (naritai desu → naritakatta desu) (*I wanted to be*); **b** kodomo no koro eiga sutā ni naritakatta desu. For other occupations replace **eiga sutā**. **3** every day, morning, every morning

Conversation: 1 Robert says he's not very good at golf but he'll give it a try; **2** He offers to teach him how to play golf and to pick him up at his apartment; **3** This Sunday at 12; **4 a** batsu/false; **b** maru/true; **c** batsu; **5 a** 12-ji ni mukae ni ikimasu; **b** Iie, kuruma de ikimasu; **c** Iie, amari jōzu dewa arimasen

9.1: a です desu; **b** かったです katta desu; **c** 食べたくない tabetakunai; **d** たくなかった takunakatta; **Your turn: a** tabetai desu; **b** banana o/ga tabetai desu; **c** tōsuto wa tabetakunai desu; **d** Kōhī wa nomitakunai desu; **e** O-sake wa nomitakunakatta desu; **f** Yūbe bīru wa nomitakunakatta desu

9.3 は、が、です; wa, ga, desu. **Your turn: a** Miki-san wa supōtsu ga amari suki ja arimasen; **b** Roger-san wa tenisu ga totemo suki desu; **c** Rie-san wa kaimono ga suki desu; **d** Ian-san wa ame ga kirai desu

9.4: a kai; **b** kaki; **c** kiki; **d** yomi; **e** nomi; **f** mi; **g** iki; **h** hataraki; **i** shi; **j** hanashi; **Your turn: a** Katie-san wa nyūsu o kikinagara ocha o nomimasu; **b** Naoe-san wa shokuji o tsukurinagara Yuki-san to (ni) hanashimasu; **c** Robāto-san wa ongaku o kikinagara kanji o kakimasu; **d** Ian-san wa asagohan o tabenagara hon o yomimasu; **e** Hondō-san wa hatarakinagara hirugohan o tabemasu

9.5: 僕はゴルフのし方を教えます Boku wa gorufu no shikata o oshiemasu; **Your turn: a** Sushi no tabekata; **b** Sushi no tsukurikata; **c** Kanji no kakikata; **d** Nihongo no yomikata; **e** Eigo no hanashikata. Full sentences all end in **o oshiemashita**, **a–d** start with Rie-san wa Katie san ni; **e** starts with Katie-san wa Rie-san ni

9.6 ロバートさんのアパートへ迎えに行きます。Robāto-san no apāto e mukae ni ikimasu. **Your turn: a** Tabe ni ikimasu; **b** Resutoran e tabe ni ikimasu; **c** Resutoran e washoku o tabe ni ikimasu; **d** Hondō-san wa Robāto-san no apāto e mukae ni ikimashita

9.7 Your turn: a Yūmeisō desu; **b** Kono eiga wa tsumaranasō desu; **c** Atama ga itasō desu; **d** Totemo utsukushisō desu ne (*or* kireisō desu ne); **e** Nihongo o hanashisō desu

9.8: a Roger likes sports best; **b** Roger is most skilful at bowling; **Your turn: a** Miki-san wa eiga ga ichiban suki desu; **b** Supōtsu ga ichiban heta desu; **c** Tenisu ga ichiban kirai desu ga …; **d** Yakyū ga ichiban tsumaranai desu

Listening 1: a A firefighter; **b** Until late in the evening; **c** Yes; **d** Work in America; **e** Tokyo English translation of Robert's speech: When I was a child I wanted to be a firefighter but, in fact, I became a journalist. Every day I work until late in the evening but the work is very enjoyable. Many times I do my work at home while having a meal but it can't be helped. In the future I want to work in America. The American lifestyle looks interesting but I like the Tokyo lifestyle best of all.

Speaking: All begin with **Katie-san wa: a** eiga ga suki desu; **b** terebi ga totemo suki desu; **c** hon ga suki ja arimasen (ja nai desu); **d** kaimono ga totemo suki desu; **e** gorufu ga amari suki ja arimasen; **f** tenisu ga jōzu desu; **g** gorufu ga heta desu; **h** yakyū ga jōzu desu; **i** ryōri ga nigate desu; **j** sūgaku ga tokui desu

Listening 2: a false; **b** true; **c** false; **d** true; **e** true

Reading and writing: a kata. Mr Hondō taught Robert how to play golf; **b** nagara. Naoe watches TV while eating her breakfast; **c** ni ikimasu. Tomorrow I will go with Katie to town to watch a film; **d** sō. A filmstar's lifestyle looks unpleasant, doesn't it?; **e** tai desu. Next year I want to go to Japan; **f** kata. I don't know how to make cakes; **g** sō: Miki looks like she will eat that sushi doesn't she (technically **tai** also fits but isn't usually used in situations when you don't know for certain what another person wants)

Start reading: a 3; **b** 7; **c** 8; **d** 9; **e** 1; **f** 15; **g** 6; **h** 10; **i** 13; **j** 11; **k** 14; **l** 4; **m** 12; **n** 5; **o** 2

Reading 1: a mountain; **b** river; **c** bamboo; **d** woman; **e** child; **f** forest; **g** stone; **h** root; **i** sun; **j** moon; **k** wood; **l** fire; **m** rice field; **n** power; **o** earth/ground; **p** water; **q** tree; **r** gold

Reading 2: a 3; **b** 5; **c** 4; **d** 2; **e** 1

Days of the week 1: (from top to bottom) sun, moon, fire, water, tree, gold, earth

Days of the week 2: Sunday c 1; Monday f 4; Tuesday e 2; Wednesday a 7; Thursday b 6; Friday g 5; Saturday d 3

Test yourself: a Ian didn't want to drink rice wine/alcohol; **b** Miki doesn't like beer very much; **c** Every morning Naoe reads the paper while drinking her coffee; **d** Roger taught Miki how to bowl; **e** Katie went to town to meet up with Rie; **f** This film looks interesting, doesn't it?; **g** Roger likes sports best; **h** Yuki Hondo wants to be a doctor in the future; **i** Robert works every day until late; **j** I went with Katie to a restaurant to eat Japanese food.

UNIT 10

Culture point: 1 a Western room; **b** Western food; **c** Japanese-style hotel; **2 a** Japanese clothes; **b** Western clothes

Vocabulary builder: a eat; **b** drink; **c** see; **d** show; **e** read; **f** speak; **g** get up

Conversation: 1 It closes at 10 a.m. and opens at 4 p.m.; **2** Men can take a bath from 5 to 7, women from 7 to 9; **3** until 9; **4** The film tonight finishes at 10.30 but the TV room closes at 10 (and there appears to be no flexibility); **5** He is surprised by the sleeping time rule of 10.30 and he didn't know that men and women have separate rooms! **6** You place these words *after* the times; **7 a** false; **b** true; **c** true; **d** false; **e** false; **8 a** 十時まで開いています。 **b** 二階にあります。 **c** 五時から七時までです。 **d** いいえ、はいてはいけません。 **e** 十時半です。

Script in **rōmaji**:

Receptionist	Irasshaimase!
Katie	Konnichiwa. Kyō yoyaku o shimashita. Katie Mears to Ian Ferguson desu ga.
Receptionist	Hai, wakarimashita. Sukoshi yūsuhosuteru no rūru o setsumei shimasu. Nihongo de ii desu ka.
Katie	Hai, ii desu.
Receptionist	Kono yūsuhosuteru wa gozen jūji made aiteimasu. Soshite mata gogo yoji kara aiteimasu. Hiruma haitte wa ikemasen.
Katie	Yoru yoji kara aiteimasu ne.

Receptionist	Hai. Soshite yūsuhosuteru no naka de wa kutsu o haite wa ikemasen.
Ian	(*Looking at his shoes*) Ā, sumimasen.
Receptionist	Sorekara ofuro no rūru desu. Dansei wa goji kara shichiji made ofuro ni haittemo ii desu. Josei wa shichiji kara kuji made desu.
Ian	Heya de tabetemo ii desu ka.
Receptionist	Tabetewa dame desu! Shokudō de tabete kudasai. Shokudō wa kuji made aiteimasu.
Katie	Wakarimashita.
Receptionist	Soshite terebi no heya wa jūji made aiteimasu. Terebi wa jūji made mitemo ii desu.
Ian	Jūji made desu ka. Demo konban no eiga wa jūji han made desu. Jūji han made mitemo ii desu ka.
Receptionist	Ikemasen. Terebi no heya wa jūji made desu. Soshite nerujikan wa jūji han desu.
Ian	(*Getting annoyed*) Jūji han desu ka. Sore wa . . .
Katie	(*Interrupting*) Wakarimashita. Heya wa doko desu ka.
Receptionist	Josei no heya wa kono kai desu. Dansei no heya wa nikai desu.
Ian	Heya wa betsubetsu desu ka. Shinjirarenai!
Receptionist	Koko wa yūsuhosuteru desu yo!
Katie	(*Quickly*) Hai, hai, wakarimashita. Arigatō.

10.1 Your turn: Answers on audio.

10.2: example sentence: I get up at about ten, then I have breakfast, then I go shopping; **a** おきて (wake up); **b** かいて; **c** まって; **d** しんで; **e** さがして

10.3 Your turn: a 毎日七時に起きて、朝ご飯を食べて、（家を）掃除します。
b 毎日十二時に昼ご飯を食べて、仕事に行きます。**c** きのう遅く起きて、コーヒーを飲んで、町に行きました。**d** 明日六時に家に帰って、晩ごはんを食べて、テレビを見ます。**e** 月曜日に日本語を勉強して、レストランへ昼ごはんを食べに行きます。

10.4 Example sentence: After I get home I read the newspaper; **Your turn: a** テレビを見てから、寝ました。**b** 昼ごはんを食べてから、いつもニュースを聞きます。**c** 母に電話してから、友達のうちに行きました。**d** 新聞を読んでから、家を掃除しました。

10.5 The receptionist says: テレビは十時まで見てもいいです。 **Your turn: 1** All begin with ここで then: **a** ねてもいいです。**b** よんでもいいです。**c** べんきょうしてもいいです。**d** テレビをみてもいいです。**e** にほんごをはなしてもいいです。**f** おんがくをきいてもいいです。**g** あそんでもいいです。**2** Ian says 十時半まで見てもいいですか。**3** You add か: **a** 窓を開けてもいいですか。**b** 窓を閉めてもいいですか。**c** この部屋に入ってもいいですか。**d** お風呂に入ってもいいですか。

10.6 Your turn: a ここで飲んではいけません。**b** 窓を開けてはいけません。**c** そのドアを開けてはいけません。**d** この部屋に入ってはいけません。**e** お風呂に入ってはいけません

10.7 Your turn: a 郵便局<ruby>郵便局<rt>ゆうびんきょく</rt></ruby>は<ruby>九時<rt>くじ</rt></ruby>から<ruby>五時<rt>ごじ</rt></ruby>までです。**b** <ruby>東京<rt>とうきょう</rt></ruby>から<ruby>京都<rt>きょうと</rt></ruby>まで<ruby>行<rt>い</rt></ruby>きました。**c** <ruby>東京<rt>とうきょう</rt></ruby>から<ruby>京都<rt>きょうと</rt></ruby>まで<ruby>新幹線<rt>しんかんせん</rt></ruby>で<ruby>行<rt>い</rt></ruby>きました。

Listening 1: a She has breakfast/drinks coffee; **b** She eats at a restaurant; **c** She goes home; **d** Any three from cleans the house, watches TV, makes dinner, works.

Katie's routine: Shichiji ni okite, asagohan ni itsumo kōhī o nomimasu. Asa tabitabi tomodachi to depāto de kaimono o shite, resutoran de shokuji o shimasu. Gogo tokidoki sūpā ni itte, soshite uchi ni kaerimasu. Uchi ni kaette kara tama ni uchi o sōji shimasu. Sorekara terebi o mite, bangohan o tsukutte, yoru shichiji kara shigoto o shimasu.

3: A 3; **B** 1; **C** 4; **D** 2; **E** 5

Script: これから、<ruby>学校<rt>がっこう</rt></ruby>の<ruby>規則<rt>きそく</rt></ruby>を<ruby>説明<rt>せつめい</rt></ruby>します。

1 アクセサリーやイヤリングなどをしてはいけません。**2** <ruby>教室<rt>きょうしつ</rt></ruby>で<ruby>昼<rt>ひる</rt></ruby>ごはんを<ruby>食<rt>た</rt></ruby>べてもいいです。**3** <ruby>学校<rt>がっこう</rt></ruby>の<ruby>中<rt>なか</rt></ruby>では<ruby>靴<rt>くつ</rt></ruby>を<ruby>入<rt>はい</rt></ruby>ってはいけません。**4** <ruby>授業<rt>じゅぎょう</rt></ruby>の<ruby>間<rt>あいだ</rt></ruby>、<ruby>トイレ<rt>といれ</rt></ruby>に<ruby>行<rt>い</rt></ruby>ってはいけません。**5** <ruby>先生<rt>せんせい</rt></ruby>と<ruby>話<rt>はな</rt></ruby>したい<ruby>場合<rt>ばあい</rt></ruby>は<ruby>職員室<rt>しょくいんしつ</rt></ruby>に<ruby>入<rt>はい</rt></ruby>ってもいいです。

4: Sequence answers from l to r: 1, 5, 4, 2, 6, 7, 3 Script: はじめまして、<ruby>石橋<rt>いしばし</rt></ruby>たけしです。これから<ruby>僕<rt>ぼく</rt></ruby>の<ruby>一日<rt>いちにち</rt></ruby>について<ruby>話<rt>はな</rt></ruby>します。<ruby>毎日<rt>まいにち</rt></ruby>、<ruby>遅<rt>おそ</rt></ruby>くまで<ruby>寝<rt>ね</rt></ruby>ています。<ruby>十一時<rt>じゅういちじ</rt></ruby>ごろ<ruby>起<rt>お</rt></ruby>きて、コーヒーを<ruby>飲<rt>の</rt></ruby>んでから、<ruby>大学<rt>だいがく</rt></ruby>に<ruby>行<rt>い</rt></ruby>きます。<ruby>大学<rt>だいがく</rt></ruby>で<ruby>友達<rt>ともだち</rt></ruby>にあって、<ruby>食堂<rt>しょくどう</rt></ruby>で<ruby>昼<rt>ひる</rt></ruby>ごはんを<ruby>食<rt>た</rt></ruby>べます。そしてたまに、<ruby>大学<rt>だいがく</rt></ruby>の<ruby>先生<rt>せんせい</rt></ruby>と<ruby>会<rt>あ</rt></ruby>って、<ruby>勉強<rt>べんきょう</rt></ruby>について<ruby>話<rt>はな</rt></ruby>します。<ruby>毎晩<rt>まいばん</rt></ruby>バンドのメンバーと<ruby>一緒<rt>いっしょ</rt></ruby>に、バンドの<ruby>練習<rt>れんしゅう</rt></ruby>します。<ruby>僕<rt>ぼく</rt></ruby>はリードギターをやっていて、ポップの<ruby>音楽<rt>おんがく</rt></ruby>を<ruby>作<rt>つく</rt></ruby>っています。バンドの<ruby>練習<rt>れんしゅう</rt></ruby>が<ruby>終<rt>お</rt></ruby>わってから、バンドのメンバーとパブに<ruby>行<rt>い</rt></ruby>って、<ruby>遅<rt>おそ</rt></ruby>くまでビールを<ruby>飲<rt>の</rt></ruby>んだり、ポテトチップスなどを<ruby>食<rt>た</rt></ruby>べたりします。<ruby>夜<rt>よる</rt></ruby><ruby>一時<rt>いちじ</rt></ruby>か<ruby>二時<rt>にじ</rt></ruby>ごろ<ruby>部屋<rt>へや</rt></ruby>に<ruby>帰<rt>かえ</rt></ruby>って、すぐ<ruby>寝<rt>ね</rt></ruby>ます。

Writing: a もって; **b** けして; **c** うたって; **d** えらんで; **e** ひいて; **f** やすんで; **g** ぬいで; **h** きめて; **i** でて; **j** つけて

Speaking: a Kono kamera o motte kudasai; **b** Denki o tsuketemo ii desu ka; **c** Denki o keshite kudasai; **d** Koko de utatte wa ikemasen; **e** Hitotsu erande kudasai; **f** Kono heya de gitā o hiitemo ii desu; **g** Yasundemo ii desu ka; **h** Kutsu o nuide kudasai; **i** Hayaku kimete kudasai; **j** Yoru dete wa ikemasen

Reading 1: a Every day I get up at 6, eat breakfast then go to work; **b** On Saturdays I get up at about 9, I drink coffee then I shop in town; **c** Yesterday I worked until late, then I went to a restaurant with a colleague; **d** In the evening I eat dinner, watch TV then go to bed late; **e** Tomorrow I will go shopping with a neighbour, return home then chill out

Start reading: a eye; **b** ear; **c** foot; **d** hand; **e** mouth/opening; **f** person; **g** big; **h** small; **i** above; **j** below; **k** middle

Reading 2: a big; **b** ear; **c** small; **d** below; **e** middle; **f** above; **g** mouth; **h** eye; **i** person; **j** foot; **k** hand

Reading 3: 1 a 4; **b** 5; **c** 7; **d** 8; **e** 1; **f** 2; **g** 3; **h** 6; **2 a** above, below, middle; **b** mouth, ear, eye, foot, hand; **c** person, woman, man, child, power; **d** small, big, few, blue, black, white, bright, like; **e** mountain, river, tree, forest, wood, bamboo, rice field, sun, moon, root; **f** water, fire, gold, earth, stone

Test yourself: a either 9 or 2; **b** either 2 or 9; **c** 7; **d** 5; **e** 4; **f** 8; **g** 1; **h** 10; **i** 6; **j** 3

Rōmaji version: **a** Yūsuhosuteru no naka de wa kutsu o _____.; **b** Gakkō de wa kutsu o _____.; **c** Dansei no ofuro wa _____ desu.; **d** Takeshi-san wa _____, jūichiji goro okimasu.; **e** Katie-san wa asa depāto de _____, resutoran de shokuji o shimasu.; **f** Soshite _____ tama ni uchi o sōji shimasu.; **g** Hiruma yūsuhosuteru ni _____.; **h** Yoru bangohan o tabete kara kompyūtā de _____.; **i** Yūbinkyoku wa _____ aiteimasu.; **j** Hondō-san wa _____ shinkansen de ikimashita.; **1** haitte wa ikemasen; **2** nuide kudasai; **3** Tōkyō kara Ōsaka made; **4** kaimono o shite; **5** osoku made nete; **6** kuji kara goji made; **7** goji kara shichiji made; **8** uchi ni kaette kara; **9** haite wa dame desu; **10** mēru o dashimasu

UNIT 11

Culture point: 1 a お母さん okāsan; **b** お父さん otōsan; **c** お兄さん onīsan; **d** お姉さん onēsan; **2** ちゃん; **3** さん; **4 a** 母; **4 b** 父; **5** Because they derive from the western names Papa and Mama; **6 a 1** お母さん okāsan, **2** お父さん otōsan, **3** えり Eri; **4** お祖父ちゃん・お祖父さん ojīchan/ojīsan; **b 1** お母ちゃん okāchan; **2** お父ちゃん otōchan; **3** お姉ちゃん onēchan; **4** おばあちゃん obāchan

Vocabulary builder: 2 All end in さん

Conversation 1: 1 On foot; **2 a** Yuki's routine – tennis club after school, twice a week cram school where studies maths and English, home about 7 p.m., eats dinner, does homework until late; **2 b** Eri's routine – goes home after school, helps mother make dinner, practises piano, eats dinner with sister, does judo twice a week at school, bed about 10 p.m.

Conversation 2: 1 Yuki: does club at school on Saturday mornings then she generally goes into town with friends and does some shopping. Sometimes she goes to see a film. On Sundays she often goes for a drive with the family and sometimes goes with Grandad for a walk; Eri: often goes to town with her mum and granddad on Saturdays to do some shopping. Sometimes she takes part in judo tournaments at school. She always spends time with the family on Sundays; **2** Eri does a little each day but hasn't done any yet this week. Yuki says that Eri doesn't like homework much and Eri says she wants Yuki to do her homework for her to which Yuki says: 'No way, do it yourself!' **3** Eri says 今ピアノを習っています; **4 a** false; **b** false; **c** true; **d** false; **e** true; **5 a** テニスクラブに参加します。 **b** 二回塾に行きます。 **c** 土曜日に時々散歩します。 **d** 大抵うちに帰って、母と一緒に晩ごはんを作ります...。 **e** 学校でします

Script in **rōmaji:**

Robert	Yuki-san, Eri-chan, jibun no ichinichi ni tsuite oshiete kudasai.
Yuki	Watashi wa mainichi aruite gakkō ni itteimasu. Gakkō no ato de tenisu kurabu ni sanka shiteimasu. Soshite maishū nikai juku ni itte, sūgaku ya eigo o benkyō shiteimasu. Shichiji goro uchi ni kaette, bangohan o tabete, soshite osoku made shukudai o shimasu.

Eri	Watashi mo aruite gakkō ni ikimasu. Gakkō no ato de taitei uchi ni kaette, haha to issho ni bangohan o tsukurimasu. Ima piano o naratteimasu kara mainichi renshū o shiteimasu. Soshite onēchan to bangohan o tabemasu. Maishū nikai gakkō de jūdō o shiteimasu. Jūji goro nemasu.
Robert	Shūmatsu ni taitei nani o shiteimasu ka.
Yuki	Doyōbi no asa gakkō de kurabu o shimasu. Soshite gogo taitei tomodachi to machi ni itte kaimono o shimasu. Tokidoki eiga o mi ni ikimasu. Nichiyōbi ni tabitabi kazoku to issho ni doraibu o shimasu. Tokidoki sofu to sampo shimasu.
Eri	Watashi wa doyōbi ni yoku haha to ojīchan to machi ni itte, kaimono o shimasu. Tokidoki gakkō de jūdō no shiai ni sanka shimasu. Nichiyōbi wa itsumo kazoku to sugoshimasu.
Robert	Eri-chan, itsu shukudai o shimasu ka.
Eri	Sō desu ne. Mainichi sukoshi shiteimasu ga konshū wa mada shiteimasen!
Yuki	Eri-chan wa shukudai ga amari suki janai desu.
Eri	Onēchan ni shukudai o shite hoshii desu.
Yuki	Dame desu yo! Jibun de shitemite kudasai.

11.1 Your turn: 1 a 今音楽を聞いています。**b** 今ニュースを聞いています。**c** テレビを見ています。**d** 日本語の新聞を読んでいます。**e** 家族と食事をしています。
2 You change います to いました。**3** present negative is て form + いません and past negative is て form + いませんでした ; **a** ゆきさんはしゅくだいをしていません。
b えりさんはテレビを見ていませんでした。

11.3 Your turn: a I walk to school every day; **b** After school I take part in the tennis club; **c** Twice a week I do judo at school.

11.5 Your turn: a is the correct translation; **b** would be 両親は日本に行きます。

11.6 Your turn: 1 a Tomorrow I'm going to try sushi; **b** Last night I tried sake; **2 a** May I try writing it in kanji?; **b** I want to try on this jacket

11.7 Your turn: 1 お姉ちゃんに宿題をしてほしいです。 **2** I want Miki to teach me Japanese; **3** に; **4 a** I want a smart jacket; **b** What do you want?

11.8 Your turn: a I am still doing my homework. **b** I haven't gone to work yet.

Listening: 1 a 1 She is drinking coffee while listening to the news; **2** Yuki is watching TV while eating breakfast; **3** Eri is doing her homework while eating toast; **b** Her husband has already set off to his company but Grandad is still sleeping; **2 1** f; **2** h; **3** a; **4** g; **5** c; **6** d; **7** i; **8** j; **9** e; **10** b

Reading 1: 1 a まだ mada; **b** もう mō; **c** もう mō or まだ mada; **d** まだ mada; **e** もう mō; **f** まだ mada or もう mō; **g** まだ mada; **h** もう mō; Meanings: **a** Roger hasn't played tennis with Miki yet; **b** Miki has already had a date with Roger; **c** Mr Hondo isn't at home now. He is already (**mō**) at work; or he is still (**mada**) at work; **d** Eri hasn't done her homework yet this week; **e** Yuki has already done her homework this week; **f** Katie's parents are still (**mada**) in Japan; or they are already (**mō**) in Japan; **g** Takeshi doesn't work yet; **h** Naoe's father no longer works. He is at home every day

Script in rōmaji: **a** Roger-san wa _____ Miki-san to tenisu o shiteimasen.; **b** Miki-san wa _____ Roger-san to dēto o shimashita.; **c** Hondō-san wa ima uchi ni imasen. _____ kaisha ni imasu.; **d** Eri-san wa konshū _____ shukudai o shiteimasen.; **e** Yuki-san wa konshū _____ shukudai o shimashita.; **f** Katie-san no goryōshin wa _____ Nihon ni imasu.; **g** Takeshi-san wa _____ shigoto o shiteimasen.; **h** Naoe-san no chichi wa _____ shigoto o shiteimasen. Mainichi uchi ni imasu.; **2 a** 7; **b** 3; **c** 1; **d** 8; **e** 5; **f** 2; **g** 4; **h** 6

Reading 2: a 7; **b** 9; **c** 10; **d** 8; **e** 3; **f** 6; **g** 2; **h** 4; **i** 5; **j** 1

Reading 3: a 2; **b** 4; **c** 5; **d** 3; **e** 1

Reading 4: a 11, 12, 13, 14, 15; **b** 20, 30, 40, 50, 60; **c** 90, 91, 92, 93, 94; **d** 33, 44, 55, 66, 77; **e** 59, 58, 57, 56, 55

Reading 5: a Tues 25th Dec; **b** Wed 17th June; **c** Sat 3rd Sept **d** Fri 21st April

Reading 6: a ¥400; **b** ¥700; **c** ¥1900; **d** ¥490; **e** ¥5000

Test yourself: 1 a At present I am eating dinner with the family; **b** I am learning the guitar; **c** I am studying (study) Japanese at university; **d** My older sister is married; **e** My Dad has gone to (and is in) America at the moment; **f** Let's try this sushi!; **g** I want you to switch off the TV; **h** Have you already eaten breakfast?; **i** No, not yet. (I haven't eaten it yet/I am not eating it yet); Rōmaji version: **a** Ima kazoku to bangohan o tabeteimasu; **b** Gitā o naratteimasu; **c** Daigaku de Nihongo o benkyō shiteimasu; **d** Ane wa kekkon shiteimasu; **e** Chichi wa ima Amerika ni itteimasu; **f** Kono sushi o tabetemimashō!; **g** Terebi o keshite hoshii desu; **h** Mō asagohan o tabemashita ka; **i** Iie, mada tabeteimasen. **2 a** Doyōbi ni itsumo karē o tabeteimasu; **b** Nihon no bīru o nondemitai desu; **c** Nihongo de kaitemite kudasai; **d** Nihongo de kaite hoshii desu; **e** ōkii kuruma ga hoshii desu; **f** Mō Hondō-san ni denwa o shimashita ka. Iie mada desu, **g** Eri-san wa mada shukudai o shitteimasen ga Yuki-san wa mada shitteimasu.

UNIT 12

Culture point: a Miki isn't shy (you know); **b** This film is interesting, (you see); the ending soften the statements.

Vocabulary: 2 a Eri can already swim. **b** Roger likes to drink beer with his friends. **c** Next year I intend to go to South America. **d** I have an interest in South America so I want to go. **e** I am learning Japanese therefore I have come to Japan. **f** What's the matter? Well, you see, I've got a headache.

Converation 1: 1 Because she can't play sports very well; **2** Watching a film, eating at a restaurant before; **3** Saturday evening

Converation 2: 1 She suggests watching baseball because she likes watching sport; **2** Eating shabu-shabu; **3** Various restaurants; **4 a** She likes watching sport; **b** He is a vegetarian; **5 a** false; **b** true; **c** true; **d** false; **e** false; **6 a** りえさんとレストラン（れすとらん）で食べて、えいがを見るつもりです。**b** スポーツ（すぽーつ）を見ることが好きだからです。**c** いいえ、できません。**c** ベジタリアン（べじたりあん）だからです。**d** すしやさんで食べるつもりです。
6 Rōmaji version: **a** Miki-san wa konban nani o suru tsumori desu ka; **b** Miki-san wa dōshite

yakyū o mitai desu ka; **c** Roger-san wa shabu shabu o taberu koto ga dekimasu ka; **d** Dōshite desu ka; **e** Doko de taberu tsumori desu ka.

6 Rōmaji answers: **a** Rie-san to resutoran de tabete, eiga o miru tsumori desu; **b** Supōtsu o miru koto ga suki da kara desu; **c** Iie, dekimasen; **d** Bejitarian da kara desu; **e** Sushiya-san de taberu tsumori desu

Script in **rōmaji**:

Miki	Moshi moshi.
Roger	Moshi moshi, Miki-san desu ka. Roger desu ga …
Miki	Roger-san! Konnichiwa.
Roger	Konnichiwa. Ano ne, konban hima desu ka.
Miki	Konban desu ka. Konban wa chotto … Rie-san to eiga o mimasu. Miru mae ni resutoran de taberu tsumori desu.
Roger	Sō desu ka. Jā, doyōbi no ban wa dō desu ka.
Miki	Doyōbi wa ii desu yo. Nani o shimashō ka.
Roger	Tenisu o shimashō ka.
Miki	Tenisu desu ka. Tenisu wa amari dekimasen.
Roger	Jā, badominton wa dō desu ka.
Miki	Nē, Roger-san, sumimasen ga supōtsu o suru koto ga amari suki ja nai desu.
Roger	(Sounding disappointed) Ā, sō desu ka.
Miki	Demo supōtsu o miru koto wa suki desu yo! Doyōbi no ban yakyūjō de yakyū o mi ni ikimashō ka.
Roger	(Brightening up) Sō shimashō!
Miki	Yakyūjō no chikaku ni iroirona resutoran ga arimasu. Yakyū o miru mae ni shabu-shabu demo tabemashō!
Roger	(Sounding doubtful) Shabu shabu wa niku desu ne. Boku wa bejitarian na no de niku o taberu koto ga dekimasen.
Miki	Sakana wa dō desu ka.
Roger	Sakana wa daijōbu desu. Taberu koto ga dekiru n desu.
Miki	Jā, yakyū no mae ni sushiya-san de tabemashō!

12.1: a eat, **b** watch/see, **c** teach, **d** go out; **e** listen; **f** buy, **g** write, **h** drink, **i** speak, **j** go

Your turn: 1 a Terebi o miru; **b** Eigo o oshieru; **c** Uchi o deru; **d** Nyūsu o kiku; **e** Terebi o kau; **f** Mēru o kaku; **g** Bīru o nomu; **h** Nihongo o hanasu; **i** Furansu ni iku; **2** Group 1 verbs: **a** かく; **b** はなす; **c** もつ; **d** およぐ; **e** あそぶ; **3** Group 2 verbs: **a** ねる; **b** おきる; **4** いく;
5 To convert from plain form to **masu** form, follow the rules in reverse and add **masu**:
for Group 1 change **u** to **i**; for Group 2 drop **ru**: **a** はなします; **b** よみます; **c** わかります;
d でかけます; **e** でます

12.3 見る前にレストランで食べるつもりです。 **Your turn: 1 a** before going to bed;
b before drinking; **2 a** Mr Hondo always reads a book before going to bed; **b** Ian ate dinner before drinking beer

12.4 Your turn: 1 a I can play tennis; **b** Rie can cook; **2 a** ロバートさんはビールを飲むことができません。 **b** りえさんは英語を話すことができます。 **c** なおえさんは少し英語を話すことができます。

12.5 Your turn: 1 Katie doesn't like cooking; **2 a** I am good at speaking Japanese but bad at reading Japanese; **b** Yuki's strong point is studying maths but her weak point is English

12.6 Your turn: a お母さんにてがみを書くつもりですか。**b** 今晩ビールを飲むつもりですか。**c** 毎日遅くまで働くつもりですか。**d** 日曜日になおえさんとゴルフをするつもりですか。**e** 今晩サッカーを見るつもりですか。

12.7: a 日本に行くので毎日日本語を勉強します (I am going to Japan so I am studying Japanese every day); **b** 先生がやさしい（です）から英語が好きです (Because the teacher is kind I like English); **c** みきさんはきれいなのでロジャーさんは好きです (Because Miki is beautiful Roger fancies her); **d** 毎日家を掃除する（します）からいつもきれいです (Because I clean the house every day it is always clean)

Listening: 1: a Miki says: Next year I want to go to South America and so I am learning Spanish at the moment; **b** She says: I really like Spanish food but I can't make it; **c** She says: Tonight I plan to meet a friend in town and eat Spanish food in a nice restaurant; **2: a** Miki's version 9 → 5 → 2 → 3 → 6; **b** Roger's version 8 → 5 → 1 → 4 → 7

Speaking: 1 a きのう家に帰る前にバーに行きました。Kinō uchi ni kaeru mae ni bā ni ikimashita; **b** 明日うちに帰る前にレストランで食べます。Ashita uchi ni kaeru mae ni resutoran de tabemasu; **c** 毎朝シャワーを浴びる前にコーヒーを飲みます。Maiasa shawā o abiru mae ni kōhī o nomimasu; **d** いつも出る（出かける）前に家を掃除します。Itsumo deru (dekakeru) mae ni uchi o sōji shimasu; **e** シャワーを浴びる前に大抵朝ごはんを食べます。Shawā o abiru mae ni taitei asagohan o tabemasu; **2 a** スポーツが下手なのでテニスクラブで参加しません。Supōtsu ga heta na no de tenisu kurabu de sanka shimasen; **b** あの・そのレストランは高いから家で食べましょう。Ano (sono) resutoran wa takai kara uchi de tabemashō; **c** ケイティさんは上手な先生なのでクラスがたのしいです。Katie-san wa jōzuna sensei na no de kurasu ga tanoshii desu

Writing: 1 a 泳ぐことができます。**b** 見ることが好きです。**c** 作るつもりです。**d** 食べることが好きです。**e** することが上手です。**f** 働くことができません。**2 a** ケイティさんは友達と遊ぶことが好きです。**b** えりちゃんは宿題をすることが好きじゃありません。**c** 日本人と会うことが面白いです。**d** なおえさんはピアノを弾くことが上手です。**e** ロジャーさんは漢字を書くことがとくいです。**a** Katie likes hanging out with friends; **b** Eri doesn't like doing homework; **c** It's interesting meeting Japanese people; **d** Naoe is good at playing the piano; **e** Roger is good at writing **kanji**

Start reading: Story 1 = c; Story 2 = d; Story 3 = a; Story 4 = b; Story 5 = e

Reading 1: a person; **b** cow; **c** shellish; **d** mouth; **e** heart; **f** water; **g** fire; **h** sun; **i** going person; **j** moon/flesh

Reading 2: a eat; **b** drink; **c** write; **d** exit; **e** enter; **f** say/words; **g** speak, talk; **h** sell; **i** read; **j** see; **k** buy; **l** understand/divide/minute; **m** listen; **n** go; **o** rest, holiday

Reading 3: a 3; **b** 4; **c** 6; **d** 7; **e** 8; **f** 1; **g** 9; **h** 10; **i** 5; **j** 2

Reading 4: a I eat breakfast; **b** Sometimes I read the newspaper; **c** Every day I listen to the news; **d** I watch TV with my father; **e** Tomorrow I will go to Japan; **f** I spoke Japanese; **g** I bought an interesting book; **h** I do the shopping on Saturdays; **i** On Sunday I sold a car; **j** Every day I try to write **kanji**

Reading and writing challenge: 来年日本に行きたいので日本語をならっています。日本語を話すことがまだあまり上手じゃありませんが日本のことにきょうみがあります。そして日本の料理もとても好きですが作ることはできません。明日ともだちと会って、ゆうめいなれすとらんで日本の料理を食べるつもりです。Rainen Nihon ni ikitai no de ima Nihongo o naratteimasu. Nihongo o hanasu koto ga mada amari jōzu ja arimasen ga Nihon no koto ni kyōmi ga arimasu. Soshite Nihon no ryōri mo totemo suki desu ga tsukuru koto wa dekimasen. Ashita machi de tomodachi to atte, yūmeina resutoran de Nihon no ryōri o taberu tsumori desu.

Test yourself: 1 a つたえます; **b** いれます; **c** だします; **d** おくれます; **e** がんばります; **f** はしります; **g** あるきます; **h** つかいます; **i** おきます; **j** あらいます; **2 a** Speaking with Japanese people is interesting; **b** I'm sick therefore I'm off work; **c** Because Katie likes Indian food, she plans to make some; **d** Roger practises everyday so he is good at tennis; **e** Miki has a headache therefore she's not drinking coffee at the moment. Rōmaji version: **a** Nihonjin to hanasu koto ga omoshiroi desu; **b** Byōki na no de shigoto o yasundeimasu; **c** Katie-san wa indo ryōri ga suki da kara sore o tsukuru tsumori desu; **d** Roger-san wa mainichi renshū o suru no de tenisu o suru koto ga jōzu desu; **e** Miki-san wa atama ga itai kara ima kōhī o nondeimasen.

UNIT 13

Culture point: 1 six times, meaning 'ward' (ku); **2** it means 'six trees'. The middle **kanji** 本 is, here, the counter for long objects such as trees; **3 a** 館 (kan) means 'building'; **b** 園 (en) means 'park'; **4 a** station (eki); **b** Tokyo; **c** east (higashi); **d** west (nishi); **e** manga (comic books)

Conversations 1: 1 Last summer, to Minneapolis, Milwaukee, Chicago; **2** Three years ago; **3** Two years, taught Japanese and travelled.

Conversaton 2: 1 Last summer when she was living in Chicago; she thought they were really brilliant; **2** Jazz; **3** After they've drunk up their wine; **4 a** false; **b** true; **c** false; **d** false; **e** false; **5 a** パーティーで会いました; **b** ラブラブボーイズです; **c** 日本語を教えたり、旅行したりしました; **d** ジャズとポップスのミックスです; **e** いいジャズクラブがあるからです

Rōmaji version:

Takeshi	Miki-san wa daigakusei ja nai desu ne.
Miki	Ē. Sannen mae ni sotsugyō shimashita kara. Soshite ninen kan Amerika de nihongo o oshietari, ryokō shitari shimashita.
Takeshi	Amerika desu ka. Boku mo Amerika ni itta koto ga arimasu. Kyonen no natsu boku no bando to rokku tsuā o shiteimashita. Totemo subarashikatta desu.
Miki	Doko de ensō shimashita ka.

Takeshi	Ē to, Minneapolis, Milwaukee, Chicago …
Miki	Chicago desu ka. Bando no namae wa nan desu ka.
Takeshi	Rabu rabu bōizu desu.
Miki	Are! Mita koto ga arimasu yo! Chicago ni sundeita toki iroirona konsāto ni ikimashita. Rabu rabu bōizu wa hontō ni subarashikatta wa!
Takeshi	Mita n desu ka. Shinjirarenai!
Miki	Nē, anō, jazu to rokku no mikkusu desu ne. Watashi wa totemo suki deshita.
Takeshi	Arigatō. Jazu ga suki desu ka.
Miki	Hai, poppusu yori jazu no hō ga suki desu.
Takeshi	Boku mo suki desu. Anō, roppongi ni totemo ii jazu kurabu ga arimasu. Kono pātī no ato de issho ni ikimashō ka.
Miki	Pātī no ato desu ka. Chotto osoi wa.
Takeshi	Jā, wain o nonde shimaimashō ka. Sorekara ikimashō.
Miki	Ii desu ne!

13.1 Your turn: 1 a 見た, looked; **b** 飲んだ, drank; **c** 忘れた, forgot; **d** 演奏した, performed; **e** 卒業した, graduated; **2 a** Last night I ate lots of sushi at the sushi bar; **b** 2 I have never been abroad; **c** Every day after eating dinner I watch TV; **d** You should drink this water; **e** At the party I drank wine and talked to friends; **f** Tokyo is bigger than London; **g** When I lived in America I spoke English every day.

13.2 Your turn: a 飲んでいる、飲んでいた; **b** 書いている、書いていた; **c** 住んでいる、住んでいた; **d** 行っている、行っていた; **e** している、していた

13.3 Your turn: a さしみを食べたことがあります; **b** 富士山を見たことがありません; **c** 日本語で（or の）てがみを書いたことがあります; **d** 日本語の新聞を読んだことがありません; **e** 南アメリカに行ったことがありません

13.4 Your turn: a ビールを飲んだ後で、すぐ寝ました; **b** 宿題をした後で、パーティーに行きました; **c** 家に帰った後で、友達に電話しました; **d** コンサートの後で、バーに行きました

13.5 Your turn: a 野菜を食べたほうがいいですよ; **b** 寝たほうがいいですよ; **c** 水を飲んだほうがいいですよ; **d** 家に帰えたほうがいいですよ; **e** メールを出した（書いた）ほうがいいですよ; Friendlier: all the same as previous except replace ですよ with でしょう

13.6 1 アメリカで　日本語を教えたり、旅行したりしました; **2** たり・たり

Your turn: a 日曜日にごろごろしたり、新聞を読んだり、メールを出したりします; **b** クリスマスにいっぱい食べたり、テレビを見たり、友達と会ったりします; **c** 朝ごはんにコーヒーを飲んだり、紅茶を飲んだりします

13.7 I prefer jazz to pop music ＝ポップスより　ジャズの方が　好きです; **Your turn: a** The train is quicker than the bus; **b** The book was more interesting than the film; **c** It is quicker to go by train.

13.8 Your turn: a When I was in America I learned English; **b** When I eat breakfast I always watch TV

13.9 Your turn: a 宿題を忘れてしまった; **b** カメラを落としてしまった; **c** ビールを飲んでしまった; **d** 疲れてしまった

13.10 Your turn: 1 a (not) at all, never; **b** not very, hardly; **c** a little; **d** sometimes; **e** loads, full amount; **f** all; **2 a** 日本語の新聞をだいぶ読みました; **b** メールをいっぱい（たくさん）出しました; **c** ごはんをぜんぶ食べてしまった

13.11 Your turn: 1 a yesterday; **b** last night; **2 a** 先週の土曜日; **b** 昨日の午後; **c** 去年の三月

Listening: 1 a 5; **b** 2; **c** 4; **d** 1; **e** 6; **f** 3

Script: **1 Man** Dōshita n desu ka. **Woman** Nodo ga itai n desu. **Man** Jā, kono kusuri o nonda hō ga ii desu yo. **2 Woman** Dōshita n desu ka. **Man** Nodo ga kawaitta n desu. **Woman** Jā, mizu o nonda hō ga ii deshō. **3 Man** Dō shita n desu ka. **Woman** Kibun ga warui n desu. **Man** Neta hō ga ii desu yo. **4 Woman** Dōshita n desu ka. **Man** kamera o otoshite shimatta n desu. **Woman** Atarashii kamera o katta hō ga ii deshō. **5 Man** Shōrai daigaku ni ikitai desu. **Woman** Jā, isshōkenmei benkyō shita hō ga ii desu yo. **6 Woman** Rainen Igirisu ni ikitai desu. **Man** Jā, korekara eigo o naratta hō ga ii desu ne.

Listening: 2 a ゆうべ、あった; **b** ジャズ、好き、だから、に、行った; **c** 飲んだり、話したり、聞いたり、した; **d** にいて、にかえった; **e** (full script): Last night I met a really nice person. Miki likes jazz so together we went to my favourite jazz club. At that jazz club we drank beer, chatted and listened to good music. We stayed at the club until late then at about 2 o'clock went home. I want to meet with Miki again!

Speaking: ゆうべ　とてもすてきな人に会あった。みきさんはジャズが好きだから緒に僕の好きなジャズクラブに行った。その　クラブくらぶでビールを飲んだり、話したり、いい音楽をきいたりした。遅くまでクラブにいて、そして二時ごろうちにかえった。

Reading 1: 1 b e h d g f c a; **2** Missing words: **a** ippai いっぱい; **b** takusan たくさん; **c** sukoshi すこし; **d** daibu だいぶ; **e** zenzen ぜんぜん; **f** amari あまり; **g** zembu ぜんぶ; **h** takusan/ippai たくさん・いっぱい

Writing: a みきさんのほうがロジャーさんよりまじめです; **b** ロジャーさんのほうがみきさんよりスポーツが上手です; **c** ゆきさんのほうがえりちゃんより背が高いです; **d** and **e** are author's personal opinion; **d** スポーツをするほうがスポーツを見るより楽しいです; **e** ビールを飲むほうが水を飲むよりいいと思います

Weather and the seasons: Story 1: e; Story 2: c; Story 3: a; Story 4: b; Story 5: d

Reading 2: a 4; **b** 5; **c** 6; **d** 8; **e** 2; **f** 12; **g** 9; **h** 3; **i** 7; **j** 10; **k** 11; **l** 1

Reading 3: a father; **b** mother; **c** younger sister; **d** younger brother; **e** older sister; **f** older brother

Reading 4: a younger brother; **b** younger sister; **c** rain; **d** snow; **e** fine; **f** spring; **g** autumn, fall; **h** mother; **i** father; **j** heaven, sky, weather; **k** summer; **l** winter; **m** older brother; **n** older sister; **o** country

Writing challenge: a 先週映画を見た。**b** 今朝七時に起きた。**c** 夕べ十二時ごろ寝た。**d** 友達に手紙を書いた。**e** 友達と音楽を聞いた。**f** 夕べビールをいっぱい飲んだ。**g** 日本語のマンガを読んだ。**h** 新しい先生に話した。**i** 部屋でインド料理を作った。**j.** きのう母と父はイギリスに帰った。**a** Senshū eiga o mita; **b** Kesa shichiji ni okita; **c** Yūbe jūniji goro neta; **d** Tomodachi ni tegami o kaita; **e** Tomodachi to ongaku o kiita; **f** Yūbe bīru o ippai nonda; **g** Nihongo no manga o yonda; **h** Atarashii sensei ni hanashita; **i** Heya de indo ryōri o tsukutta; **j** Kinō haha to chichi wa Igirisu ni kaetta

Test yourself: a 先週映画を見た。**b** 今朝七時に起きた。**c** 夕べ十二時ごろ寝た。**d** 友達に手紙を書いた。**e** 友達と音楽を聞いた。**f** 夕べビールをいっぱい飲んだ。**g** 新しい先生に話した。**h** 部屋でインド料理を作った。**i** きのう父と母はイギリスに帰った。**a** Minami Amerika ni itta koto ga arimasu; **b** Rabu rabu bōizu no ongaku o kiita koto ga arimasen; **c** Rokku no hō ga jazu yori suki desu; **d** Gakusei no toki konsāto ni takusan ikimashita; **e** Ōsutoraria ni sundeita toki Eigo o yoku hanashimashita (ga yoku dekimashita); **f** Yūbe osoku neta kara (no de) tsukarete shimatta; **g** Kono kamera no hō ga sono kamera yori ii to omoimasu; **h** Takeshi-san to hanashita ato de Miki-san wa Roger-san ni denwa shimashita; **i** Shūmatsu ni kaimono o shitari, eiga o mitari shimasu

UNIT 14

Culture point: 1 a 上 meaning above, top; **b** 人 meaning person; **2 a** 4; **b** 1; **c** 5; **d** 2; **e** 3

Conversation 1: 1 He tried to find another job in Tokyo; **2** She thinks it's a shame, she wants to carry on working in Japan but she thinks she will go to China; **3** Get married; **4** In Japan, before a transfer you're supposed to hold a farewell party; **5** She's pleased and says it can be a farewell and wedding party; **6 a** false; **b** false; **c** true; **d** false; **e** true; **7 a** 八月に行くつもりです; **b** 転勤することになったからです; **c** ざんねんですがいいチャンスです (or similar answer); **d** 来月中国に行くかもしれません; **e** パーティーをするつもりです

Rōmaji script:

Katie	Zannen desu ga Ian wa mō sugu Chūgoku ni tenkin suru koto ni narimashita.
Rie	Chūgoku desu ka. Ii chansu desu ne.
Katie	Tokyo de hoka no shigoto o mitsukeyō to shimashita ga shigoto wa zenzen arimasen deshita.
Rie	Katie-san wa dō shimasu ka.
Katie	Sō desu ne. Mada Nihon de hatarakitai desu ga watashi mo Chūgoku ni ikō to omoimasu.
Rie	Zannen desu ne. Nan nenkan Nihon ni sundeimashita ka.
Katie	Ian wa ni nenkan desu. Watashi wa sannen kurai da to omoimasu.
Rie	Itsu tenkin shimasu ka.
Katie	Ian wa raigetsu Chūgoku ni iku kamo shiremasen ga mada hakkiri wakarimasen. Soshite watashi wa hachigatsu ni ikō to omoimasu.

Rie	Chūgoku de nani o suru tsumori desu ka.
Katie	Mada wakarimasen ga watashitachi wa kekkon suru koto ni shimashita.
Rie	Hontō desu ka. Omedetō gozaimasu. Jā, Chūgoku ni iku mae ni pātī o shimashō ne! Nihon de wa tenkin suru mae ni 'sayōnara pātī' o okonau koto ni natte imasu yo!
Katie	Ii desu ne. Sayōnara to kekkon no pātī o shimashō!

14.1 行こう let's/will go; 見つけよう let's/will find; **Your turn: a** みよう let's watch; **b** きこう let's listen; **c** かこう let's write; **d** あおう let's meet; **e** いこう let's go; **f** やすもう let's rest; **g** はなそう let's talk; **h** およごう let's swim; **i** みせよう let's show; **j** まとう let's wait;

14.2 Your turn: a I will watch the film; **b** Shall I go to bed?

14.3 Your turn: 1 a 私も中国に行こうと思います; **b** 八月に行こうと思います; **2 a** 来年日本に行こうと思う（と思います）; **b** 母は来年ヨーロッパに行こうと思っている（と思っています）; **c** 新しい車を買おうと思う（と思います）; **d** たけしさんはみきさんにまた会おうと思っている（と思っています）

14.4 Your turn: a ピアノを習おうとしている（しています）; **b** そのレポートを書こうとした（しました）; **c** 父は新しいジャケットを買おうとした; **d** 去年日本に行こうとした

14.5 イアンさんは来月中国に行くかもしれません; **Your turn: a** 2; **b** 4; **c** 1; **d** 4; **e** 3

14.6 結婚することにしました。 **Your turn: a** I will go for a coffee (e.g. when ordering from a menu); **b** I decided to take a day off work tomorrow; **c** Let's (decide to) travel through Europe – a decision is being made but don't need to include the word 'decide' in English; **d** As a rule I take a walk every morning

14.7 イアンはもうすぐ中国に転勤することになりました。 **Your turn: a** It has been arranged (for me) to meet Mr Hondo tomorrow; **b** It has been decided (for me) to travel to England with my family (family decision, no one 'taking credit'); **c** In Japan, before you get in the bath, you are supposed to wash (custom)

Listening: 1 a On Monday it was decided that she would go to a baseball game with her family; **b** Tuesday and Wednesday; **c** On Thursday it was unexpectedly arranged for her to take part in a judo contest; **d** Next week she will almost definitely be free all week; **e** About one hour; **f** 練習をしようとしていましたが; **g** やきゅうゲームに行くことになりました; **h** 来週は一週間きっとひまだと思います; **2 a** shinkansen (bullet train) 5 hours; **b** train, 6 hours; **c** on foot, 3 months; **d** by plane, 1 hour; **e** by car, 1 day

Speaking: a ニュースを聞こうか。 **b** メールを書こうか。 **c** 映画館の前で会おうか。 **d** 今パーティーに行こうか。 **e** 休もうか。 **f** 日本語で話そうか。

Reading 1: a ことになっています。 **b** ことにしました。 **c** ことになりました。 **d** ことになっています。 **e** ことにしています。

Reading and writing: You: すみませんが、日本語は　あまりべんきょうしません
でした。べんきょうをしようとしていましたが、とてもいそがしかったです。
月曜日に　営業部長と　食事をすることになりました。そして、火曜日も
水曜日も　おそくまで　会社で　はたらきました。木曜日に、とつぜん私は
なごやにしゅっちょうすることになりました。来週は　一週間　きっと、ひまだ
と思います。だから、毎日二時間ぐらいは　べんきょうをしようと思います。

Rōmaji versions: Eri: Sumimasen ga konshū piano no renshū jikan wa amari arimasen
deshita. Renshū o shiyō to shiteimashita ga iroirona mondai ga arimashita. Getsuyōbi ni
kazoku to yakyū gēmu ni iku koto ni narimashita. Soshite kayōbi mo suiyōbi mo shukudai
ga takusan arimashita. Mokuyōbi ni totsuzen watashi wa jūdō no shiai ni sanka suru koto
ni narimashita. Raishū wa isshūkan kitto hima da to omoimasu. Dakara mainichi ichi jikan
gurai wa renshū o shiyō to omoimasu.

Sumimasen ga konshū Nihongo wa amari benkyō shimasen deshita. Benkyō o shiyō to
shiteimashita ga totemo isogashikatta desu. Getsuyōbi ni eigyō butchō to shokuji o suru
koto ni narimashita. Soshite kayōbi mo suiyōbi mo osoku made kaisha de hatarakimashita.
Mokuyōbi ni totsuzen watashi wa Nagoya ni shutchō suru koto ni narimashita. Raishū wa
isshūkan kitto hima da to omoimasu. Dakara mainichi ni jikan gurai wa benkyō o shiyō to
omoimasu.

Reading 2: a 10; **b** 2; **c** 7; **d** 3; **e** 5; **f** 4; **g** 1; **h** 8; **i** 9; **j** 6

Reading 3: a 12; **b** 1; **c** 15; **d** 2; **e** 7; **f** 16; **g** 10; **h** 11; **i** 14; **j** 4; **k** 3; **l** 9; **m** 6; **n** 13; **o** 8; **p** 5

Test yourself: a 買いたいと思います; **b** 行こうと思います; **c** 会うつもりです; **d** 会お
うとしました; **e** 習うことにします; **f** 帰るかもしれません; **g** 見に行くでしょう;
h 来ようと思います; **i** 飲むことにしています; **j** 休むつもりでは（じゃ）ありません
(you can also say 休まないいつもりです)

Rōmaji versions: **a** atarashii kamera o (kaimasu). (I hope to buy a new camera); **b** Rainen
Chūgoku ni (ikimasu). (I think I will go to China next year); **c** Ashita tomodachi ni (aimasu).
(I intend to meet my friend tomorrow); **d** Kinō tomodachi to (aimasu). (I tried to meet up
with my friend yesterday); **e** Itariago o (naraimasu). (I have decided to learn Italian); **f** Kono
eiga wa omoshirokunai no de uchi e (kaerimasu). (This film isn't interesting so he might go
home); **g** Kitto ashita no yakyū no shiai o (mi ni ikimasu). (I bet he goes to see the baseball
match tomorrow); **h** Kyō asobi ni (kimasu). (I think I will come and visit today); **i** Mainichi
mizu o takusan (nomimasu). (As a rule I drink lots of water every day); **j** Raishū shigoto o
(yasumimasu). (I don't plan to be off work next week)

UNIT 15

Culture point: 1 a 市 meaning city; **b** You have seen it in 外国人 (non-Japanese person/
foreigner) and 外 (outside); **c** outside the city; **2** You have learned うち – these two words
can share the same kanji with いえ meaning house and うち meaning home.

Conversation 1: He tells her she shouldn't say that sort of thing

Conversation 2: 1 Before it gets hot/while it's not hot; **2** She tells him not to make excuses

Conversation 3: 1 It is in plain speech because they are all are of a similar age and know each other well; **2** She must tell Roger about Takeshi; **3** She thinks they are both nice people; **4 a** true: **b** false; **c** false; **d** false; **e** true; **5 a** 中国に行きたいからです。**b** 中国に行く前に結婚したいです。**c** 急に結婚したら、よくないと思っています。**d** 三人で映画を見たり、いいレストランで食べたり、いろいろなバーで飲んだりしました。**e** みきさんは二人の人とデートしたからです。(other answers possible)

Rōmaji scripts:

Conversation 1:

Eri	Nē, Katie-san, chansu ga attara, Chūgoku e asobi ni ittemo ii desu ka.
Tatsuya	Eri-chan! Dame desu yo. Sonna koto o itte wa ikenai desu yo.
Katie	Daijōbu desu. Moshi chansu ga attara, zehi gōkazoku to Chūgoku e asobi ni kite kudasai.
Eri	Arigatō! Tanoshimi ni shiteimasu.
Tatsuya	Nē, Eri, Chūgoku ni ikitakattara, sono mae ni mainichi piano no renshū o shinakereba narimasen yo!
Eri	(*In a resigned voice*) Hai.

Conversation 2:

Naoe	Itsu kekkon o suru tsumori desu ka.
Ian	Mada hakkiri wakarimasen ga, dekitara Chūgoku ni iku mae ni kekkon shitai to omoimasu.
Naoe	Sō desu ka. Tenki ga atsukunai uchi ni kekkon shita hō ga ii desu ne.
Ian	Shikashi kyū ni shitara yokunai to omoimasu.
Naoe	Ian-san, iiwake shinai de kudasai!

Conversation 3:

Robert	Nē, Miki-san, Takeshi-san wa anata no koto ga totemo suki da to omou yo.
Rie	Takeshi-san? Rabu rabu bōizu no Takeshi-san? Roger-san to dō shita no?
Robert	Roger-san? Roger-san to mo dēto o shita no?
Miki	Sō nē Takeshi-san mo Roger-san mo totemo ii hito da to omou. Itsumo tanoshiku sugoshiteiru wa.
Rie	Demo Roger-san wa anata ga hontō ni suki yo. Takeshi-san no koto o iwanakereba naranai to omou wa.
Miki	Daijōbu yo. Yūbe sannin de asonda kara. Eiga o mitari, oishii resutoran de tabetari, iroirona bā de nondari shita no. Totemo tanoshikatta.
Robert	Miki-san! Futari no hito to dēto o shinai hō ga ii yo.
Miki	Heiki yo. Shinpai shinai de. Ā, futari ga kita. (*Roger and Takeshi enter the room together*) Roger-san, Takeshi-san, konban wa! Yūbe hontō ni arigatō!
Rie and Robert	Shinjirarenai!

15.1 Your turn: 1 a 話さない；**b** 読まない；**c** 聞かない；**d** 遊ばない；**e** 見ない；**f** 食べない；**g** 見せない；**2** 会わない；**3 a** 話さないでください。**b** 読まないでください。**c** 聞かないでください。**d** 遊ばないでください。**e** 見ないでください。**f** 見せないでください。

15.2 Your turn: a ビールを飲まないで、家に帰りました。**b** みきさんに電話をしないで、レストランに行きました。

15.3 Your turn: a tabako o suwanai de hoshii desu; **b** kaigishitsu ni hairanai de hoshii desu; **c** bīru o zembu nonde shimawanai de hoshii desu
a タバコを吸わないでほしいです; **b** 会議室に入らないでほしいです; **c** ビールを全部飲んでしまわないでほしいです

15.4 Your turn: a 食べなかったです; **b** 買わなかったです

15.6 Your turn: a You/I must study; **b** You/I must go to work; **c** You/I must drink (take) the medicine; **d** You/I must give up smoking; **e** You/I must write the report; **f** You change なりません to ならない（です）

15.7 Your turn: Answers a–d begin with 'it's all right if you don't/you don't have to'; **a** study Japanese this week; **b** write that report; **c** speak Japanese; **d** buy that expensive camera; **e** I don't feel well so is it alright if I don't go to work?

15.8 Your turn: 1 a You'd better not drink that beer; **b** You shouldn't buy that camera; **2** a–c all end in ほうがいいです; **a** 今晩ロジャーさんに会わない; **b** 今日会社（仕事）を休まない; **c** 社長にメールを出さない

15.9 Your turn: I played golf while it wasn't raining *or* I played golf before it rained.

15.10 Your turn: 1 a 面白かったら; **b** 面白くなかったら; **c** きれいだったら; **d** 行ったら; **e** 好きだったら; **2 a** 日本に行ったら富士山を見たいです; **b** よく勉強したら、日本語を話すことができます; **c** きれいじゃなかったら、デートをしたくないです; **d** すもうが好きだったら、今晩の試合をみてください; **e** その映画は面白かったら、全部見たでしょう・だろう

Listening: a Splendid; **b** Met lots of people, learned lots of things; **c** Next month; **d** There are still things they want to do and see; **e** contact them

Rōmaji version of speech: Kyō wa Katie to watashitachi no tame ni konna ni seidai na sōbetsukai to kekkon zenyasai o hiraite kudasatte arigatō gozaimasu. Totemo kansha shiteimasu. Nihon ni iru aida, takusan no hitotachi ni ai, takusan no koto o benkyō shimashita. Nihon no minasan wa totemo shinsetsu de taihen osewa ni narimashita. Raigetsu Chūgoku e iku koto ni narimashita ga, mada shitai koto ya mitai tokoro ga atta node, sukoshi zannen desu. Demo, mata itsuka Nihon ni kite, minasan to aitai desu. Iroiro to arigatō gozaimashita. Moshi Chūgoku ni kuru chansu ga attara, zehi renraku shite kudasai. Arigatō gozaimashita.

English translation: Thank you for having/organizing such a splendid farewell and pre-wedding party for me and Katie today. We really appreciate it. While we were in Japan, we met many people and learned many things. People in Japan were very kind and you have really looked after us. We will go to China next month but we still had lots of things we want to do and places we want to see, so it is a bit of a shame. But we want to come to Japan again one day and we want to see you all. Thank you for everything. If you have a chance to come to China, be sure to contact us. Thank you.

Writing: Make changes to these parts; the rest remains the same: 今日は私のためにこんなにせいだいなそうべつかい（パーティー）をひらいてくださって、ありがとうございます。来月 own country へ帰ることになりましたが ... もし own country に来るチャンスがあったら、ぜひ連絡してください。

Reading 1: **a** 16; **b** 15; **c** 2; **d** 9; **e** 3; **f** 6; **g** 10; **h** 8; **i** 12; **j** 14; **k** 4; **l** 7; **m** 5; **n** 13; **o** 1; **p** 11

Reading 2: **a** 2; **b** 3; **c** 1; **d** 4; **e** 7; **f** 5; **g** 6; **h** 10; **i** 9; **j** 8; **k** 12; **l** 11; **m** 13; **n** 16; **o** 15; **p** 14; **q** 20; **r** 19; **s** 18; **t** 17

Test yourself: **a** Please don't go into that meeting room; **b** I think that that film wasn't interesting; **c** I went to work (to the company) without eating breakfast; **d** I want you not to write that report; **e** I must ring Mr Hondo; **f** You don't have to attend the meeting; **g** You shouldn't smoke cigarettes; **h** I played golf while it wasn't raining (before it rained); **i** While Ian was cooking Katie was reading a book; **j** If you come to China, please make contact.

Appendices

Telling the time

 15.11 Here are the times in five-minute segments. Listen to the audio and practise saying them.

English time	Japanese time	Alternative
1.05 (five past one)	ichiji gofun	
1.10 (ten past one)	ichiji juppun	
1.15 (quarter past one)	ichiji jū gofun	
1.20 (twenty past one)	ichiji nijuppun	
1.25 (twenty-five past one)	ichiji nijū gofun	
1.30 (half past one)	ichiji sanjuppun	ichiji han
1.35 (twenty-five to two)	ichiji sanjū gofun	niji nijū gofun mae
1.40 (twenty to two)	ichiji yonjuppun	niji nijuppun mae
1.45 (quarter to two)	ichiji yonjū gofun	niji jū gofun mae
1.50 (ten to two)	ichiji gojuppun	niji juppun mae
1.55 (five to two)	ichiji gojū gofun	niji gofun mae

Summary of numbers – 100s and 1000s

100	hyaku	1000	sen (issen)
200	nihyaku	2000	nisen
300	sambyaku	3000	sanzen
400	yonhyaku	4000	yonsen
500	gohyaku	5000	gosen
600	roppyaku	6000	rokusen
700	nanahyaku	7000	nanasen
800	happyaku	8000	hassen
900	kyūhyaku	9000	kyūsen

Verb table

Here is a list of all the main verbs that have been included in this course. They are not included in the vocabulary lists so use this appendix when you need to find a verb in English or Japanese. They are organized first by group (Group 1, Group 2, **Shimasu** verbs, Irregular) then alphabetically within group. Group 1 and irregular verbs are listed in **masu** and dictionary form, the rest in **masu** form only – to change to dictionary form look back to the Language discovery section in Unit 12; to change into other forms refer to the Index of grammar and structures.

GROUP 1

aimasu (au)	*meet*
araimasu (arau)	*wash*
asobimasu (asobu)	*play*
dashimasu (dasu)	*send, take out, submit*
erabimasu (erabu)	*choose*
(ame ga) furimasu (furu)	*(rain) falls*
hairimasu (hairu)	*enter*
(kutsu o) hakimasu (haku)	*wear (shoes)*
hanashimasu (hanasu)	*talk, speak*
hatarakimasu (hataraku)	*work*
hikimasu (hiku)	*pull, play*
hirakimasu (hiraku)	*organize, hold*
kaimasu (kau)	*buy*
kakimasu (kaku)	*write, draw*
keshimasu (kesu)	*switch off, erase*
kikimasu (kiku)	*listen*
kowashimasu (kowasu)	*break*
machimasu (matsu)	*wait*
mochimasu (motsu)	*hold*
naraimasu (narau)	*learn*
narimasu (naru)	*become, get, will be*
nomimasu (nomu)	*drink*
nugimasu (nugu)	*take off*
okonaimasu (okonau)	*hold (an event)*
okurimasu (okuru)	*send, post, mail*
omoimasu (omou)	*I think*
otoshimasu (otosu)	*lose, drop*
oyogimasu (oyogu)	*swim*
sagashimasu (sagasu)	*look for*
shinimasu (shinu)	*die*
shiru (shirimasu/shitteimasu)	*know*

sugoshimasu (sugosu)	*spend time*
tabako o suimasu (suu)	*smoke cigarettes*
tsukimasu (tsuku)	*arrive*
tsukurimasu (tsukuru)	*make, build*
utaimasu (utau)	*sing*
wakarimasu (wakaru)	*understand*
yasumimasu (yasumu)	*rest, take holiday*
yomimasu (yomu)	*read*

GROUP 2

(shawā o) abimasu	*take a shower*
aiteimasu	*is open*
dekakemasu	*go out, set off*
dekimasu	*can do*
demasu	*leave, exit, go out*
kaerimasu	*return*
kimemasu	*decide*
mimasu	*watch, see, look*
misemasu	*show*
mitsukemasu	*find*
mukaemasu	*meet, receive, collect (someone)*
nemasu	*go to bed*
okimasu	*get up*
oshiemasu	*teach*
shitteimasu	*know*
sundeimasu	*live*
tabemasu	*eat*
tsukaremasu	*tired*
tsukemasu	*switch on*
wasuremasu	*forget*
yamemasu	*give up*

SHIMASU (SURU) VERBS

benkyō shimasu	*study*
denwa shimasu	*make a phone call*
doraibu shimasu	*drive (go for a drive)*
ensō shimasu	*perform*
gorogoro shimasu	*chill out, laze around*
gorufu o shimasu	*play golf*
kaimono shimasu	*do shopping*
kansha shimasu	*appreciate*
kekkon shimasu	*get married*
renraku shimasu	*make contact*

renshū shimasu	*practice, practise*
ryokō shimasu	*travel, take a trip*
sakkā shimasu	*play football*
sampo shimasu	*go for a walk*
sanka shimasu	*take part in*
setsumei shimasu	*explain*
shigoto shimasu	*work (do a job)*
shinpai shimasu	*worry*
shokuji shimasu	*have a meal*
shukudai shimasu	*do homework*
shusseki shimasu	*attend*
shutchō shimasu	*take a business trip*
sōji shimasu	*do the cleaning*
sotsugyō shimasu	*graduate*
tenkin shimasu	*transfer*
yoyaku shimasu	*make a reservation*

IRREGULAR VERBS

asobi ni ikimasu (iku)	*go and visit*
asobi ni kimasu (kuru)	*come and visit*
ikimasu (iku)	*go*
kimasu (kuru)	*come*
shimasu (suru)	*do, make, play*

Index of grammar and structures

Japanese–English vocabulary

ā, sō desu ka	oh, really?
aida (ni)	while, during
akarui	bright, cheerful
aki	fall/autumn
amari (+ negative)	not very, hardly
ame	rain
Amerika	America
Amerikajin	American (person)
anata no koto	you (lit. your things)
anata	you
anatatachi	you (plural)
ane	older sister
ani	older brother
aneki	older sister (boys use)
aniki	older brother (boys use)
anō (ne)	hey, erm (friendly)
ano, are	that, that one (over there)
aoi	blue
apāto	apartment
are	that (one) over there
are	hey!, what!
arigatō gozaimasu	thank you
arimasu (1)	have, possess
arimasu (2)	there is, there are (non-living things, inanimate)
aruite	on foot
Aruzenchin	Argentina
asa	morning
asagohan	breakfast
ashita	tomorrow
asoko	over there
atama	head
atarashii	new
atatakai	warm
ato de	after
atsui	hot
badominton	badminton
bai bai	bye-bye
banana	banana
bando	band
bangohan	evening meal
basutei	bus stop
Beikoku	America
bejitarian	vegetarian
bengoshi	lawyer

benkyō	studying
betsubetsu	separately
bijutsu	art
bijutsukan	art gallery
bīru	beer
boku	I (male)
bōringu	bowling (ten-pin)
bōringu jō	bowling alley
budō	martial arts
Burajiru	Brazil
chadō	tea ceremony
chairo	brown
chansu	chance
chichi	my dad
chiisai	small
chikaku	near to
Chūgoku	China
da	is (informal of **desu**)
dai	large machinery
daibu(n)	greatly, quite a lot
daigaku	university
daigakusei	university student
daijōbu	fine
dame	no good, don't!
dandan	gradually
dansei	men, male
dare	who
dare ka	someone
dare mo	no one (+ negative)
darō (plain of deshō)	will probably
de	at/in (after place)
de gozaimasu	= **desu** (humble polite form)
dejikame	digital camera
demo	but
demo	something like or something
denchi	batteries
denki	lights, electricity
densha	train
depāto	department store
deshō	will probably
desu	am, is, are
dēto	date
dewa arimasen	is not, am not, are not
dō	how, what way

dō desu ka	how about … ?	hagaki	postcard
doa	door	haha	mum (own)
Doitsu	Germany	hai	yes
doko	where	haiyū	actor
doko made	where to	hajimemashite	how do you do?
dono, dore	which, which one	hakkiri	clearly
dōro	street, road	hakubutsukan	museum
dōshite	why	hana	nose
doyōbi	Saturday	hare	fine, sunny
dōzo yorosh(i)ku	pleased to meet you	haru	spring
		hashi	bridge
e = ni	to (a place)	hashi	chopsticks
ētto	er, erm	hayai	quick, early
eiga	movie, film	hayaku	early, quickly
eiga sutā	film star	hazukashigari (na)	shy, seems shy
eigakan	cinema	hazukashii	embarrassed
Eigo	English	heiki	it's cool, ok
eigyō buchō	sales manager	heta	no good at
Eikoku	England	heya	room, bedroom
en	yen (Japanese currency)	hidari (gawa)	left (side)
		hiki (piki, biki)	small animals
Fujisan	Mount Fuji	hikui	low/small
Furansu	France	hima (na)	free
Furansu no	French (items)	hiroi	spacious, big (places)
furui	old (things)	hirugohan	lunch
futari	two (people)	hiruma	daytime, during the day
futatsu	two items	hitotsu	one item
futatsu me	second	hitotsu me	first
futsū	average	hodōkyō	footbridge
fuyu	winter	hoka no	other
fuyukai (na)	unpleasant, disagreeable	hon (pon, bon)	long (cylindrical items)
		hontō	real
ga	but	hontō ni	really
gaikoku	abroad, foreign country	hoshii	want
gakkō	school	hoteru	hotel
gekijō	theatre	hyaku	hundred
getsu	month		
getsuyōbi	Monday	ichi jikan	one hour
ginkō	bank	ichiban	most, number one
ginkōin	bank worker	ichinichi (1)	a (typical) day
gitā	guitar	ichinichi (2)	all day
go	five	Igirisu	England
gogo	afternoon, pm	ii (yoi)	good, nice
gohan	rice	iie	no
gokazoku	family (others)	iiwake	excuse
gokyōdai	siblings (others)	ikebana	flower arranging
goro	about (used with times)	ikura	how much?
gorufu	golf	imasu	there is, there are
goryōshin	parents (others)		(animals and people)
goshujin	husband (others)	imōto	younger sister (own)
gozen	am, morning	imōtosan	younger sister (others)
gozonji desu ka	do you know? (respect)	Ingurando	England
gurai	about	inu	dog

ippai	loads, full amount	kashu	singer
irasshaimase	welcome, may I help you?	kayōbi	Tuesday
iroiro (na)	various	kaze	wind
isha	doctor	kazoku	family (own)
issho ni	together	keisatsukan	policeman
isshūkan	one week, per week	keitai (denwa)	mobile (phone)
itai	hurts	kēki	cake
Itaria	Italy	kekkon	marriage
itsu	when	kesa	this morning
itsuka	some time, one day	ki	tree
itsumo	always	kinjo no hito	neighbour
itsutsu	five items	kinō	yesterday
iya (na)	awful	kinpatsu	blonde
		kinyōbi	Friday
ja mata ne	see you!	kippu	ticket
jā	ok, right, in that case	kirai (na)	hate
jānarisuto	journalist	kirei (na)	beautiful; clean
jazu	jazz	kiri	fog
ji	o'clock	kiro	kilo
jibun (no)	oneself (one's own)	kissaten	coffee shop
jimusho	office	kitte	stamps
jin	person (nationality)	ko	round objects
jissai wa/jitsu wa	in fact	kōcha	black tea
josei	women, female	kochira	this (person)
jōzu (na)	good at, skilful	kodomo no koro	childhood
juku	cram school	kōhī	coffee
		koko; soko; asoko	here; there; over there
ka	? (spoken question mark)	kokonotsu	9th (date)
kaban	bag	kompyūtā	computer
kado	corner	konban	tonight
kai	floors	konbanwa	good evening
kai	number of times	kongetsu	this month
kaigi	meeting	konkai	this floor
kaigishitsu	meeting room	konna ni	such
kaimono	shopping	konnichiwa	hello
kaisha	company	kono, kore	this, this one
kaisha no eigyō buchō	company sales manager	konsāto	concert
kaishain	company employee	konshū	this week
kamera	camera	korejji	college
kameraman	photographer	kōsaten	crossroads
kami	hair	koto	Japanese harp
kami	paper	kudasai	may I have …?
kaminari	thunder	kumori	cloudy
kamo shiremasen	might	kurabu	club
kanai/tsuma	wife (own)	kurasu	class
kangoshi	nurse, medical carer	kurisumasu	Christmas
Kankoku	Korea	kuroi	black
kanojo	she	kuruma	car
kao	face	kusuri	medicine
kara	from	kutsu	shoes
kara	therefore, so	kyō	today
kare	he	kyōdai	siblings (own)
karera	they	kyōmi ga aru	have an interest

kyonen	last year	nan/nani	what
kyū ni	suddenly	nanatsu	seven items
		nani ka	something
machi	town	nani mo + negative	nothing
mada	not yet, still	natsu	summer
mado	window	naze	why
mae (ni)	before	ne	isn't it, right?
mae	in front of	nē	look (letting someone know something)
magaru	turn		
mai	square-ish, flat-ish	nerujikan	sleep time
maiasa	every morning	ni	at/for/on/in
mainichi	every day	ni tsuite	about
maishū	every week	nichi	day
maitsuki	every month	nichiyōbi	Sunday
majime (na)	serious, conscientious (person)	nigate	poor at
		nigiyaka (na)	lively, bustling
marui	round	Nihon	Japan
massugu	straight ahead	Nihongo	Japanese
mata	again	nikai	second floor
me	eyes	niku	meat
meishi	business card	nin	people (counter)
Mekishiko	Mexico	ninen kan	two-year period
mēru	email	ningyō	doll
michi	road, way	niwa shigoto	gardening
migi (gawa)	right (side)	no	's (possessive)
mijikai	short	no de	therefore, so
mikkusu	mix	nō gekai	brain surgeon
minami	south	nochi	later
minasan	everyone	Nyū Jīrando	New Zealand
mittsu	three items	nyūsu	news
mizu	water		
mo	also	obāchan	gran
mo … mo	both … and	obāsan	grandmother
mō	already (no longer)	ōdan hodō	pedestrian crossing
mō sugu	soon	ofuro	bath
mokuyōbi	Thursday	o-hashi	chopsticks
mondai	problem	ohayō gozaimasu	good morning
moshi	if	ojīchan	grandad
mukae	to meet, collect (someone)	ojīsan	grandfather
		okagesama de	I'm fine, thank you
mukaigawa	opposite	okāchan	mum
musuko	son (own)	okāsan	mother (others)
musukosan	son (other)	ōkii	big (objects)
musume	daughter (own)	okusan	wife (others)
musumesan	daughter (others)	omedetō gozaimasu	congratulations
muttsu	six items	omoshiroi	interesting, funny, fun
		omoshirosō	looks interesting
n desu	you see	onēchan	older sister (informal)
n ja nai deshō ka	probably (polite)	onēsan	older sister (others)
nagai	long	onīchan	older brother (informal)
nagara	while	onīsan	older brother (others)
naka	inside, in	origami	paper folding
namae	name	o-sake	rice wine

osaki ni	*before you*
osewa	*help, care for*
osoi	*late, slow*
osoku	*late*
osoku made	*until late*
Ōsutoraria	*Australia*
otonashii	*quiet* (person)
otōchan	*dad*
otōsan	*father* (others)
otōto	*younger brother* (own)
otōtosan	*younger brother* (others)
oyasumi nasai	*good night*
pātī	*party*
poppusu	*pop music*
Porutogaru	*Portugal*
pūru	*swimming pool*
rabu rabu bōizu	*Love Love Boys* (band name)
raigetsu	*next month*
rainen	*next year*
raishū	*next week*
repōto	*report*
resutoran	*restaurant*
ringo	*apple*
roketto kagakusha	*rocket scientist*
rokku tsuā	*rock tour*
roku	*six*
Roppongi	*trendy area of Tokyo*
rūru	*rules*
ryokō	*travel, trip*
ryōri	*cooking, cuisine*
ryōshin	*parents* (own)
sai	*years old*
sakana	*fish*
sake	*rice wine*
sakkā	*soccer, football*
sakka	*writer*
samui	*cold*
sannen	*three years*
sashimi	*raw fish slices*
satsu	*book* (counter)
sayōnara	*goodbye*
se	*height/back*
se ga takai	*tall*
seidai na	*splendid*
seikatsu	*lifestyle*
sen	*thousand*
sengetsu	*last month*
senshū	*last week*
sensu	*folding fan*

setsumei	*explanation*
shabu-shabu	*table-top dish of thinly sliced beef*
shachō	*company director, president*
shiai	*tournament, contest*
shikakui	*square*
shikata	*how to do/play*
shikata ga arimasen	*it can't be helped*
shimatta (shimau)	*gone and ..., completely*
shinbun	*newspaper*
shingō	*traffic lights*
shinjirarenai!	*I can't believe it!*
shinkansen	*bullet train*
shinsetsu (na)	*kind*
shita	*below, under*
shitsurei shimasu	*excuse me for interrupting*
shitteimasu	*I know*
shōbōshi	*firefighter*
shodō	*calligraphy*
shokuji	*meal*
shokudō	*dining room, canteen*
shōrai (ni)	*in the future*
shū	*week*
shufu	*housewife*
shujin	*husband* (own)
shukudai	*homework*
shūmatsu	*weekend*
shumi	*hobby*
shusseki suru	*attend*
soba	*alongside, by*
sōbetsukai	*farewell party*
sobo	*grandmother* (own)
sofu	*grandfather* (own)
sōji	*cleaning*
soko	*there*
soku	*pairs* (footwear)
sonna ni	*(not) especially (+ negative)*
sono, sore	*that, that one*
sorekara	*and then*
sorosoro	*shortly, soon*
soshite	*and/also*
subarashii	*wonderful, great*
sūgaku	*maths*
sugu	*straightaway*
suiyōbi	*Wednesday*
suki	*like*
sukoshi	*a little*
sumimasen	*excuse me, sorry*
sūpā	*supermarket*
Supein	*Spain*
supōtsu	*sports*

sushiya-san	sushi bar	uchūhikōshi	astronaut
suzushii	cool/fresh	ue	above, on top
		ushiro	behind
tabitabi	many times	utsukushii	beautiful
tachi	makes certain words plural		
		washoku	Japanese food
taitei	generally, usually	watashi	I
takai	expensive	watashi no	my
takai	high/tall	watashitachi	we
takusan	a lot		
tama ni	occasionally	ya	and (when giving examples)
tamago	egg		
tame ni	for	yakyū	baseball
tanoshii	enjoyable, pleasant	yakyūjō	baseball stadium
tegami	letter	yasai	vegetables
teishoku	set meal	yasashii	kind, gentle
tenki	weather	yattsu	eight items
terebi	television	yo	you know, I tell you
to	and	yoko	beside, side
to	with	yohō	forecast
tō	ten items	yōkoso	welcome
tō	large animals (counter)	yoku	often, well
toire	toilet	Yōroppa	Europe
tokei	watch (clock)	yoru	evening
toki	when	yottsu	four items
tokidoki	sometimes	yoyaku	reservation, booking
tokoro	place	yūbe	last night
tokui	good at	yūbinkyoku	post office
tomodachi	friend	yukata	cotton kimono
tonari	next to, next door	yuki	snow
tōsuto	toast	-yuki	bound for
totemo	very	yūmei (na)	famous
totsuzen	unexpectedly	yūsuhosuteru	youth hostel
tsugi	next		
tsuki	month	zannen	shame, pity
tsuma	wife (own)	zasshi	magazine
tsumaranai	boring	zehi	be sure to
tsumori	intend to do	zembu	all
		zembu de	altogether, in total
uchi	home	zenyasai	pre-event party
uchi (ni)	while	zenzen	not at all (+ negative)

English–Japanese vocabulary

a (typical) day	ichinichi	baseball stadium	yakyūjō
a little	sukoshi	bath	ofuro
a lot	takusan	batteries	denchi
about (used with times)	goro	be sure to	zehi
about, concerning	ni tsuite	beautiful	utsukushii
about, roughly	gurai	beautiful; clean	kirei (na)
above, on top	ue	beer	bīru
abroad, foreign country	gaikoku	before	mae (ni)
actor	haiyū	before you	osaki ni
after	ato de	behind	ushiro
afternoon, pm	gogo	below	shita
again	mata	beside	yoko
all	zembu	big (objects)	ōkii
all day	ichinichi	big (places)	hiroi
alongside, by	soba	black	kuroi
already (no longer)	mō	black tea	kōcha
also	mo	blonde	kinpatsu
altogether, in total	zembu de	blue	aoi
always	itsumo	book (counter)	satsu
am, is, are	desu	boring	tsumaranai
America	Amerika, Beikoku	both … and	mo … mo
American (person)	Amerikajin	bound for	-yuki
and	to	bowling (ten-pin)	bōringu
and (examples)	ya	bowling alley	bōringu jō
and/also	soshite	brain surgeon	nō gekai
and then	sorekara	Brazil	Burajiru
apartment	apāto	breakfast	asagohan
apple	ringo	bridge	hashi
Argentina	Aruzenchin	bright, cheerful	akarui
art	bijutsu	brown	chairo
art gallery	bijutsukan	bullet train	shinkansen
astronaut	uchūhikōshi	bus stop	basu-tei
at/for/on/in	ni	business card	meishi
at/in (after place)	de	bustling, lively	nigiyaka (na)
attend	shusseki suru	but	demo
Australia	Ōsutoraria	but	ga
autumn	aki	bye bye	bai bai
average	futsū		
awful	iya (na)	cake	kēki
		calligraphy	shodō
bad at	heta (na), nigate	camera	kamera
badminton	badominton	car	kuruma
bag	kaban	chance	chansu
banana	banana	cheerful	akarui
band	bando	childhood	kodomo no koro
bank	ginkō	China	Chūgoku
bank worker	ginkōin	chopsticks	o-hashi, hashi
baseball	yakyū	Christmas	Kurisumasu

cinema	**eigakan**	enjoyable, pleasant	**tanoshii**
class	**kurasu**	er, erm	**ētto**
cleaning	**sōji**	Europe	**Yōroppa**
clearly	**hakkiri**	evening	**yoru**
cloudy	**kumori**	evening meal	**bangohan**
club	**kurabu**	every day	**mainichi**
coffee	**kōhī**	every month	**maitsuki**
coffee shop	**kissaten**	every morning	**maiasa**
cold	**samui**	every week	**maishū**
collect (someone)	**mukae**	everyone	**minasan**
college	**korejji**	excuse	**iiwake**
company	**kaisha**	excuse me for interrupting	**shitsurei shimasu**
company director	**shachō**	excuse me, sorry	**sumimasen**
company employee	**kaishain**	expensive	**takai**
company sales manager	**kaisha no eigyō buchō**	explanation	**setsumei**
computer	**kompyūtā**	eyes	**me**
concert	**konsāto**		
congratulations	**omedetō gozaimasu**	face	**kao**
conscientious (person)	**majime (na)**	fall/autumn	**aki**
contest	**shiai**	family (others)	**gokazoku**
cooking, cuisine	**ryōri**	family (own)	**kazoku**
cool/fresh	**suzushii**	famous	**yūmei (na)**
cool, ok	**heiki**	fan (folding)	**sensu**
corner	**kado**	farewell party	**sōbetsukai**
cotton kimono	**yukata**	father (others)	**otōsan**
cram school	**juku**	father (own)	**chichi**
crossroads	**kōsaten**	film, movie	**eiga**
		film star	**eiga sutā**
dad	**otōchan**	fine	**daijōbu**
date	**dēto**	fine, sunny	**hare**
daughter (others)	**musumesan**	firefighter	**shōbōshi**
daughter (own)	**musume**	first	**hitotsu me**
day	**nichi**	fish	**sakana**
daytime, during the day	**hiruma**	five	**go**
department store	**depāto**	five items	**itsutsu**
digital camera	**dejikame**	floors	**kai**
dining room, canteen	**shokudō**	flower arranging	**ikebana**
do you know? (polite)	**gozonji desu ka**	fog	**kiri**
doctor	**isha**	football (soccer)	**sakkā**
dog	**inu**	footbridge	**hodōkyō**
doll	**ningyō**	for	**tame ni**
door	**doa**	forecast	**yohō**
disagreeable	**fuyukai (na)**	four items	**yottsu**
during	**aida**	France	**Furansu**
		free	**hima (na)**
early	**hayaku, hayai**	French (items)	**Furansu no**
egg	**tamago**	Friday	**kinyōbi**
eight items	**yattsu**	friend	**tomodachi**
electricity	**denki**	from	**kara**
email	**mēru**	front of	**mae**
embarrassed	**hazukashii**	future (in the)	**shōrai (ni)**
England	**Eikoku, Igirisu, Ingurando**		
		gardening	**niwa shigoto**
English (language)	**Eigo**	generally, usually	**taitei**

Germany	**Doitsu**	I'm fine, thank you	**okagesama de**
golf	**gorufu**	if	**moshi**
gone and …	**shimatta (shimau)**	in fact	**jitsu wa**
good at	**tokui**	inside, in	**naka**
good at, skilful	**jōzu (na)**	intend to do	**tsumori**
good evening	**konbanwa**	interest (have an)	**kyōmi (ga aru)**
good morning	**ohayō gozaimasu**	interesting, funny, fun	**omoshiroi**
goodnight	**oyasumi nasai**	is	**desu, da**
good, nice	**ii (yoi)**	isn't it, right?	**ne**
goodbye	**sayōnara**	it can't be helped	**shikata ga arimasen**
gradually	**dandan**	Italy	**Itaria**
gran	**obāchan**		
grandad	**ojīchan**	Japan	**Nihon**
grandfather	**ojīsan**	Japanese	**Nihongo**
grandfather (own)	**sofu**	Japanese food	**washoku**
grandmother	**obāsan**	Japanese harp	**koto**
grandmother (own)	**sobo**	jazz	**jazu**
great	**subarashii**	journalist	**jānarisuto**
greatly, quite a lot	**daibu**		
guitar	**gitā**	kilo	**kiro**
		kind	**shinsetsu (na)**
hair	**kami**	kind, gentle	**yasashii**
hate	**kirai (na)**	Korea	**Kankoku**
have an interest	**kyōmi ga aru**		
have, possess	**arimasu**	large animals (counter)	**tō**
he	**kare**	large machinery	**dai**
head	**atama**	last month	**sengetsu**
height/back	**se**	last night	**yūbe**
hello	**konnichiwa**	last week	**senshū**
help, care for	**osewa**	last year	**kyonen**
here	**koko**	late	**osoku**
hey!, what!	**are**	late, slow	**osoi**
hey, erm (friendly)	**anō (ne)**	later	**nochi**
high/tall	**takai**	lawyer	**bengoshi**
hobby	**shumi**	left (side)	**hidari (gawa)**
home	**uchi**	letter	**tegami**
homework	**shukudai**	lifestyle	**seikatsu**
hot	**atsui**	lights, electricity	**denki**
hotel	**hoteru**	like	**suki**
hour	**jikan**	lively, bustling	**nigiyaka (na)**
housewife	**shufu**	loads, full amount	**ippai**
how about … ?	**dō desu ka**	long	**nagai**
how do you do?	**hajimemashite**	long (cylindrical items)	**hon (pon, bon)**
how much?	**ikura**	looks interesting	**omoshirosō**
how to do/play	**shikata**	low/small	**hikui**
how, what way	**dō**	lunch	**hirugohan**
hundred	**hyaku**		
hurts	**itai**	magazine	**zasshi**
husband (others)	**goshujin**	many times	**tabitabi**
husband (own)	**shujin**	marriage	**kekkon**
		martial arts	**budō**
I	**watashi**	maths	**sūgaku**
I (male)	**boku**	may I have … ?	**kudasai**
I can't believe it!	**shinjirarenai!**	meal	**shokuji**

meat	niku	often, well	yoku
medicine	kusuri	oh really?	ā, sō desu ka
meet, collect (someone)	mukae	ok, right, in that case	jā
meeting	kaigi	old (things)	furui
meeting room	kaigishitsu	older brother (own)	ani, aniki
men, male	dansei	older brother (informal)	onīchan
Mexico	Mekishiko	older brother (others)	onīsan
might	kamo shiremasen	older sister (own)	ane, aneki
mix	mikkusu	older sister (informal)	onēchan
mobile (phone)	keitai (denwa)	older sister (others)	onēsan
Monday	getsuyōbi	on foot	aruite
month	getsu, tsuki	one hour	ichi jikan
morning	asa	one item	hitotsu
morning, am	gozen	one week, per week	isshūkan
most, number one	ichiban	oneself (one's own)	jibun (no)
mother (others)	okāsan	opposite	mukaigawa
mother (own)	haha	other	hoka no
Mount Fuji	Fujisan	over there	asoko
movie, film	eiga		
mum	okāchan	pairs (footwear)	soku
museum	hakubutsukan	paper	kami
my	watashi no	paper folding	origami
		parents (others)	go-ryōshin
name	namae	parents (own)	ryōshin
near to	chikaku	party	pātī
neighbour	kinjo no hito	pedestrian crossing	ōdan hodō
new	atarashii	people (counter)	nin
New Zealand	Nyū Jīrando	per week	isshūkan
news	nyūsu	person (nationality)	jin
newspaper	shinbun	photographer	kameraman
next	tsugi	place	tokoro
next month	raigetsu	pleased to meet you	dōzo yorosh(i)ku
next to, next door	tonari	policeman	keisatsukan
next week	raishū	poor at	nigate
next year	rainen	pop music	poppusu
nine items	kokonotsu	Portugal	Porutogaru
ninth (date)	kokonoka	post office	yūbinkyoku
no	iie	postcard	hagaki
no good at	heta	president (company)	shachō
no good, don't!	dame	probably	deshō, darō (plain)
no one	dare mo (+ negative)	probably (polite)	n ja nai deshō ka
nose	hana	problem	mondai
not (isn't …)	dewa/ja arimasen		
not at all	zenzen (+ negative)	question mark	ka
not especially	sonna ni (+ negative)	quick	hayai
not very, hardly	amari (+ negative)	quickly	hayaku
not yet, still	mada	quiet (person)	otonashii
nothing	nani mo + negative		
number of times	kai	rain	ame
nurse, medical carer	kangoshi	raw fish slices	sashimi
		real	hontō
o'clock	ji	really	hontō ni
occasionally	tama ni	report	repōto
office	jimusho	reservation, booking	yoyaku

restaurant	**resutoran**	sports	**supōtsu**
rice	**gohan**	spring	**haru**
rice wine	**o-sake, sake**	square	**shikakui**
right (side)	**migi (gawa)**	square-ish, flat-ish	**mai**
road, way	**michi**	stamps	**kitte**
rock tour	**rokku tsuā**	straight ahead	**massugu**
rocket scientist	**roketto kagakusha**	straightaway	**sugu**
room, bedroom	**heya**	street, road	**dōro**
round	**marui**	studying	**benkyō**
round objects	**ko**	such	**konna ni**
rules	**rūru**	suddenly	**kyū ni**
		summer	**natsu**
's (possessive)	**no**	Sunday	**nichiyōbi**
Saturday	**doyōbi**	supermarket	**sūpā**
school	**gakkō**	sushi bar	**sushiya-san**
second	**futatsu me**	swimming pool	**pūru**
second floor	**nikai**		
see you!	**ja mata ne**	tall	**takai, se ga takai**
separately	**betsubetsu**	tea ceremony	**chadō**
serious (person)	**majime (na)**	television	**terebi**
set meal	**teishoku**	ten items	**tō**
seven items	**nanatsu**	thank you	**arigatō gozaimasu**
shame, pity	**zannen**	that (one) over there	**ano, are**
she	**kanojo**	that, that one	**sono, sore**
shoes	**kutsu**	theatre	**gekijō**
shopping	**kaimono**	there	**soko**
short	**mijikai**	there is, there are	**arimasu** (non-living things, inanimate)
shortly, soon	**sorosoro**		
shy, seems shy	**hazukashigari (na)**	there is, there are	**imasu** (animals and people)
siblings (others)	**gokyōdai**		
siblings (own)	**kyōdai**	therefore, so	**kara, no de**
side	**yoko**	they	**karera**
singer	**kashu**	this (person)	**kochira**
six	**roku**	this; this one	**kono; kore**
six items	**muttsu**	this floor	**konkai**
sleep time	**nerujikan**	this month	**kongetsu**
slow	**osoi**	this morning	**kesa**
small	**chiisai**	this week	**konshū**
small animals	**hiki (piki, biki)**	thousand	**sen**
snow	**yuki**	three items	**mittsu**
soccer (football)	**sakkā**	three years	**sannen**
someone	**dare ka**	thunder	**kaminari**
something	**nani ka**	Thursday	**mokuyōbi**
something like	**~ demo**	ticket	**kippu**
sometime, one day	**itsuka**	to (a place)	**e, ni**
sometimes	**tokidoki**	toast	**tōsuto**
son (other)	**musukosan**	today	**kyō**
son (own)	**musuko**	together	**issho ni**
soon	**mō sugu**	toilet	**toire**
sorry	**sumimasen**	tomorrow	**ashita**
south	**minami**	tonight	**konban**
spacious, big (places)	**hiroi**	tournament, contest	**shiai**
Spain	**Supein**	town	**machi**
splendid	**seidai na**	traffic lights	**shingō**

train	densha	when	itsu (question word)
travel, trip	ryokō	when	toki
tree	ki	when I was a child	kodomo no koro
Tuesday	kayōbi	where	doko
turn	magaru	where to	doko made
two (people)	futari	which, which one	dono, dore
two items	futatsu	while	nagara, uchi (ni),
two-year period	ninen kan		aida (ni)
under	shita	who	dare
unexpectedly	totsuzen	why	dōshite, naze
university	daigaku	wife (others)	okusan
university student	daigakusei	wife (own)	kanai/tsuma
unpleasant, disagreeable	fuyukai (na)	will probably	deshō, darō (plain)
usually	taitei	wind	kaze
until late	osoku made	window	mado
		winter	fuyu
various	iroiro (na)	with	to
vegetables	yasai	women, female	josei
vegetarian	bejitarian	wonderful, great	subarashii
very	totemo	writer	sakka
want	hoshii	years old	sai
warm	atatakai	yen (currency)	en
watch (clock)	tokei	yes	hai
water	mizu	yesterday	kinō
we	watashitachi	you	anata, anata no koto
weather	tenki	you (plural)	anatatachi
Wednesday	suiyōbi	you know, I tell you	yo
week	shū	you see	n desu
weekend	shūmatsu	younger brother (others)	otōtosan
welcome	yōkoso	younger brother (own)	otōto
welcome, may I help you?	irasshaimase	younger sister (others)	imōtosan
well	yoku	younger sister (own)	imōto
what	nan/nani	youth hostel	yūsuhosuteru